THE GOSPEL OF
JUSTIFICATION IN CHRIST

THE GOSPEL OF
JUSTIFICATION IN CHRIST

Where Does the Church Stand Today?

Edited by

Wayne C. Stumme

William B. Eerdmans Publishing Company
Grand Rapids, Michigan / Cambridge, U.K.

© 2006 Wm. B. Eerdmans Publishing Co.

Wm. B. Eerdmans Publishing Co.
255 Jefferson Ave. S.E., Grand Rapids, Michigan 49503 /
P.O. Box 163, Cambridge CB3 9PU U.K.

Printed in the United States of America

10 09 08 07 06   7 6 5 4 3 2 1

Library of Congress Cataloging-in-Publication Data

Stumme, Wayne C.
   The Gospel of justification in Christ: where does the church stand today? /
   edited by Wayne C. Stumme.
      p.   cm.
   Includes bibliographical references
   ISBN-10: 0-8028-2690-3 / ISBN-13: 978-0-8028-2690-9 (pbk.: alk. paper)
   1. Justification (Christian theology) — History of doctrines.
   I. Stumme, Wayne, 1929-

   BT764.3.G67   2006
   234'.7 — dc22

                                                            2005033664

www.eerdmans.com

Contents

Contents

Preface

"There never was and there never can be any true Christian Church without the doctrine of justification. In this sense it is indeed the *articulus stantis et cadentis ecclesiae*" (CD IV/1, 523). Few in the churches today would dispute this conviction of the premier theologian of the twentieth century, Karl Barth.

The essays and sermons in this book are attempts to probe that theological convergence and reflect on its consequences. Where indeed does the Church "stand" today with respect to this doctrine? The presentations in this volume demonstrate the extent to which the churches of our time are able to stand *together* in confessing this fundamental truth of the faith. The authors come from the Catholic, Episcopal, Lutheran, and Reformed (Presbyterian, Reformed Church in America, and the United Church of Christ) traditions. Through a long process of ecumenical conversation, their churches have achieved a significant level of theological agreement concerning justification. Few representatives of these Christian communities, however, have concluded their engagement with a doctrine so central and challenging. In the words of one essayist, they now also find it necessary to engage in "mutual affirmation and admonition" on the basis of the common understanding they have reached. Evidence of such ecclesial self-examination and insightful critique of ecumenical partners is abundantly present in these pages.

A number of the presentations consider the significance for the unity of the Church of the recent Joint Declaration on the Doctrine of Justification signed by the Lutheran World Federation and the Roman Catholic Church. The Declaration, itself the product of many years of ecumenical dialogue, came to this conclusion: "Together we confess: By grace alone, in faith in Christ's saving work and not because of any merit on our part, we are accepted by God and receive the Holy Spirit, who renews our hearts while equipping and calling us to good works" (JD, 15). While grateful to God for this step forward in the long journey toward the visible oneness of Christians, several presenters also want to identify unresolved theological issues and shared tasks.

Again, if the doctrine of justification, so essential for the unity of the Church in truth, is also gospel, what can that mean for the life and mission of the churches today? As they confess this good news, the churches, at the same time and in their own ways, stand *with* a world aware of its diversity, conflict, suffering, and unfulfilled longing. One essay in this collection, for example, recounts the story of the relation between the American social gospel movement and its critics and its historical indifference to the doctrine of justification. Another presenter asks what meaning the Christian confession of the God who justifies sinners in Christ might have for the encounter with the religions (Judaism, Islam, Buddhism, and Hinduism). A concluding essay argues that the doctrine of justification is "supremely pastoral" and demonstrates its function in the "cure of souls" as practiced within and for the Church of forgiven sinners.

Yet all theological effort, as Barth has reminded us and the essayists do not forget, exists for the sake of the Church's proclamation. Two sermons related to the theme are included. There something of the wonder and the joy, the liberation and the promise of life that the gospel of justification holds forth, comes to moving expression. In this connection one recalls the life vocation of Professor Gerhard Forde of Luther Seminary in Saint Paul, Minnesota, whose powerful and eloquent exposition of this doctrine has influenced several generations of Lutheran pastors. Illness prevented him from contributing to this volume, but his deeply informed and persuasive insistence on the power of justifying grace to awaken faith through the word of preaching continues to inspire all who have read his books or heard him speak. Gerhard Forde died in August of 2005; his voice is silenced, but his witness to the gospel of Christ continues.

These essays and sermons were delivered at a conference that met to address the theme of this book. It was the tenth of a series of biennial theology and mission conferences organized by the Institute for Mission in the USA, an agency of partnership in mission within the Evangelical Lutheran Church in America, based at Trinity Lutheran Seminary in Columbus, Ohio. Most of these events (all of which were held at Luther Seminary) dealt with theological topics suggested by the theology of Karl Barth. For nearly twenty years these conferences have sought to encourage conversation with this eloquent theologian of grace. Many pastors and professors and lay persons would attest to the benefit for their own ministries of this engagement with the teacher of Basel. It is noteworthy that several of the presenters in this conference found Barth's own formulation of the theme of particular value. In the volume on reconciliation in his great *Church Dogmatics,* Barth wrote:

> The *articulis stantis et cadentis ecclesiae* is not the doctrine of justification as such, but its basis and culmination: the confession of Jesus Christ, in whom are hid all the treasures of wisdom and knowledge (Colossians 2:3); the knowledge of his being and activity for us and to us and with us. It could probably be shown that this was also the opinion of Luther. If here, as everywhere, we allow Christ to be the center, the starting-point and the finishing point, we have no reason to fear that there will be any lack of unity and cohesion, and therefore of systematics in the best sense of the word. (CD IV/1, 527-28)

Here as well the authors of this volume found the unifying center of their efforts.

The conference at which these lectures and sermons were given was hosted by Luther Seminary. Generous contributions from institutions, judicatories, congregations, and individuals representing a number of denominations were evidence of the ecumenical support for this event. To all of them we are most grateful. Special thanks goes to the staff of the Institute for Mission; Bishop Kenneth Sauer, who succeeded me as director; and the gifted associates of the Institute — Phyllis Dawson, Carol Dixon, and Vijayarani Benjamin. Their efforts and encouragement were crucial for the success of this as well as earlier conferences.

Perhaps these words (as slightly modified) from the Official Common Statement of the Joint Declaration on Justification can serve to express the expectations and hopes of all who contributed to this book:

> The two [and more!] partners in dialogue are committed to continued and deepened study of the biblical foundations of the doctrine of justification. They will also seek further common understanding of the doctrine of justification. . . . Lutherans and Catholics [and other Christians!] will continue their efforts ecumenically in their common witness to interpret the message of justification in language relevant for human beings today, and with reference both to individual and social concerns of our times. (JD, 42)

Soli Deo gloria!

Saint Paul, Minnesota   WAYNE C. STUMME

Affirmations and Admonitions:
Lutheran and Reformed

Gabriel Fackre

Reflecting the secular theology of 1960s, the German industrial missioner, Horst Symanowski, declared that in the sixteenth century

> Luther's question . . . "How can I find a gracious God?" . . . unleashed crusades and started wars. It drove man and would not let him sleep. But how many people today are awakened to rise and seek an answer to that question? . . . Another question does drive us . . . unsettles us, agitates whole peoples, and forces us into anxiety and despair: How can I find a gracious neighbor?[1]

What counts is not the rupture of the vertical relation between the soul and God, but the horizontal split between East and West, rich and poor, male and female, black and white that causes our generation to lie awake at night. Many of us believed this dictum with its sharp juxtaposition, caught up as we were in the turn toward Harvey Cox's "secular city."[2]

Now here we are, strangely enough, returning to Luther's ques-

---

1. Horst Symanowski, *The Christian Witness in an Industrial Society*, trans. George H. Kehm, Introduction by Robert Starbuck (Philadelphia: Westminster, 1964), p. 50.

2. Touted on the original cover as "A celebration of its liberties and an invitation to its discipline." Harvey Cox, *The Secular City: Secularization and Urbanization in Theological Perspective* (New York: Macmillan, 1965).

1

tion. Even Cox has had second thoughts about secularity, with his discovery of the continuing power of evangelical piety and Pentecostalism. How can we not rethink the oversimplifications of the sixties? Especially so when the religious fervor of radical Islam that promises paradise by suicide attack is dramatically affecting East and West, rich and poor, male and female, and all the ethnic polarizations entailed. The two alienations — vertical vis-à-vis God, and horizontal vis-à-vis neighbor — are not the Symanowski either-or.

Interestingly, while Luther's question was being sidelined by those of us consumed by the secular agenda of that time, others were less convinced of its irrelevance. The Lutheran–Roman Catholic dialogue on Luther's question began in this country in the year *The Secular City* was published.[3] And the dialogue, expanded internationally, bore fruit ("strange fruit" by the standards of secularity), as in the remarkable agreement on the importance of, and answer to, Luther's question in the recent Lutheran–Catholic Joint Declaration on the Doctrine of Justification.[4]

Significantly, the Lutheran and Reformed traditions were also in conversation about the doctrine of justification and related matters in the same secular period, and have been since, exploring their own historic disagreements.[5] My comments on this occasion rise from a fifteen-year involvement at the North American end of the Lutheran-Reformed exchange, and some engagement with the Lutheran-Catholic dialogue, in both cases, but also with an eye on Symanowski's still-important question. Drawing on those involvements, I'll reflect on justification from a "world-formative" Reformed perspective (Nicholas Wolterstorff's characterization).[6] At the same time, I have come to

---

3. See H. George Anderson, T. Austin Murphy, and Joseph A. Burgess, eds., *Justification by Faith: Lutherans and Catholics in Dialogue VII* (Minneapolis: Augsburg, 1985), pp. 8-9.

4. The Lutheran World Federation and the Roman Catholic Church, *Joint Declaration on the Doctrine of Justification*, English Language Edition (Grand Rapids: Eerdmans, 2000).

5. The history is recorded in an account from the last round. See Keith F. Nickle and Timothy Lull, eds., *A Common Calling: The Witness of Our Reformation Churches in North America Today* (Minneapolis: Augsburg, 1993), pp. 9-21.

6. Nicholas Wolterstorff, *Until Justice and Peace Embrace* (Grand Rapids: Eerdmans, 1983), pp. 3-22.

appreciate, from participation in these fora, the temptations and limitations of my own tradition.[7] The Yes-and-No of the matter is nicely captured in the phrase coined in the 1988-1997 North American Lutheran–Reformed Conversation, "mutual affirmation and mutual admonition," my organizing principle here.[8]

A full-orbed doctrine of justification, the fruit of such mutual learnings, is critical to Christian witness today. It will make us attend to the issues Symanowski accused its proponents of ignoring. And it will speak to the current zealotries in works-righteousness, both the flight from justification to justice so influential still in mainline church secular mission theory, and the teaching in some Muslim circles that paradise can be won by the "works-righteousness" of suicide bombing. In such a time how can we not fling joyfully in the air the good news that the gracious God has found us, enabling us to seek a gracious neighbor?

Mutual Affirmation

In the 1973 Leuenberg Agreement that now brings eighty national churches, Lutheran and Reformed, into full communion, the lead section on "The Common Understanding of the Gospel" begins with "The Message of Justification as the Free Grace of God":

> The gospel is the message of Jesus Christ, the salvation of the world. . . . The true understanding of the gospel was expressed by the . . . Reformation in the doctrine of justification. . . . In this message, Jesus Christ is acknowledged as the one in whom God became [human] . . . as the crucified and risen one who took God's judgment upon himself, and in so doing demonstrated God's love to sinners. . . . Through his Word, God by his Holy Spirit calls all . . .

---

7. The figure is used in the joint Lutheran-Reformed statement, *A Common Calling*, p. 40.

8. For a development of that formula in recent Lutheran negotiations see Gabriel Fackre and Michael Root, *Affirmations and Admonitions: Lutheran Decisions and Dialogue with Reformed, Episcopal, and Roman Catholic Churches* (Grand Rapids: Eerdmans, 1998). The material in this work appeared initially as the 1997 Hein-Fry lectures, published in *Currents in Theology and Mission* 24, no. 2 (April 1997).

to repent and believe, and assures the believing sinner of . . . righteousness in Jesus Christ. Whoever puts . . . trust in the gospel is justified in God's sight for the sake of Jesus Christ and set free from the accusation of the law. . . . This message sets Christians free for responsible service in the world. . . . The message of God's free grace is the measure of all the church's preaching.[9]

In 1983, Lutheran and Reformed churches in this country made their own proposal of full communion, beginning also with a "Joint Statement on Justification." Its key sentences declare:

Both Lutheran and Reformed churches are evangelical. We are rooted in, live by, proclaim, and confess the gospel of the saving act of God in Jesus Christ. . . . The gospel is the good news that for us and for our salvation God's Son became human in Jesus the Christ, was crucified and raised from the dead. By his life, death, and resurrection he took upon himself God's judgment on human sin and proved God's love for sinners, reconciling the entire world to God. . . . Those trusting in this gospel, believing in Christ as Savior and Lord, are justified in God's sight. . . . This gospel sets Christians free for good works and responsible service in the whole world. . . . Both the Lutheran and Reformed traditions confess this gospel in the language of justification by grace through faith alone. This doctrine of justification was the central theological rediscovery of the Reformation; it was proclaimed by Martin Luther and John Calvin and their respective followers.[10]

Out of the latter came the full communion agreement voted in 1997 by the Evangelical Lutheran Church in America and three churches in the Reformed tradition in North America.[11] Of such is the *mutual affirma-*

9. "Leuenberg Agreement," in James E. Andrews and Joseph Burgess, eds., *Invitation to Action: The Lutheran-Reformed Dialogue, Series III, 1981-1983,* A Study of Ministry, Sacraments, and Recognition (Philadelphia: Fortress, 1984), pp. 67-68.

10. Andrews and Burgess, eds., *Invitation to Action,* p. 9.

11. So noted in *A Common Calling,* pp. 10-13. Before the final vote on full communion among the participating denominations — the Evangelical Lutheran Church in America, the Presbyterian Church, USA, the Reformed Church in America, and the United Church of Christ — a listing of fourteen shared affirmations included in the 1983 North American Lutheran–Reformed agreement, on which the

tion that has Lutheran-Reformed ecclesial currency both here and overseas.

On the face of it, the mutuality appears to be that of Reformation traditions bound by the *sola fide* that distinguishes them from the Roman Catholic tradition with its absence of the interpretive "alone." But something more is going on here. The Reformation consensus on subjective soteriology focal in the *sola fide* is grounded in an agreement on a deeper common *trinitarian-christological* premise. Justification writ small — the forgiveness brought by grace through faith to the sinner through the Holy Spirit — is grounded in justification writ large — the Father sending the Son to take upon himself our judgment. As expressed in the North American statement just cited:

> This gospel is the good news that for us and for our salvation God's Son became human in Jesus Christ, was crucified and raised from the dead. By his life, death and resurrection he took upon himself God's judgment on human sin and proved God's love for sinners, reconciling the entire world to God.[12]

From there both statements move to the application of the benefits of the saving work of Christ to the faithful by the Holy Spirit, as in the Leuenberg formulation.

> Through his Word, God by his Holy Spirit calls all . . . to repent and believe, and assures the believing sinner of . . . righteousness in Christ. Whoever puts . . . trust in the gospel is justified in God's sight for the sake of Jesus Christ. . . .[13]

What is striking to me is that the breakthrough agreement just reached between Lutherans and Roman Catholics on the doctrine of justification is constructed in the same way. I believe, and have argued elsewhere,[14] that the 1999 Augsburg accord was made possible by

---

1997 proposal was premised, were added to the published "A Formula of Agreement." They appeared originally in *Invitation to Action*, pp. 2-3. Item c. is "Affirm the doctrine of justification by faith as fundamental," p. 2.

12. *Invitation to Action*, p. 9.

13. "Leuenberg Agreement," in *Invitation to Action*, p. 67.

14. "The Joint Declaration and the Reformed Tradition," in *Ecumenical Perspectives on the Joint Declaration*, ed. William Rusch (Collegeville, Minn.: Liturgical

turning first and foremost to the *trinitarian-christological* foundation of the doctrine of justification, as in its defining paragraph:

> The Father sent his Son into the world to save sinners. The foundation and presupposition of justification is the incarnation, death and resurrection of Christ.[15]

This Lutheran-Roman Catholic agreement then goes on to link objective and subjective soteriology:

> Justification means that Christ himself is our righteousness, in which we share through the Holy Spirit in accord with the will of the Father. Together we confess: By grace alone, in faith in Christ's saving Work, and not because of any merit on our part, we are accepted by God and receive the Holy Spirit, who renews our hearts while equipping and calling us to good works.[16]

Surely, this mutuality of affirmation in all three traditions has important implications for future relations among us, as well as with other Christian traditions.[17] And the trinitarian-christological foundation with its focus on the divine Life Together speaks profoundly to Symanowski's reminder of the contemporary agony of life apart — East and West, black and white, male and female, rich and poor. Convergence here could make for the kind of common witness so needed as the Christian community faces together the ideologies and antagonisms of the hour.

Press, 2002). I have drawn on research on the historic Reformed position on justification done for this chapter in the present inquiry into Lutheran-Reformed convergences and divergences.

15. *The Joint Declaration on the Doctrine of Justification*, p. 15.

16. *The Joint Declaration on the Doctrine of Justification*, p. 15.

17. For responses from other traditions, see Geoffrey Wainwright's Methodist perspective, "Rechtfertigung: lutherisch oder katholisch?" *Kerygma und Dogma*, 45 Jahrgang, Heft 3, Juli/September 199, and Henry Chadwick's, "The Implications of the Joint Declaration on Justification: An Anglican Perspective," *Ecumenical Perspectives on the Joint Declaration. The Journal of Ecumenical Studies* 38, no. 1 includes the papers from the 2001 Annual Conference of the North American Academy of Ecumenists on the Joint Declaration, with a version of the Wainwright paper, another Anglican perspective by William Petersen, an Orthodox point of view by Lucian Turcesco, an "African Response" by Mutombo Nkulu-N'Sengha, and other commentary.

To press the trinitarian-christological reading of justification even one step further, into subjective soteriology, note that the commonalities being discussed today increasingly relate justification to "union with Christ." In an important recent article in the *International Journal of Systematic Theology*, Bruce Marshall contends that Luther's view of that union can bridge church-dividing differences on the doctrine, as "the coherence of the forensic and the transformative is as much a problem for Lutherans as for anyone else."[18] He argues, following the new Finnish school of Luther interpretation in dialogue with Eastern Orthodoxy, that in the structure of Luther's teaching, as well as in occasional references, justification is correlated with deification, based on a union with Christ that comprehends both imputation and impartation.

"Union with Christ" is a key theme *also* in Calvin. With him, participation in Christ is basic to receiving the benefits of Christ for "as long as Christ remains outside of us, and we are separated from him, all that he has done for the salvation of the human race remains useless. . . ."[19] There are differences here, of course, for the Reformed stress on union with the second Person of the Trinity is through the human nature, as Lewis Smedes has argued in his insightful study of Reformed teaching on our union with Christ,[20] whereas other traditions stress union with the Person through the divine nature. The commonality, however, constitutes yet more grounds for mutuality of affirmation among those probing the trinitarian-christological depths of the doctrine and relating it to today's issues.

In Lutheran-Reformed matters, for all the agreement on the doc-

18. Bruce Marshall, "Justification as Declaration and Deification," *International Journal of Systematic Theology* 4, no. 1 (March 2002): 4.

19. John Calvin, *Institutes of the Christian Religion*, Vol. I, trans. Henry Beveridge (Grand Rapids: Eerdmans, 1957), Book III, Chapter I, 1, 463.

20. Lewis Smedes, *All Things Made New: A Theology of Man's Union with Christ* (Grand Rapids: Eerdmans, 1970), esp. pp. 23-30. The Mercersburg theologians to be discussed shortly, the Reformed tradition's premier ecumenists, show how key this was to Calvin's teaching on the Lord's Supper, for "those benefits could never reach us if Christ did not first make himself ours. . . ." For the Reformed, the accent is on the flesh of Christ in our "mystical union" with him, and thus on the human nature, given the problematic of human disobedience that had to be overcome by Christ's active and passive obedience and thus the narrative of cross and resurrection, not only the incarnation.

trine of justification, the partners in dialogue did not shy away from significant historic and continuing disagreements. (Nor did, of course, the participants in the Lutheran-Catholic exchange.) But the present partners look at them through a lens different from that of earlier inspection teams. The North American conversation named it as a new kind of "confessional hermeneutics":

> Throughout this document we employ the principle of "mutual affirmation *and* mutual admonition" to make the different theological emphases of traditions fruitful for each other and for the common witness in the wider church.[21]

That is, the differences are construed as occasions for mutual warnings and corrections within the context of commonalities, looking toward a fuller grasp of the doctrine. Ecumenist Harding Meyer highlights this development, speaking of the formula as an important ecumenical breakthrough, for "a clearly *positive function* is being attributed to the differences, the function of mutual admonition, or mutual correction, of being 'no trespassing signs.'"[22]

To discern the admonitory witness of each tradition regarding divergences in the doctrine of justification, we must first identify overall aspects of each tradition that shape those distinctives, ones discernible in a range of topics from Christology and soteriology, through ecclesiology and sacramentology to ethics and election. They can be characterized as (1) the Reformed accent on the divine *sovereignty* "over," vis-à-vis the Lutheran accent on the divine *solidarity* "in, with and under," and (2) the Reformed emphasis on the *sanctification* of the believer vis-à-vis the Lutheran emphasis on the *simultaneity* of sinfulness and justification of the believer *(simul iustus et peccator)*. First, we examine this back-and-forth in general terms, then relate the differing perspectives to their function in the doctrine of justification.

---

21. *A Common Calling,* p. 66.

22. Harding Meyer, "*A Common Calling* in Relation to International Agreements," *Ecumenical Trends* 23, no. 8 (September 1994): 4/116–5/117. See also his comments in Harding Meyer, *That All May Become One: Perceptions and Models of Ecumenicity* (Grand Rapids: Eerdmans, 1999), pp. 127-28 and *passim*.

Sovereignty and Solidarity

A familiar way of distinguishing the Reformed emphasis on the divine "sovereignty" over us and the Lutheran accent on the divine "solidarity" with us is the contrast between the former's *finitum non capax infiniti* and the latter's *finitum capax infiniti,* whether the Infinite is "haveable, graspable," or not, in Dietrich Bonhoeffer's graphic language in his debate with Barth on this matter.[23] The two different accents against the background of critical commonalities can be clearly tracked in Lutheran-Reformed disputes about the Eucharist, as laid out by the nineteenth-century Mercersburg theologian, John Williamson Nevin, in his influential 1846 work, *The Mystical Presence* (just republished and appreciatively edited by Augustine Thompson, O.P.). In it he shows that both the Reformed and the Lutheran traditions teach Christ's unique presence in the Lord's Supper. Calvin's view, which shaped the Reformed Church's confessional statements on the Eucharist, declares that we partake there of the veritable flesh and blood of Christ:

> As such it is a real communion with the Word made flesh, not simply with the divinity of Christ, but with his humanity also; since both are inseparably joined together in his person. . . .[24]

Nevin distinguishes this view from the memorialist notion (held, he declares, by pietists and rationalists in both Reformed and Lutheran congregations), which interprets holy communion as

> a sign only by which the memory and heart may be assisted in calling up what is past and absent for the purposes of devotion [or] . . . a pledge simply of our own consecration [or] an occasion, by which the soul of the believer may be excited to pious feelings or desires [or] . . . a simple *legal* union . . . of advantages secured by his mediatorial work. . . .[25]

23. See Dietrich Bonhoeffer, *Act and Being,* trans. Bernard Noble (New York: Harper & Bros, 1961), pp. 90-91.

24. John Williamson Nevin, *The Mystical Presence: A Vindication of the Reformed or Calvinistic Doctrine of the Holy Communion,* ed. Augustine Thompson, O.P. (Eugene, Ore.: Wipf and Stock Publishers, 2001), p. 53.

25. Nevin, *The Mystical Presence,* pp. 52, 53.

However, he points out, both Reformed and Lutheran official texts and traditions hold that we have otherwise in the Eucharist

> the very life of the Lord Jesus himself . . . with Christ himself in his whole being so that we may be said to be fed and nourished by his very flesh and blood. The communion is truly and fully with the *Man* Christ Jesus.[26]

Herein is the conjunction with the Lutheran view with respect to its stress on the "real presence."

After the affirmation comes Nevin's distinction of the Reformed and Lutheran sacramentology. In the latter case

> his body is received by the worshiper *orally* . . . and so not by believers simply, but by unbelievers also, to their own condemnation [given] the ubiquity of Christ's glorified body. Bread and wine retain their own nature, but Christ . . . present in his human nature in all places where he may please to be imparts his true flesh and blood *in, with and under* the outward signs to all communicants, whether with or without faith. . . .[27]

Nevin contrasts this view with the Reformed accent on the divine sovereignty over us, holding that the body of Christ is in heaven. How then is the sacrament a communion with the real presence?

> The body of Christ is in heaven, the believer on earth; but by the power of the Holy Ghost, nevertheless, the obstacle of such vast local distance is overcome, so that in the sacramental act . . . the very body and blood of Christ are at the same time inwardly and supernaturally communicated to the worthy believer. . . .[28]

Because of the work of the Holy Spirit in the eating and drinking, and the rejection of conventional corporeality, the Reformed tradition

---

26. Nevin, *The Mystical Presence,* pp. 53, 54. These are Nevin's descriptions of the Reformed view and, by implication, of every "high" doctrine of the Eucharist — Lutheran, Roman Catholic, Anglican, and Orthodox. The distinctions have yet to be discussed.

27. Nevin, *The Mystical Presence,* p. 55.

28. Nevin, *The Mystical Presence,* p. 56.

speaks of Christ's presence as a *"spiritual* real presence" [i.e., a presence rendered by the Holy Spirit, not by our finite capacities] entailing no less "a participation in the Saviour's life . . . subsisting in a true bodily form, the living energy, the vivific virtue, as Calvin styles it of Christ's flesh. . . ."[29]

What is going on here, for our purposes, is the appearance of Reformed and Lutheran distinctives in the often-tortured formulations of the mode of Christ's presence in the Eucharist. The Reformed stress on the divine sovereignty appears as an effort to avoid any tendency to domesticate deity, in this case in the sacramental means of grace, and that with an eye on what it perceived to be Lutheran tendencies. Given the philosophical and scientific premises of the day, this tradition with its accent on sovereignty deployed the notion of the divine-human Person of Jesus lifted on high to the "right hand of the Father," then sought to find a way to declare for a real partaking of the body and blood of that Person by recourse to the Holy Spirit's evocation of faith and a lifting of the believer to the locale of participation. Meanwhile, the Lutheran tradition was determined to assert the "haveability" of Christ, wary of those who so distanced the divine sovereignty from the givens that Christ was absent, not present in the Eucharist, and this with an eye on what it perceived to be Reformed tendencies. Hence, given again the philosophical and scientific worldviews of the day, the introduction of the idea of the ubiquity of Christ and the removal of all doubt of divine access to us in the givens, faith or no faith, with the formula of "in, with and under."

The respective accents on sovereignty and solidarity recur in other aspects of each tradition. For example, Reformed sovereignty expresses itself in its history of rewriting its confessions and catechisms, on the grounds that no human formulation captures the majesty of divine truth, and that the God both above and out ahead calls for fresh credos according to new times and circumstances. The Lutheran accent on the solidarity of Christ with us in his church expresses itself in the honoring of historic givens, whether it be the ancient creeds or the Reformation confessions, deposits of faith not to be rewritten or altered.[30]

---

29. Nevin, *The Mystical Presence*, p. 57.

30. As observed by Karl Barth: "Our fathers had good reason for leaving us *no* Augsburg Confession, *no* Formula of Concord, *no* 'Symbolic Books' which might

We might dwell on what each has to learn here from the other in all these latter concerns. In sacramentology, the relativizing of theories of the "how" of Christ's presence, as in much current ecumenical study and statement,[31] and the correctives to the reductionist tendencies of each tradition? Or in the confessional arena, the need for the Reformed churches to be wary of so relativizing the creedal givens and altering historic confessions that the culture then begins to define the faith rather than the other way around? And the Lutheran temptation to be so wary of change that it is not open to the "new light and truth that can break forth from God's Holy Word"?[32] Or take note of important efforts to bridge the gap by fresh formulations of consensus, as Michael Root notes about the Leuenberg accord, stating as it does that Christ "gives himself unreserved to all who receive the bread and wine: faith receives the Lord's Supper for salvation, unfaith for judgment" and "We cannot separate communion with Jesus Christ in his body and blood from the act of eating and drinking."[33] However, we reserve the mutualities of counsel for our dealing with justification, albeit anticipated by the kind of mutual corrigibility in these areas.

Sanctification and Simultaneity

These two accents enter decisively into the two traditions' understanding of justification, so I will deal with them principally at that juncture. However, they manifest themselves in other areas of both doctrine and practice, whenever a sanctifying "growth in grace" is stressed, or

---

later, like the Lutheran, come to possess the odor of sanctity. . . . It *may* be our doctrinal task to make a careful revision of the theology of Geneva or the Heidelberg Catechism or the Synod of Dort or . . . it *may* be our task to draw up a new creed. . . ." *The Word of God and the Word of Man,* trans. Douglas Horton (Boston: Pilgrim Press, 1928), pp. 229, 230.

31. As in the North American Lutheran–Reformed "Joint Statement on the Sacrament of the Lord's Supper," which asserts that "Both Lutheran and Reformed Churches affirm that Christ himself is the host at his table. Both churches affirm that Christ himself is truly present and received in the Supper. Neither communion professes to explain how this is so." *Invitation to Action,* p. 14.

32. So the counsel of the Reformed pastor, John Robinson, as he sent the Pilgrims on their way.

33. Michael Root, *Affirmations and Admonitions,* p. 92.

wherever sobriety about claims to advances in piety and morality is focal. Their respective theologies of history are a showcase of the differences. Reinhold Niebuhr's comments on both and his effort to integrate them in his own thought are an interesting illustration of admonitory mutuality. Such was no accident, for Niebuhr's own church tradition (the Evangelical Synod of North America, and, later, the Evangelical and Reformed Church, each shaped by both Reformed and Lutheran traditions) was one in which the accents on sovereignty and simultaneity converged, a fact often unnoticed in evaluation of Niebuhr's thought.[34]

Niebuhr credited the Reformed tradition with stewarding in teaching (much flawed in practice) the "prophetic" critique of institutions based on "the majesty of God" that stood in judgment over all human achievements, and also the "possibilities of justice in every historical situation. . . . The possibilities of realizing a higher justice are indeterminate."[35] Niebuhr also affirmed the Lutheran *simul iustus et peccator* as applied to history, that is, "history negates the Kingdom of God . . . grace is in contradiction to nature. . . . Christ is what we cannot be . . . the power of God is against us in judgment and mercy";[36] sin continues at every level of historic advance, threatening it with corruption and increasing the possibilities of evil as well as good.

Niebuhr saw these two accents as correcting each other's reductionist tendencies. He admonished the Calvinist tradition about its

34. A case I have tried to make in Fackre and Root, *Affirmations and Admonitions,* pp. 37-43. Recent portrayals of Niebuhr's thought, notably Richard Fox's *Reinhold Niebuhr: A Biography* and Stanley Hauerwas, *With the Grain of the Universe,* are innocent of these influences and replete with caricatures of his theology. For a responsible reading of Niebuhr with a corrective of the many misconstruals of Niebuhr by Fox see the recently republished work of Charles Brown, *Niebuhr and His Age: Reinhold Niebuhr's Prophetic Role and His Legacy,* New Edition (Harrisburg, Pa.: Trinity Press International, 2002), pp. 266-70, 291-92. My own effort to interpret Niebuhr in the Marty and Peerman "Promise Series" is *The Promise of Reinhold Niebuhr* (Philadelphia: J. J. Lippincott, 1970; rev. ed., Lanham, Md.: University Press of America, 1994). A detailed analysis of Hauerwas's treatment of Niebuhr is available from the writer. A portion of it appears in "Was Reinhold Niebuhr a Christian?" in the October 2002 issue of *First Things.*

35. Reinhold Niebuhr, *The Nature and Destiny of Man: A Christian Interpretation: Human Destiny,* vol. 2 (New York: Charles Scribner's Sons, 1945), pp. 284, 192.

36. Niebuhr, *The Nature and Destiny of Man,* vol. 2, p. 204.

temptation and tendency to expect too much of history, as illustrated by both its theocratic and utopian pretensions. It needs the Lutheran wisdom about the persistence of sin in every historical advance. And he admonished the Lutheran tradition about its inordinate suspicion concerning the possibilities of history and thus its temptation to withdraw into apolitical or pietist sanctuaries.[37] Better what he called "the double aspect of grace, the twofold emphasis on the obligation to fulfill the possibilities of life and upon the limitations and corruptions in all historical realizations. . . ."[38] With this duality in mind we turn to the mutual admonitions of each tradition on the doctrine of justification.

Justification: Accents and Admonitions

Reformed Sovereignty

A Reformed response to the Lutheran-Catholic Joint Declaration on the Doctrine of Justification illustrates one of the various ways in which its accent on the divine sovereignty affects its reading of justification.[39] Like the Declaration, Reformed teaching presses the doctrine beyond its usual locus in subjective soteriology into its source in the sovereign purposes of God and their execution. As noted, it is this same *trinitarian-christological* framework that was critical to the Lutheran-Catholic agreement. Indeed, the Declaration's use of John 3:16 as its leading biblical warrant is the same text Calvin uses to frame his understanding of the doctrine. Thus, in the scholastic language of the day, Calvin says:

> The efficient cause of our eternal salvation the Scripture uniformly declares to be the mercy and free love of the heavenly Father toward us; the material cause to be Christ with the obedience by which he purchased righteousness for us; and what can be the for-

37. See also Wolterstorff on the "avertive" tendency in Lutheranism, *Until Justice and Peace Embrace*, pp. 5, 10, 16.

38. Niebuhr, *The Nature and Destiny of Man*, vol. 2, p. 211.

39. A theme developed in Gabriel Fackre, "A Reformed Perspective on the Joint Declaration on the Doctrine of Justification," in William Rusch, ed., *Ecumenical Perspectives on the Joint Declaration*.

mal or instrumental cause but faith? John includes the three in one sentence when he says, "God so loved the world, that he gave his only begotten Son, that whosoever believeth in him should not perish but have everlasting life."[40]

Elsewhere he makes the same point.

> The efficient cause of our salvation is placed in the love of the Father; the material cause in the obedience of the Son; the instrumental cause in the illumination of the Spirit, that is, in faith. . . .[41]

This holistic, or "narrative" understanding of justification, as Markus Barth describes it,[42] appears also in the Reformed Confessions:

French Confession
Articles XVII and XX: We believe that by the perfect sacrifice that the Lord Jesus offered on the cross, we are reconciled to God, and justified before him . . . by his death we are fully justified, and through him only can we be delivered from our iniquities and transgressions . . . we are made partakers of this justification by faith alone.[43]

Belgic Confession
Article XXIII, "Our Justification Consists in the Forgiveness of Sin and the Imputation of Christ's Righteousness" . . . the . . . Apostle saith, *that we are justified freely by his grace, through the redemption which is in Jesus Christ.* And therefore we always hold fast this foundation, ascribing all glory to God . . . relying and resting on the obedience of Christ crucified alone, which becomes ours when we believe in him.[44]

---

40. Calvin, *Institutes of the Christian Religion,* Vol. II, Book III, Chapter XIV, 15, 85.

41. Calvin, *Institutes of the Christian Religion,* Vol. II, Book III, Chapter XIV, 15, 88.

42. See Markus Barth, *Justification: Pauline Texts Interpreted in the Light of Old and New Testaments* (Grand Rapids: Eerdmans, 1971), p. 21.

43. "The French Confession of Faith, 1559," in Arthur Cochrane, ed., *Reformed Confessions of the 16th Century* (Philadelphia: Westminster, 1956), p. 151.

44. "The Belgic Confession of Faith, 1561," in *Reformed Confessions of the 16th Century,* p. 204.

Second Helvetic Confession

Chapter XV, "Of the Justification of the Faithful." . . . *We are justified on account of Christ* . . . we are justified, that is, absolved from sin and death by God the Judge. . . . "Since all have sinned and fall short of the glory of God they are justified by his grace as a gift through the redemption which is in Christ Jesus." . . . Properly speaking, therefore, God alone justifies us, and justifies us on account of Christ, not imputing sins to us, but imputing righteousness to us . . . we receive this justification, not through any works, but through faith in the mercy of God and in Christ. . . .[45]

Karl Barth's version of this encompassing Reformed view of justification gives pride of place to "justification writ large," pointing to

the divine verdict in Jesus Christ by which man is justified. This justifying sentence of God is his decision in which man's being as the subject of that act ["sin as the human act of pride"] is repudiated, his responsibility for that act, his guilt is pardoned, canceled and removed, and there is ascribed to him instead a being as the subject of pure acts of thankfulness for this liberation.[46]

Associated with this press of the doctrine toward its roots in the sovereign divine purposes is the Reformed stress on election. Whether it is Dort's doctrine of double predestination or Barth's christological reading of election, Reformed eyes look first to what the majestic God eternally wills and historically executes, not to what our (graced) responses might be at the receiving end. They see, first and foremost, the *non capax* of the divine initiative, the kingly rule of Christ.

Lutheran Solidarity

And historic Lutheran eyes? Surely, from Luther forward, they are not fixed, first and foremost on issues of predestination and election, but on the *pro me* of justification:

45. "The Second Helvetic Confession, 1566," in *Reformed Confessions of the 16th Century*, pp. 255, 256.
46. Karl Barth, *Church Dogmatics*, VI/1, trans. Geoffrey Bromiley (Edinburgh: T. & T. Clark, 1956), p. 145.

No good work can rely upon the Word of God or live in the soul, for faith alone and the Word of God rule in the soul. Just as the heated iron glows like fire because of the union of fire with it, so the Word imparts its qualities to the soul. . . . Wherefore the afflicted and troubled conscience hath no remedy against desperation and eternal death, unless it takes hold of the promise of grace freely offered in Christ. . . . When sin is pardoned and the conscience delivered from the burden and string of sin, then may a Christian bear all things easily; because he feeleth all things within sweet and comfortable, therefore he doeth and suffereth all things willingly.[47]

The focus on the appropriative aspect of justification is apparent in the historic conflicts with Roman Catholicism as to whether the reception of grace is by faith alone, or by the Roman Catholic stress on the believer's "faith, hope, and love"; whether in a forensic declaration of pardon, on the one hand, or by the infusion of grace, on the other; whether the believer can be assured of salvation through that faith or whether some doubt lingers. The accent on subjective soteriology continues in the Lutheran tradition, from pietism to existentialist developments, from Kierkegaard's "subjectivity" to Bultmann's decision of faith.

Why are the dynamics of appropriation so focal? Can it be the mark left by Luther's own personal struggle, "How can *I* find a gracious God?" While such may have played a role, I believe the stress on the appropriative is to be traced to the *solidarity* accent we have been noting. The haveable Christ of Lutheran sensibility turns our attention to the action of grace "in, with and under" the givens of justifying faith. The Lutheran *capax* is to the fore. The assurance of pardon of the sinner is crucial. The promises of God must be trusted to be fulfilled as a "real presence" of Christ in the believer. As noted, the Finnish school of Luther research associates this with justification and thus its affinities to the Eastern motif of deification.[48] While sounding like the sus-

---

47. Martin Luther, "Freedom of a Christian," "Commentary on Galatians," in John Dillenberger, ed., *Martin Luther* (Garden City, N.Y.: Doubleday, 1961), pp. 58, 102, 112.

48. For overviews of the Finnish school and related interpretations of *theosis* in Luther's theology, see Tuomo Mannermaa, "Theosis as a Subject of Finnish Luther Research," *Pro Ecclesia* 4, no. 1 (Winter 1995): 37-48 and Risto Saarinen, "Salva-

pect teaching of Andreas Osiander, Robert Jenson argues that "this is not a dissolution in God or even any usual sort of mysticism or idealism, for the Christ who is one with me so that I am one with God is precisely Christ in 'flesh and bones.'"[49] Again, it means in ethics that we do not need to "work at" loving, for love rises spontaneously from faith, as we are graced to be a veritable Christ to our neighbor.

In recent Lutheran theology, especially in its evangelical catholic wing, and also in the Lutheran-Catholic dialogue, the theme of solidarity is at work with reference to baptism and justification. The grace of justification is seen to begin in baptism, reflecting the solidarity of Christ with the church, and thus at this doorway

> . . . God chooses to use the bath and the proclamation of the triune name as together one instrument of grace. The transformation God works by this instrument is *justification*. Since the Pauline connection of faith and justification is maintained, baptism is "the sacrament of faith."[50]

Mutual Admonitions

Accents bring in their wake admonishments. As judgment begins with ourselves, we heed first the needed Lutheran critique of Reformed sovereignty gone amok in matters of justification. While Luther held to the doctrine of predestination (as in *The Bondage of the Will*), the doctrine of double predestination is rejected in the Formula of Concord,[51]

tion in the Lutheran-Orthodox Dialogue: A Comparative Perspective," *Pro Ecclesia* 5, no. 2 (Spring 1996): 202-13.

49. Robert Jenson, *Systematic Theology*, vol. 2 (New York: Oxford University Press, 1999), p. 297.

50. Robert Jenson, "Baptism," in Carl Braaten and Robert Jenson, *Christian Dogmatics*, vol. 2 (Philadelphia: Fortress, 1984), p. 324. For the writer's interpretation of the role of *finitum capax infiniti* in Jenson's theology, see "The Lutheran *Capax* Lives," in *Trinity, Time and Church, Festschrift for Robert Jenson*, ed. Colin Gunton (Grand Rapids: Eerdmans, 2000), pp. 94-102. For the linkage of baptism and justification see also *Joint Declaration on the Doctrine of Justification*, 4/4, pp. 20-22.

51. "Formula of Concord: Epitome, Article XI: Election," in *The Book of Concord: The Confessions of the Evangelical Lutheran Church*, ed. Robert Kolb and Timothy Wengert, trans. Charles Arand, Eric Gritsch, Robert Kolb, William Russell, James Schaaf, Jane Strohl, and Timothy J. Wengert (Minneapolis: Fortress, 2000), pp. 516-20.

the historic Lutheran stress being on the doxological and existential understanding of election: thanks expressed by believers for the grace given. Thus Lutherans are rightly wary of the speculative use of the doctrine that moves from the personal to the pre-temporal. Speculation goes where no human belongs, into the inner recesses of the divine mind, as evidenced in both the theories of double predestination and its presumed opposite, universalism. This Lutheran critique is expressed in the North American Lutheran–Reformed agreement:

> Reformed Christians may have to hear the warning against illicit speculation, a weak ecclesiology, the temptation to want to know more than what is revealed in Jesus Christ and thus the danger of triumphalist, moralistic judgmental distortion of the gospel message.[52]

That includes the dangers of abstract doctrines of either predestination or universalism, on the one hand, or an antisacramental memorialism on the other.

Concerns about the effects of an overemphasis on sovereignty are also echoed in Lutheran critiques of the third use of the law as it is found in traditional Reformed teaching. The third use of the law with its urgings and calls to obedience can be an invitation to works-righteousness and a sign of the absence of Christ, as surely as the charge of the absence of Christ is heard in sacramental debates.

The Lutheran-Reformed study, *A Common Calling*, balances its warnings about Reformed temptations with those appropriate to Lutherans:

> Lutherans may need to hear the warnings against complacent self-assurance, pious passivity, and the danger of overlooking the importance of the responding life of faith among the elect lived in and for, not only against, the world.[53]

In another vein, Barth, criticizing the "the older Protestantism" for its anthropocentric preoccupation with "the individual experience of grace . . . filled out psychologically and biographically," remarks, "We only ask in

---

52. *A Common Calling*, p. 55.
53. *A Common Calling*, p. 55.

passing whether and to what extent Luther's well-known question in the cloister . . . contributed if only by way of temptation to this trunca-tion. . . ."[54] And yet again, the Reformed stress on the divine sovereignty over all our givens will be wary of a too-simple linkage of justification with the waters of a baptism that excludes the place of faith in this means of grace or denies the freedom of God to work beyond those means.[55]

The Reformed accent on the divine sovereignty has implications for current ecumenical debate on its status as *the* article on which the church stands or falls. In a recent Reformed response to the Lutheran-Catholic Joint Declaration, Alan Falconer points out that in classical formulations and in current bilateral dialogues "the Reformed tradi-tion has not found it congenial to identify an *articulus stantis et cadentis ecclesiae,* but has focused on Jesus Christ as mediator and reconciler, from which a trinitarian theology is developed, and as a consequence, an understanding of justification and sanctification of Christians."[56] Here is a Reformed move to locate the teaching of justification in the context of *soli Deo gloria,* and thus relate the doctrine of justification to the wider trinitarian-christological context, as Lutherans indeed sought to do by defining justification in that context in the recent Augsburg accord.

And yet again on divine sovereignty, the earlier counsel of Reinhold Niebuhr is apt, for he faults the Lutheran side of his own tra-dition for a preoccupation with personal justification that leads to quietism and accession to the political status quo for lack of account-ability to the kingship of Christ over society as well as the soul.

Reformed Sanctification

Commenting on Calvin's teaching about sanctification vis-à-vis justifi-cation in his First Catechism, with Calvin's *Institutes* as a backdrop, John

---

54. Barth, *Church Dogmatics* IV/1, p. 150.

55. So too the ecumenical document BEM, which insists that "The necessity of faith for the reception of the salvation set forth and embodied in baptism is ac-knowledged by all churches." *Baptism, Eucharist and Ministry* (Geneva: World Council of Churches, 1982), p. 3.

56. Alan Falconer, "Confessing the One Faith," *Reformed World* 53, no. 1 (March 2002): 33.

Hesselink remarks, "For Calvin, however, *sanctification* is just as important as justification; and both are derived from our union with Christ."[57] Calvin describes this parity as the fruit of a "double grace." The Christ to whom we are joined by faith brings to us, and in us, holiness of life:

> Christ justifies no man without sanctifying him . . . never the one without the other . . . we are justified not without, yet not by works . . . while we acknowledge that faith and works are necessarily connected, we, however, place justification in faith, not works.[58]

The sanctified life entails not only the spontaneous and ecstatic flow of love from faith, but also a willed obedience to the divine law. As Randall Zachman comments,

> Although the conscience is freed from the law with regard to its justification before God, it is not freed with regard to its sanctification, for the law still exhorts and teaches believers to be conformed to the goal of their calling.[59]

This struggle forward is reflected in a variety of ways in Reformed history, as different as John Bunyan's *Pilgrim's Progress* and the much-discussed *ordo salutis* in Reformed scholasticism.

Sovereignty joined to sanctification in the Reformed tradition issues, as has been noted, in a "world-formative" perspective.[60] From Geneva forward it has sought to call social, economic, and political institutions to account before sovereign norms, with the possibilities of sanctifying growth in public arenas. A characteristic formulation of this conjunction is the Reformed teaching of the kingly rule of Christ (the third office of Christ in Calvin's *munus triplex*) over the voting booth and counting house.[61] Karl Barth's interpretation of sanctification writ large, comparable to his view of justification writ

---

57. I. John Hesselink, *Calvin's First Catechism: A Commentary* (Louisville: Westminster/John Knox, 1997), p. 105.

58. Calvin, *Institutes of the Christian Religion*, Vol. II, Book III, Chapter XV/1, 99, 98.

59. *Calvin's First Catechism*, pp. 206-7.

60. *Until Justice and Peace Embrace*, passim.

61. W. A. Visser 't Hooft, *The Kingship of Christ: An Interpretation of Recent European Theology* (New York: Harper & Bros., 1948).

large, is yet another way in which the tradition has exhibited its world-embracing accent.[62]

Lutheran Simultaneity

From Luther's *Bondage of the Will* forward, Lutherans, on the other hand, remind us of our captivity to sin even as we labor under the sovereign God for a sanctified world. As he argues against Erasmus, the fall is a state not to be ignored by Pelagianisms, semi or otherwise:

> "As it is written," he [Paul] says, "'None is righteous, no, not one, no one understands, no one seeks for God. All have turned aside, together they have become worthless. . . .'" Here give me a "suitable interpretation" if you can! Invent tropes, allege that the words are obscure or ambiguous, and defend free choice against these damning sentences if you dare![63]

And don't think the problem is over when the Christian enters the kingdom of grace by baptism and faith. Those so justified must still deal with the persistence of sin in the life of the redeemed. As the Smalcald Articles express it,

> while the Holy Spirit is there to "daily cleanse," repentance continues until death, for all through life it contends with the sins that remain in the flesh. As St. Paul testifies in Romans 7:23, he wars with the law in his members. . . . As . . . St John writes, "If we say we have no sin, we deceive ourselves and the truth is not in us."[64]

---

62. "The sanctification of man, his conversion to God, is like his justification, a new determination, which has taken place *de iure* for the world and therefore for all men." Karl Barth, *Church Dogmatics* IV/2, ed. G. W. Bromiley and T. F. Torrance (Edinburgh: T. & T. Clark, 1958), pp. 511 and passim. Barth adds, of course, "*De facto*, however, it is not known by all men, just as justification has not *de facto* been grasped and acknowledged and known and confessed by all men, but only by those who are awakened to faith" (p. 511).

63. "The Bondage of the Will," in Timothy F. Lull, *Martin Luther's Basic Theological Writings* (Minneapolis: Fortress, 1989), p. 184.

64. The Smalcald Articles, 526, 527.

It is no accident that confession of sin, private and public, is a vital part of the Lutheran tradition; the Johannine words are often part of the call to repentance. Lutheran piety of this kind is a living out of the *simul iustus et peccator* of its doctrine. This emphasis on the simultaneity of sin and a declared righteousness brings with it a sobriety about claims to sanctification. While the faithful are in a new state in which sin is "ruled,"[65] the battle continues to the end. As the Lutheran segment of the Joint Declaration puts it:

> Lutherans understand this condition of the Christian as being "at the same time righteous and sinner." Believers are totally righteous, in that God forgives their sins through Word and Sacrament and grants the righteousness of Christ, which they appropriate through faith. . . . Looking at themselves through the law, however, they recognize that they remain totally sinners. Nevertheless, the enslaving power of sin is broken on the basis of the merit of Christ. It no longer is a sin that "rules" the Christian, for it is itself "ruled" by Christ with whom the justified are bound by faith.[66]

Mutual Admonitions

Lutheran sobriety has a lot to teach the rest of us, the Reformed tradition included. While from Calvin forward the Reformed tradition has also stressed the fall, salvation by faith alone and not by human works, and the persistence of sin in the life of the believer, its accent on the possibilities of grace through its sanctifying power have opened it to certain temptations and tendencies. Those include too-simple assumptions about unimpeded progress in the Christian life, and the self-righteous fury that keeps company with these claims, notable in the intolerant and uncharitable treatment of those not part of the church deemed to be made up alone of "the visible saints" as described in some streams of the Reformed tradition.[67] An example of the Re-

65. Thus the Smalcald Articles: "The Holy Spirit does not permit sin to rule . . . ," 527. The Lutheran interpretation of justification in the Joint Declaration uses the metaphor, citing Apology II, *Book of Concord*, as its warrant (4.4. 29, p. 21).

66. *Joint Declaration on the Doctrine of Justification* 4.4.29, p. 21.

67. See Alan P. F. Sell, *Saints: Visible, Orderly and Catholic: The Congregational Idea of the Church* (Allison Park, Pa.: Pickwick Press, 1986).

formed impulse gone amok is the reinterpretation by Robert Schuller of justification by faith as "possibility thinking," echoing the "positive thinking" of Norman Vincent Peale, both pastors of a Reformed Church. (Lutheran Martin Marty, when asked by Schuller for a comment on his book *Self-Esteem: The New Reformation*, gently inquired, "Is not this a philosophy which makes room for God more than a theology which incorporates psychology?")[68]

Reformed piety and ecclesiology must heed the Lutheran admonition to be wary of the organic metaphor in describing the Christian life, a process of growth in which the sanctified life moves naturally to fuller and fuller realization, or so stressing the possibilities of life in Christ that its impossibilities are discounted. Rather, the Christian life struggles against sin at every stage of advance, its power increasing commensurate with that advance. Lutherans can remind the Reformed of the dangers of spiritual pride that go with sanctification, given the simultaneity of sin and righteousness, and the importance of the rite of confession of sin, too often diminished or disappearing as the accent on sanctification is immoderately pressed. In its extreme form, a doctrine of the church as visible saints, piety-cum-morality credentialing the very being of the church, is a constant temptation for the Reformed tradition. It may come in traditionalist form as the limitation of the church only to those purified by a "born-again" experience or in modern form only to "the company of the committed," those who pass the test of justice-seeking and peacemaking. In both cases, the church as a company of sinners, existing by the mercy of God and sustained by the means of grace, is lost from view. This Lutheran wisdom about our limitations also needs to be carried over into Reformed social theory, injecting a critical principle into social expectations warning of utopianism on the one hand and theocratic temptations on the other, the Lutheran two-kingdom theory warning in both cases of the dangers of too-simple association of Christ with expectations and structures in corporate life.

68. Quoted in the Introduction by Schuller, who replied, "Perhaps, I wouldn't be surprised" [!], since he sees his ministry to be with "unbelievers . . . who may not be ready to believe in God." Robert Schuller, *Self-Esteem: The New Reformation* (Waco, Tex.: Word, 1982), pp. 11, 12. While Schuller credits Marty in the Acknowledgments with being his mentor, it's hard to believe he got Marty's Lutheran point about Schuller's "Babylonian captivity" of the gospel of justification.

In the admonitory point-counterpoint, Reformed will have their warnings about the dangers of a too-simple rendering of the simultaneity of sin and righteousness. The stress on the constancy of battle in the Christian life can be such that the transformative powers of grace are denied, and its possibilities ignored. There is advance in the journey of faith, and a right to hope for growth in grace. Because of this confidence in a "double grace," an empowering sanctification inextricable from a pardoning justification, thankful obedience to the third use of the law is not a concession to works-righteousness but a living out of the partnership of gift and claim, acknowledging the imperative that rises from the indicative. And given the inextricability of justification and sanctification, how would this not also play out ecclesially? The church at every level of its life is called to holiness within its own life and in its relationship to society. Insofar as our understanding of justification excludes a passion for justice, or the call of the church to seek a gracious neighbor as well as a gracious God, we stand indicted by Symanowski's dictum. The church is a company of sinners called to saintliness with mandates and hopes for impacting society, resisting all quietisms and accessions to the status quo.[69] Justification in its fullness includes overcoming the alienations of East and West, male and female, black and white, a struggle for the poor and accountability of the rich, in the grateful obedience of the sinner who has received the Word of God's gracious mercy in faith.

Conclusion

Where does the Church stand today on the gospel of justification? If the rich ecumenical advances in mutuality so noted, and so possible as grounded in a trinitarian-christological Life Together, are an index, it stands ready to make a more faithful witness to the wider world. How desperately that word is needed! Needed because the challenge of works-righteousness is as claimant as ever. Needed because "life apart" is as much with us as in Symanowski's time. Needed because the temptation to sever justification from justice is unrelenting. Needed because the advances in acknowledged mutualities of both af-

---

69. Niebuhr, *Nature and Destiny of Man*, vol. 2, pp. 190-98.

firmation and admonition have yet to be fully "received" and imple-
mented in the life of congregations and larger church bodies. May this
gathering be one small step toward a more vigorous partnership in
sharing the good news of justification in Jesus Christ.

The Significance of the Joint Declaration on the Doctrine of Justification and the Next Steps in Ecumenical Dialogue

Margaret O'Gara

I have been in Augsburg, Germany, only once, but it was a trip that was important for me. I went on a personal pilgrimage to Augsburg in the pouring rain one mid-October day in 1999 so that I could visit the Church of Santa Anna, where the Joint Declaration on the Doctrine of Justification would soon be signed two weeks later.[1] I would be celebrating that event at another place, at Gettysburg Seminary in Pennsylvania during a special conference to mark the Joint Declaration. But I wanted to visit Augsburg myself in order to pray in thanksgiving for this great step of convergence and reconciliation between Roman Catholics and Lutherans, a step that Pope John Paul II called a "milestone" in our path toward healing the divisions within the Church of Christ.

It is not necessary to review the steps that led, on 31 October 1999, to the signing of the Joint Declaration on the Doctrine of Justification, in which at the world level the Roman Catholic Church and the Lutheran World Federation expressed a basic consensus on the doctrine of justification and said that the condemnations of the sixteenth century on this doctrine no longer apply to our ecumenical partner today. I remain convinced that the Joint Declaration represents a significant step in the dialogue between Roman Catholics and Lutherans,

---

1. Lutheran World Federation and the Roman Catholic Church, *Joint Declaration on the Doctrine of Justification* (Grand Rapids and Cambridge, U.K.: Eerdmans, 2000).

with implications as well for our many other partners in the ecumenical movement. With the Joint Declaration, the two church communions not only reached a consensus on a central doctrinal teaching that was formerly thought to be church-dividing, but they also acted on its implications, formally signing and declaring together the meaning of this consensus. I have also been struck with the liturgical celebration of the Joint Declaration at many gatherings for worship. When people start praying in gratitude for a step of reconciliation between our two church communions, it seems like another significant sign of reception of the ecumenical movement.

But not everyone was pleased with the Joint Declaration on the Doctrine of Justification. Both before and after the signing in Augsburg, a small but persistent group of people, both Roman Catholics and Lutherans, continued to criticize the Joint Declaration for what it said, what it did not say, and the procedures by which all of this had been said or not said. They remind me somewhat of the farmer who was taken to the zoo to see a giraffe. He looked at the giraffe for a while; then he shook his head firmly and said, "I don't believe it." Some critics simply shake their heads at the Joint Declaration and conclude they don't believe it, either.

What don't they believe? I think that their criticisms fall roughly into two categories, and in this presentation I want to address each of these categories. First, some critics seem to think that a consensus on justification could never be reached between Roman Catholics and Lutherans because Roman Catholic and Lutheran teachings were, and continue to remain, radically contradictory. Second, other critics believe that a consensus on justification is possible in principle, but that the Joint Declaration has not in fact achieved this consensus because the deep differences between Roman Catholic and Lutheran teachings on certain points have not in fact been resolved.

Let me address each of these kinds of criticisms.

Making the first criticism, some people seem to think that a consensus on issues that have been church-dividing between Roman Catholics and Lutherans is simply impossible. This was undoubtedly the viewpoint of some, though not all, of the theologians from Germany who campaigned against the Joint Declaration during the last stages of its preparation. From an entirely different kind of source, this criticism comes as well from the English feminist theologian Daphne Hampson, who argues that the two systems of thought are radically contradictory to each other, like a whale and an elephant. While the Joint Declaration claims "to express what is essentially the same truth in different ways," she writes, "sometimes it is very difficult to see how this can be said to be the case."[2] She wonders, given the differences between Lutheran and Roman Catholic teaching, "whether something meaningful can be said in common."[3] Reflecting on this position, Bruce Marshall observes, "Opponents of the agreement . . . often seem to suppose that 'consensus' — at least when it comes to Lutheran-Catholic dialogue — requires virtual uniformity of concept and formulation."[4] In fact, he continues, even when Lutherans and Roman Catholics say the same thing, "objectors suspect that they have not in fact succeeded in agreeing."[5] This reminds me of the description offered by Karl Rahner of the neurotic fear that we may be in agreement.

As a Roman Catholic, I find this first kind of criticism quite surprising, since Roman Catholics are convinced that it is possible to express our common faith in different ways. In his famous opening address to the Second Vatican Council, Pope John XXIII distinguished between "the substance of the ancient doctrine of the deposit of faith" and "the way in which it is presented."[6] In 1973, the Congregation for the Doctrine of the Faith taught, in *Mysterium ecclesiae,* that sometimes a dogmatic truth at first expressed incompletely might later be given a "fuller and more perfect expression."[7] In fact, the Congregation believed that the meaning in dogmatic formulations cannot change but that the formulations of this meaning might need to be changed or adapted to new times and cultures precisely in order to clarify and deepen the original meaning.[8]

With this last point, the Congregation mirrors the insight of the

---

2. Daphne Hampson, "Whales and Elephants," *The Tablet* 255 (31 March 2001): 446.

3. Hampson, "Whales and Elephants," p. 447.

4. Bruce Marshall, "The Argument Is Over," *The Tablet* 255 (7 April 2001): 481.

5. Marshall, "The Argument Is Over," p. 481.

6. John XXIII, "Opening Speech to the [Second Vatican] Council," in *The Documents of Vatican II,* ed. Walter M. Abbott (New York: America Press, 1966), p. 715.

7. Congregation for the Doctrine of the Faith, "*Mysterium ecclesiae,*" *The Tablet* 227 (14 July 1973): 667.

8. "*Mysterium ecclesiae,*" p. 668.

Second Vatican Council, which taught that the Church can grow in its understanding "of the realities and the words which have been handed down" from the apostles.[9] The Council explains this growth in understanding by using the analogy of a conversation, in which God continues to converse with the Church over the centuries. So, it explains, "the Church constantly moves forward toward the fullness of divine truth until the words of God reach their complete fulfillment in her."[10] Roman Catholics have sometimes called this process the development of dogma, but I think it is more helpful to speak of the development or growth — not of dogma — but of understanding. It is we who grow, not the dogmas. Karl Rahner reminds Roman Catholics that they too can use the term *sola scriptura,* can speak of the Scriptures as the unnormed norm, the *norma non normata,* since "no later dogmas are independent of Scripture and not subordinated to it." He continues, ". . . everything in the later utterances of faith must be measured by Scripture *(sola Scriptura),* since it is in Scripture that the one whole apostolic faith has been objectivated and has given itself, and laid down for all future times. . . ."[11]

So Roman Catholics believe that we can express the same faith in different ways but that these different ways sometimes represent a growth, an enrichment, that allows new facets of the mystery of our faith to be seen and received within the Church. In fact, I think that Lutherans would agree here with Roman Catholics in seeing the great conciliar definitions of the early centuries of the Church as consonant with the Scriptures, not adding to the truth given in the Scriptures. But, as Roman Catholics and Anglicans in dialogue together have expressed it, the great conciliar definitions were not simply repeating the words of the Scriptures, they were "also both delving into their deeper significance and unravelling their implications for Christian belief and practice."[12] I think Lutherans and Roman Catholics today share a re-

9. Vatican II, *Dei verbum,* in *The Documents of Vatican II,* ed. Walter M. Abbott (New York: America Press, 1966), #8.

10. *Dei verbum,* #8.

11. Karl Rahner, "Scripture and Tradition," in *Sacramentum Mundi,* vol. 6 (New York: Herder and Herder, 1970), p. 56.

12. Anglican–Roman Catholic International Commission [ARCIC], "Elucidation: Authority in the Church I," *The Final Report* (London: SPCK and Catholic Truth Society, 1982), #2.

newed esteem for the way that the early conciliar definitions were a translation and defense of the gospel in new cultural settings.

When they think about this process today, Roman Catholics relate it to the ongoing work of evangelization within the many cultures of the world. Precisely in order to proclaim and defend the gospel in every culture, the Church again and again finds that it must translate the gospel's meaning so that the gospel can be understood and received by its hearers. Is it any wonder that, as the Church strives to follow the Lord's Great Commission to make disciples of all nations, it seeks again and again, under the guidance of the Holy Spirit, "undiscovered riches and truths" in the Scriptures "in order to illuminate the faith according to the needs of each generation"?[13] Theologians call this "inculturation," but the story of Pentecost already gives us the image of expressing the same faith in different ways, when "in our own languages we hear them speaking about God's deeds of power" (Acts 2:11).

Let me summarize my two points here. As a Roman Catholic, I regard it as a basic part of Christian faith that it is possible to express our common faith in different ways. How could we go and make disciples of all nations if we could not express the gospel's meaning in a variety of cultures and times? And from this another point follows: as we move through time and expand into all the cultures of the world, the Holy Spirit sometimes helps the Church to grow in its understanding of the gospel, discovering new rich aspects it had never noticed until faced with a new situation for proclamation.

Now I think that these insights are both important for ecumenical dialogue. First, I think that sustained, patient dialogue among Christians of different church traditions sometimes manifests that they have expressed the same faith in different ways. While each proclaims the same Lord, they have found different formulations to speak of him. In fact, says Karl Rahner, ecumenical dialogue presupposes this insight. Ecumenical dialogue among Christians presupposes, he notes, that the same faith can be expressed in many different formulations and that Christians, in dialogue, may sometimes discover that their different formulations proclaim the same faith.[14] But my second in-

---

13. "Elucidation: Authority in the Church I,"#2.

14. Karl Rahner, "Some Problems in Contemporary Ecumenism," *Theological Investigations*, vol. 14, trans. David Bourke (New York: Seabury, 1976), pp. 248-51.

sight also applies to ecumenical dialogue. While proclaiming the gospel through the centuries, different Christian traditions have also grown in their understanding of it, discovering new rich aspects not noticed in earlier periods or former cultures. Often we have thought these different rich aspects of the gospel were contradictory. But sustained, patient dialogue among Christians sometimes discovers that these differences are not contradictory but complementary, not church-dividing but enriching, in fact an opportunity for an exchange of gifts.

The Joint Declaration illustrates both of these insights. First, it claims that Lutherans and Roman Catholics confess the same faith about justification although in different ways, because it claims a consensus on basic truths of the doctrine of justification. Finding new common language, it asserts: "Together we confess: By grace alone, in faith in Christ's saving work and not because of any merit on our part, we are accepted by God and receive the Holy Spirit, who renews our hearts while equipping and calling us to good works."[15] Furthermore, it teaches that the condemnations of the sixteenth century no longer apply to each other's teaching on justification today. And second, the Joint Declaration shows that we have each grown in our understanding of justification, developing distinctive rich emphases in our explications of the doctrine. It lists all seven areas of these differences. For example, while Lutherans emphasize that God's justifying grace does not depend on its life-renewing effects in us, Roman Catholics emphasize the transforming effects of this grace. While Roman Catholics emphasize the responsibility of persons for their actions, Lutherans emphasize that our righteousness is always complete since it is a sharing in the righteousness of Christ. But these differences in explication, the Joint Declaration teaches, "are no longer the occasion for doctrinal condemnations."[16] Since we can see divisive questions and the condemnations in a new light, Lutherans and Roman Catholics can find in each other's emphases a difference that is real but need not be church-dividing. In short, through the Joint Declaration, Roman Catholics and Lutherans found that they could confess a common faith about the

15. Lutheran World Federation and the Roman Catholic Church, *Joint Declaration on the Doctrine of Justification*, #15.
16. *Joint Declaration on the Doctrine of Justification*, #5.

doctrine of justification and could therefore now see their differences as enriching, not church-dividing.

The significance of the Joint Declaration for the imperative to proclaim the gospel in every culture became clearer to me when I participated in a recent conference on the interpretation of justification for our time. Sponsored by the Lutheran World Federation, the conference brought participants from five continents to Wartburg Theological Seminary in Iowa to discuss the meaning of the doctrine of justification in different cultural contexts. In that setting, the achievement of a differentiated consensus between Lutherans and Roman Catholics in the Joint Declaration was used as the model for the conference's whole project of interpretation within the Lutheran world family, as well as a pattern for the direction of the next steps in the mutual reconciliation among Christian communions. Explaining this approach, one group of conference participants wrote, "The Joint Declaration . . . states the common core of the doctrine to which all agree, and then describes the ways the two traditions accent and interpret that common core and take into account the concerns of the other tradition. The differences in theology, language and accents are understood as complementary and not as excluding one another. The truth of our fundamental doctrine includes more diversity than either of our traditions has thought in the past."[17]

When I speak of confessing a common faith but in different ways, do I mean that our words or convictions do not matter, that ecumenism means a kind of relativism? This is in no way my meaning. I agree with Pope John Paul II in his encyclical on ecumenism when he warns us against such relativism, teaching that ecumenical dialogue must avoid "all forms of reductionism or facile 'agreement'" in our dialogue. But if we find that we have different doctrinal formulations, he continues, we must "determine whether the words involved say the same thing."[18] As an example, he points to recent agreements over Christology between Roman Catholics and the Eastern Orthodox. Ecumenical dialogue, he explains, "makes surprising discoveries possible. Intolerant polemics and controversies have made incompatible asser-

17. "Justification Today: The Hermeneutical Challenge," unpublished report of the hermeneutics working group at the conference "Justification Today: Its Meaning and Implications," sponsored by the Lutheran World Federation at Wartburg Theological Seminary, Dubuque, Iowa, 13-18 April 2002.

18. John Paul II, *Ut Unum Sint*, in *Origins* 25 (1995):49, 51-72; see #38.

tions out of what was really the result of two different ways of looking at the same reality." So, he explains, "one of the advantages of ecumenism is that it helps Christian Communities to discover the unfathomable riches of the truth."[19] This is very different from relativism. Hence, he concludes in this encyclical that "authentic ecumenism is a gift at the service of truth."[20]

I have been discussing the first criticism of the Joint Declaration. Now let me turn to the second one. Some people argue that, although the Joint Declaration could in principle have reached a real agreement on justification, in fact it failed to achieve such an agreement. Or, put more gently, although the consensus in the Joint Declaration shows that our differences are no longer church-dividing, the different perspectives of Lutherans and Roman Catholics on several issues show that "problems . . . still remain," to cite Avery Dulles.[21] Further, Dulles concludes, "it would be too much to claim that the inveterate disagreements between Lutherans and Catholics on justification have been overcome."[22] I want to respond to this second kind of criticism, and I will focus on the issue most frequently targeted with this complaint, the teaching on *simul iustus et peccator*.

First, remember the context for the discussion of *simul iustus et peccator* in the sixteenth century. Otto Hermann Pesch notes the real fear, evidenced in the Lutheran Confessions, that "the medieval scholastic theologians and their adherents" were underestimating the power of sin,[23] a power that continues even in the baptized. The word "inclination" to sin seemed to the Reformers a pale reflection of the havoc this power could wreak even among the baptized unless they were never considered apart from Christ; and so the Reformers taught *simul iustus et peccator*. On the other hand, Pesch continues, the bishops of Trent "feared that Lutheran doctrine could weaken ethical endeavour."[24] Mistakenly thinking that the Reformers equated faith with mere intellectual

19. *Ut Unum Sint*, #38.
20. *Ut Unum Sint*, #38.
21. Avery Dulles, "Justification: The Joint Declaration," *Josephinum Journal of Theology* 9, no. 1 (2002): 111.
22. Dulles, "Justification: The Joint Declaration," p. 118.
23. Otto Hermann Pesch, "Amazing Grace," *The Tablet* 255 (14 April 2001): 532.
24. Pesch, "Amazing Grace," p. 532.

assent, the bishops at Trent "underlined the necessity of doing good works" and the power of God's transforming grace given to accomplish them, and so emphasized sanctification and renewal of the inner person by grace.[25] In short, says Pesch, the sixteenth century presented "a new pastoral situation in which one side" had "reason to fear laziness and laxity about sin, and the other side to fear laziness and distrust about grace."[26] But ecumenists, Pesch argues, must "respect the concerns, the anxieties and pastoral sorrows of both sides."[27] Because the Joint Declaration achieved such respect and followed its implications, the partners involved have succeeded in achieving a real agreement, Pesch concludes. Dulles, however, notes that Roman Catholics still do not call concupiscence "sin," although he believes that the "traditional disagreements" on *simul iustus et peccator* "have been significantly narrowed" by the Joint Declaration.[28]

While the Joint Declaration made it clear that, on *simul iustus et peccator,* a common confession could be shared while different emphases remained, the official Vatican response to the proposed Joint Declaration seemed to call a sudden halt to the anticipated celebration of agreement. On 25 June 1998, this response declared in its first section that there is a consensus on justification and said that the Catholic Church was ready to go forward to a signing of the proposed Joint Declaration.[29] Yet it also added that it could not yet speak of a consensus such as would eliminate every difference between Catholics and Lutherans on justification. In its second section — misleadingly called "Clarifications" — the Vatican response said that difficulties remain that prevent the affirmation of total consensus: "it remains difficult to see how in the current state of the presentation given in the joint declaration, we can say that this doctrine on *simul iustus et peccator* is not touched by the anathemas of the Tridentine decree on original sin and justification."[30] The "Clarifications" sec-

---

25. Pesch, "Amazing Grace," p. 532.

26. Pesch, "Amazing Grace," p. 533.

27. Pesch, "Amazing Grace," p. 533.

28. Dulles, "Justification: The Joint Declaration," p. 113.

29. Vatican, "Official Catholic Response to Joint Declaration," *Origins* 28 (1998-99): 13-32; see "Declaration."

30. Vatican, "Official Catholic Response to Joint Declaration"; see "Clarifications," #1.

tion of the Vatican document named a few other areas needing further elaboration and even raised a question about the authority of the consensus reached by the Lutheran World Federation. At the same time, it said, the Roman Catholic Church is ready to sign the document.

The Lutheran World Federation felt very upset by this Vatican response. I can see why: one Lutheran told me it was as though he were ready to start down the aisle with his chosen bride to make their wedding vows, and suddenly his betrothed turned to him and said that she had a different understanding of "'til death do us part" than he did! At least it would seem as though maybe the wedding should be postponed for an interlude of reflection and discussion. And that, of course, is exactly what happened. The plans for signing the Joint Declaration were put on hold, and a year of intense negotiation and discussion began.

I do not wish to defend this Vatican written response. I think it was a badly written document, confusing and inwardly inconsistent. Even for Roman Catholics — familiar with the system used by this document, with a first declaratory section and then a longer second section listing issues for future work — even for Roman Catholics, the document was contradictory and embarrassing. And it was even stranger that such a document would be presented to our Lutheran dialogue partners: it was as though the Vatican were speaking in code, a code difficult to follow for even experienced Roman Catholic theologians but simply inscrutable for others. At the meeting of the Lutheran–Roman Catholic International Commission on Unity, it was interesting that no Roman Catholic tried to defend this document. Several called for a new document to be written that would clarify the Vatican's confusing response.

I think the consternation caused by this Vatican document was especially painful for the German Lutherans favoring the Joint Declaration, such as the staff at the Ecumenical Institute in Strasbourg. Despite many *ad hominem* attacks leveled against them, they had spent a year defending the Joint Declaration and insisting on the good intentions of the Vatican. Now, after this exhausting year of controversy for supporters of the Joint Declaration, the Vatican was fulfilling their worst fears and acting just as badly as attackers of the Joint Declaration had been predicting all year. With friends like this, it must have seemed to Lutherans supporting the Joint Declaration, who needs enemies?

I will not rehearse in detail all the steps of that year: the letter of Joseph Ratzinger that appeared in the *Frankfurter Allgemeine Zeitung* underlining his support of the consensus reached by the Joint Declaration;[31] the follow-up letter from Edward Cassidy of the Pontifical Council for Promoting Christian Unity reaffirming the difference between the two sections of the Vatican Response and expressing his eagerness to go forward to a signing;[32] the informal meeting of Ratzinger with two German bishops and a few consultants in Regensburg, exploring the possibility of a new short document that would reassure both sides that the Declaration could be signed with integrity; the series of meetings and drafting sessions between the Vatican and the Lutheran World Federation that led finally to a resolution of the confusing hesitations. More important than reviewing the details of these steps, we should rather be asking two theological questions: What does this mean for the agreement on *simul iustus et peccator?* And what does it mean for future ecumenical work?

What was the concern of the Vatican in raising its question about the *simul iustus et peccator?* Was it a disagreement about whether baptized believers have a disordered desire even after baptism? No, the Joint Declaration had made clear that Lutherans and Roman Catholics both agreed with this. Was it to question the description of the consequences of this desire? No, both had agreed without controversy that "the power of sin" is "still pressing its attacks."[33] They had also agreed that the justified cannot rely on themselves but "must all through life constantly look to God's unconditional justifying grace."[34] And finally they had agreed that such constant looking to God takes the form of daily prayer for forgiveness, continual conversion, and penance. David Yeago points out that none of these common affirmations was questioned by the Vatican response. Instead, the Vatican was probably uneasy about the *simul iustus et peccator* because it feared Lutherans were

31. Joseph Ratzinger to the Editor, *Frankfurter Allgemeine Zeitung,* 11 July 1998.

32. Edward Cassidy to Ishmael Noko, 30 July 1998.

33. Lutheran World Federation and the Roman Catholic Church, *Joint Declaration on the Doctrine of Justification,* #28.

34. *Joint Declaration on the Doctrine of Justification,* #28.

somehow denying that justification brings about — as the Council of Trent had said — a real "renewal and sanctification of the inner man."[35]

In the Roman Catholic theological tradition on which the Vatican response draws, Roman Catholics find it more familiar to say that sin "properly speaking" is taken away by baptism.[36] They know that an inclination toward sin remains, but "they do not see this inclination as sin in an authentic sense."[37] But they recognize an inclination toward sin remaining in the baptized person, and they call this inclination "concupiscence."[38]

Of course the Lutherans had already acknowledged the point on inner renewal earlier in the Joint Declaration, noting that the Holy Spirit "renews our hearts while equipping and calling us to good works."[39] This is common Lutheran teaching, and is affirmed again when the Joint Declaration notes that God's forgiving action and the imparting of new life in Christ happen "at the same time."[40] But when Lutherans speak of *simul iustus et peccator*, the Declaration explains, they want to emphasize that we have no claim at all on God's favor and love, but depend on God's mercy.[41] Looking at themselves through the law, the justified recognize that they remain sinners, even though now their sin is "ruled" by Christ.[42] Furthermore, Lutherans wish to emphasize the gravity of the daily struggle in which the justified find themselves, and they wish to highlight how only Christ's saving work keeps the justified from being separated from God.

These points were already in the Joint Declaration. The *simul iustus et peccator* was presented as a Lutheran emphasis, not contradicting the concerns of the Catholic tradition. But through the further discussions of

35. David Yeago, "On Interpreting the 'Response of the Catholic Church to the Joint Declaration of the Catholic Church and the Lutheran World Federation on the Doctrine of Justification,'" unpublished background paper for Lutheran–Roman Catholic International Commission on Unity, 1998.

36. Vatican, "Official Catholic Response to Joint Declaration," "Clarifications," #1.

37. *Joint Declaration on the Doctrine of Justification*, #30.

38. Vatican, "Official Catholic Response to Joint Declaration," "Clarifications," #1; cf. *Joint Declaration on the Doctrine of Justification*, #30.

39. *Joint Declaration on the Doctrine of Justification*, #15.

40. *Joint Declaration on the Doctrine of Justification*, #22.

41. Yeago, "On Interpreting the 'Response of the Catholic Church,'" p. 6.

42. *Joint Declaration on the Doctrine of Justification*, #29.

the extra final year, I think that the Lutheran tradition was able to offer its Roman Catholic dialogue partner a deeper gift of understanding.

Does the doctrinal teaching expressed by the Council of Trent summarize the whole of the Roman Catholic tradition on sin and the justified? Of course not. Roman Catholics also read the scriptural texts cited in the "Annex" to the Joint Declaration.[43] They also have this prayer in their weekly or daily Eucharist: "O Lord, I am not worthy to receive you, but only say the word and I shall be healed." They also have a heritage of saints and spiritual writers who think, not in the categories of the Council of Trent, but in the categories of prayer or biblical theology that were also the more familiar style of writing for Luther. Otto Hermann Pesch speaks of Luther's style here as more existential, rather than the sapiential style of Thomas Aquinas,[44] whose distinctions and categories on sin and grace Trent distantly echoes. During the discussions of the long year of waiting, what I think happened is that the Roman Catholic Church, after a period of repentance and conversion, was also able to see the *simul iustus et peccator* "in a new light."[45] It was able to receive this tradition — a truly Lutheran tradition, yet not unrecognizable to Roman Catholics — it was able to receive this tradition as its own. I would say: this was a gift worth waiting for. Even more now at this difficult time, when the Roman Catholic Church in the United States has struggled deeply over the problem of sin among the baptized in the sexual abuse crisis, recognition of the depths of this tradition of *simul iustus et peccator* might have a special value for Roman Catholics.

Hence in the "Annex" statement that accompanied the final signing of the Joint Declaration, something new has been learned about *simul iustus et peccator*, and it has been learned by the Roman Catholic partner. In the "Annex," the two partners together recall a series of biblical texts that underline our continuing sinfulness. The "Annex" observes, "Yet we would be wrong were we to say that we are without sin,

---

43. *Joint Declaration on the Doctrine of Justification*, "Annex to the Official Common Statement," #2A.

44. Otto Herman Pesch, "Existential and Sapiential Theology — the Theological Confrontation between Luther and Thomas Aquinas," in *Catholic Scholars Dialogue with Luther*, ed. Jared Wicks (Chicago: Loyola University Press, 1970), pp. 182-93.

45. *Joint Declaration on the Doctrine of Justification*, #7.

which we learn from 1 John 1:8-10," and notes the words of Psalm 19, "'Cleanse me of many secret faults.'" We must pray, like the tax collector, "God, be merciful to me, a sinner" (Luke 18:13). Both of our liturgies contain such exhortations, notes the "Annex,"[46] and of course our mystical traditions of spirituality contain it as well. Thérèse of Lisieux felt herself to be the greatest sinner, as have other holy saints before her. Eastern Catholics confess themselves to be the greatest sinner each time they prepare to receive communion. The "Annex" notes that both Lutherans and Roman Catholics hear the exhortation, "Therefore, do not let sin exercise dominion in your mortal bodies, to make you obey their passions" (Rom. 6:12). The "Annex" comments, "This recalls to us the persisting danger that comes from the power of sin and its action in Christians." And then it adds this interesting sentence: "To this extent, Lutherans and Catholics can together understand the Christian as *simul iustus et peccator,* despite their different approaches to this subject as expressed in J[ustification] D[eclaration] nos. 29-30."[47]

What has happened here? While the Joint Declaration has presented the *simul iustus et peccator* as a Lutheran emphasis, in the "Annex" the two partners together are able to recognize it as a common heritage. In other words, the Lutheran tradition has finally been successful in offering its partner a gift earlier refused: the recognition of the *simul iustus et peccator* as truly expressing the mystery of the power of evil and the triumph of grace daily in our lives. Again I say: this was a gift worth waiting for. In the "Annex," the Roman Catholic Church in a surprising way is able to affirm this tradition as, not merely acceptable, but somehow its own.

I think it is ironic that a breakthrough on sin should be at the heart of the misunderstandings and negotiations between Lutherans and Roman Catholics. In many ways, the reactions of our two communions show how real the *simul iustus et peccator* is, not only in our personal lives but also in the lives of our two communions. While each of our communions wants to move toward the unity that Christ wills, we seem to be making the journey with reluctance, fear, and frequent trips back in the opposite direction as well as with new hearts and new minds. I mentioned earlier Karl Rahner's description of the neurotic

---

46. *Joint Declaration on the Doctrine of Justification,* "Annex," #2A.
47. *Joint Declaration on the Doctrine of Justification,* "Annex," #2A.

fear that we may be in agreement. Sometimes it seems easier to feel such neurotic fear and to look eagerly for another barrier to erect, another objection to cite, that will slow down the steps toward unity. This, I believe, is the part of sin among the baptized from which we must repent. In his encyclical on ecumenism, John Paul II says that the Second Vatican Council called for both personal conversion and communal conversion to the unity of the Church.[48] The cantankerous and fearful reactions of both our churches to each other during our year of waiting demonstrated to me how deeply our repentance must go before we are ready for an exchange of gifts. Before the gifts, we must have the repentance. And both, as we now confess together, are the work of the grace won by Christ.

It is time to conclude. In this presentation, I have wished to speak in grateful support of the achievement of the Joint Declaration, which I have done in two parts. First, in response to criticisms that it is not possible to express the common faith in different ways, I have argued to the contrary that this possibility is a basic conviction of Roman Catholics and implicit at least among all Christians who believe in evangelization. Second, in response to criticism that Lutherans and Roman Catholics could have reached agreement but in fact failed to do so when they signed the Joint Declaration in 1999, I have argued to the contrary that especially on the sensitive issue of *simul iustus et peccator,* the Joint Declaration with its "Annex" reveals a surprising retrieval of this insight by the Roman Catholic Church from its own liturgical, biblical, and spiritual traditions, a retrieval made possible by its patient and fraternal dialogue with Lutherans.

In closing, I offer both Lutherans and Roman Catholics the challenge presented by Bruce Marshall, a Lutheran who underlines the significance of the Joint Declaration on the Doctrine of Justification. Addressing Lutherans, he says, "Rome's acceptance of . . . [our predecessors'] teaching [on justification] forces us to decide whether we will go on seeking new ways to disagree about justification, so that this separation may endure, or whether we will do our part to end it."[49] In my judgment, this is a decision that faces us all.

---

48. John Paul II, *Ut Unum Sint,* #15.
49. Bruce Marshall, "The Argument Is Over," *The Tablet* 255 (7 April 2001): 481.

Continuing the Conversation: Deeper Agreement on Justification as Criterion and on the Christian as *simul iustus et peccator*

Michael Root

Can we move beyond the Joint Declaration on the Doctrine of Justification (JDDJ)[1] and what would it mean to do so? For some, these are the wrong questions. They believe that the JDDJ already goes too far, claiming a greater degree of agreement than actually exists, or they claim that the JDDJ in fact doesn't go anywhere at all and is only "a public relations document."[2] I believe, however, that we can move beyond the JDDJ in two senses. First, we can move beyond the debate over its acceptance and gain a certain critical distance. The JDDJ is not a perfect text, but I would hope we could recognize its flaws and limitations without calling into question that which the text embodies: a consensus in basic truths of the doctrine of justification sufficient to say that remaining differences need not be communion-hindering or church-dividing.

1. The official English translation of the JDDJ is in The Lutheran World Federation and The Roman Catholic Church, *Joint Declaration on the Doctrine of Justification* (Grand Rapids: Eerdmans, 2000). It has been widely reprinted, however, and all references to it will be by paragraph number.
2. J. A. Nestingen, "Anti-JDDJ: Visions and Realities," *dialog* 39 (2000): 140.

Portions of this essay appeared in "Beyond the Joint Declaration on the Doctrine of Justification: The Shape of Continuing Discussion on Justification," in *Kirche in ökumenischer Perspektive: Kardinal Walter Kasper zum 70. Geburtstag*, ed. P. Walter, K. Krämer, and G. Augustin (Freiburg: Herder, 2003), pp. 354-67. I have preserved some of the style of the original oral presentation.

We can also move beyond the JDDJ in another sense. The JDDJ was never intended to be the end of theological debate about how best to understand our justification in Christ. The ratifications by each of the two churches included calls for further discussion of certain difficult points of the doctrine of justification. The ratifying resolution of the Council of the Lutheran World Federation noted "the need for further common investigation . . . of the controverted topics within the doctrine of justification that arose during the reception process."[3] The Vatican Response of June 1998, while superseded by the affirmation in June 1999 of the Official Common Statement with its Annex, nevertheless indicated points at which at least some Catholics have difficulties with the JDDJ. We need to move beyond the JDDJ in order to examine the nature and significance of remaining misunderstandings or disagreements.

In this contribution, I will look all too briefly at two issues often mentioned as requiring further discussion: the doctrine of justification as criterion of Christian speech and practice, and the Christian as justified and a sinner at the same time, *simul iustus et peccator*. In each case, my argument will be the same. I do not believe that major substantive differences stand between Lutherans and Catholics (or, more broadly, between Protestants and Catholics) in relation to either topic. I believe the issues are far more ones of mutual understanding and of ecumenical outlook and perspective. Much depends on how one approaches the questions at hand.

How do we go about discussing and assessing ecumenical proposals and texts? Do we simply compare the JDDJ with what we understand to be the position of our own tradition (or, even more narrowly, with the language of our tradition), without allowing new proposals to supplement or even to call into some question at least the fullness of understanding in our own tradition or the language of our own tradition? Do we simply engage in an exercise in comparative doctrine, with our own traditions as immovable benchmarks? Comparison with the received doctrinal documents of our traditions is a necessary moment in any evaluation, but if it is the last word, then the ecumenical enterprise is simply hopeless.

---

3. Lutheran World Federation, *Our Continuing Journey: Documentation from the 1998 Meeting of the Council of the Lutheran World Federation*, LWF Documentation 43 (Geneva: Lutheran World Federation, 1998), p. 157.

Can we face the possibility, raised more broadly, but not with direct application to the doctrine of justification, by Ephraim Radner in his disturbing book *The End of the Church,* that the division of the Western church has led to a deep and general impoverishment of all Western traditions?[4] Are all discussions of justification since the Reformation distorted and one-sided, deformed by the way in which Christian identity has come to be understood in an essentially contrastive way? To be a Lutheran is not to be a Roman Catholic, and so Catholic elements are consciously avoided, even at the cost of a true and full picture of the gospel.

A significant limitation of the JDDJ is that it does not explicitly call either tradition to a serious re-examination of how it has thought about justification. The closest it comes to such a call is the statement that the condemnations of the past "remain for us 'salutary warnings' to which we must attend in our teaching and practice" (§42). That rather neglected statement means that each tradition remains committed not only to the condemnations within its own documents, but is now committed even more, I would say, to attending to the condemnations of the other tradition as warnings about how its own assertions can be misunderstood or misapplied. Are Catholics willing to hear Lutheran condemnations originally directed at what were understood to be Catholic teachings as at least warnings about how Catholic teachings have been heard by non-Catholics and thus warnings about how they can be misunderstood? In their recent textbook on the Lutheran Confessions, Günther Gassmann and Scott Hendrix note: "As soon as evangelical pastors stepped into the pulpit, they began to complain that people misunderstood justification by faith to mean they no longer had to repent, obey the Commandments, or do good works. To prevent this misunderstanding is a main goal of the confessions, and this goal influences to a large extent how they speak about the Christian life."[5] Even if Lutherans believe that Catholic criticisms have often been based on a misunderstanding of Lutheran language and concerns, can we take these criticisms to heart at least as indicating signifi-

---

4. E. Radner, *The End of the Church: A Pneumatology of Christian Division in the West* (Grand Rapids: Eerdmans, 1998).

5. G. Gassmann and S. Hendrix, *Fortress Introduction to the Lutheran Confessions* (Minneapolis: Fortress, 1999), p. 173.

cant problems of communication, problems we have experienced within our own churches? Can Lutherans hear a salutary warning even in the condemnations of Trent related to merit (canons 26 and 32)? Is there here a salutary warning to Lutherans not to neglect the reality toward which the concept of merit is meant to point, the "holiness without which no one will see the Lord (Heb. 12:14)," the fit that will exist between eschatological perfection and the Kingdom of Heaven? Lutherans may still want to say (as I would) that the term "merit" is so open to misunderstanding, even so suggestive of misunderstanding, that it creates more problems than it solves — a claim advanced by the Catholic theologian Otto Hermann Pesch.[6] But in light of the sort of Lutheran difficulties attested by Hendrix and Gassmann, we Lutherans should be a bit charitable in our assessments of others. A test of the true reception of the JDDJ will be whether Lutherans and Catholics will be able to hear salutary warnings in the condemnations embedded in the doctrinal texts of the other.[7]

We will have moved beyond the JDDJ when we are able to move beyond the Declaration's tendency to accept each tradition simply as it stands, to engage in a merely comparative approach. The need to move beyond such comparative approaches is not a matter merely of ecumenical goodwill, nor even a matter simply of the pursuit of church unity, as important as such a pursuit is. It is even more fundamentally a matter of the pursuit of the truth, most specifically, of the truth of the gospel. Precisely in relation to the question of truth, we perhaps come to an ecumenical crossroads. Is the truth most often found in a sharp contrast of opposing views, a contrast embodied in divided church traditions, in traditions in fact defined by division? Or is truth more often found in a dialectic that seeks to comprehend varying viewpoints, not denying their specificity, but also not allowing them to become self-enclosed, isolated wholes? I said that here was *perhaps* an ecumenical crossroads, for in fact truth is *perhaps* best

6. O. H. Pesch, "The Canons of the Tridentine Decree on Justification: To Whom Did They Apply? To Whom Do They Apply Today?" in *Justification by Faith: Do the Sixteenth Century Condemnations Still Apply?* ed. K. Lehmann, trans. M. Root and W. G. Rusch (New York: Continuum, 1997), p. 198.

7. I have explored this question further in relation to merit in "Aquinas, Merit, and Reformation Theology after the Joint Declaration on the Doctrine of Justification," *Modern Theology* 20 (2004): 5-22.

served by different approaches at different times. In relation to the questions of justification now before us, however, I believe the apprehension of the truth is best served by a perspective that tries to transcend earlier oppositions. Let me try to illustrate, if not demonstrate, this belief in relation to the two issues earlier mentioned: the criteriological role of justification and the Christian as *simul iustus et peccator*.

Justification as Criterion

In paragraph 18 of the JDDJ, Catholics and Lutherans agree that "The doctrine of justification . . . is more than just one part of Christian doctrine. It stands in an essential relation to all truths of faith, which are to be seen as internally related to each other. It is an indispensable criterion which constantly serves to orient all the teaching and practice of our churches to Christ." Agreement thus exists that the doctrine of justification is a criterion of the gospel that cannot be dispensed with, i.e., a criterion that is to be applied to any statement or practice. Any statement or practice that contradicts the doctrine of justification cannot claim to be Christian.

What appears to be a disagreement between Lutherans and Catholics immediately follows: "When Lutherans emphasize the unique significance of this criterion, they do not deny the interrelation and significance of all truths of faith. When Catholics see themselves as bound by several criteria, they do not deny the special function of the message of justification." This sentence articulates what each side wants to emphasize in this context: the Lutheran insistence on the unique role of justification and the Catholic insistence that justification is one of a number of criteria of Christian belief and practice. Note that these two assertions are not, taken at face value, mutually exclusive; they need not express a true disagreement. One could hold them both to be true. To say that justification as a criterion has a unique significance is not to say that other criteria do not exist. I would myself affirm both the Lutheran and Catholic sides of this difference.

Do we have here a true incompatibility? How can that be in doubt, after the vehement debate on just this topic? The root of these questions lies in the striking lack of conceptual clarity that has permeated the debate about the doctrine of justification as a criterion. Lutheran claims about the criteriological status of the doctrine of justification have for the most part been so unclear that one cannot confidently decide what is at stake. If we are to move beyond the JDDJ on this topic and toward greater agreement, the first step must be greater conceptual precision on what is being debated.

Unclarity has reigned in three areas. First, a debate about the doctrine of justification as criterion requires some agreement on what range of topics are directly included within the doctrine of justification. What is in fact operating as a criterion? If this question is not clearly settled, we may be comparing apples and oranges. Unfortunately, justification often functions as an accordion concept, expanding and shrinking as the occasion demands. Lutherans have a tendency when called upon to defend their statements about the centrality of justification to begin with a specific definition of the article and then to expand it when pressed to include the entirety of soteriology. Eberhard Jüngel says, for example, "The Easter hymn summarizes it [justification] most powerfully and profoundly: If he had not risen, the world would have perished. If you have grasped that, you have grasped the doctrine of justification."[8] In light of this statement, does justification mean anything more specific than "Jesus saves"? Jüngel in another context states that God's word to Cain that he will place a mark upon Cain so that others will not kill him is "the first word of justification, the first text that deals with the justification of the sinner."[9] Here, justification seems to mean even something less than "Jesus saves." Heike Schmoll of the *Frankfurter Allgemeine*, recently awarded an honorary doctorate by the University of Tübingen, regularly summarizes the doctrine of justification as a general anthropological truth, without any reference to God's act in Christ.[10] Without some clear account of just what is meant by justification, arguments about the doctrine's function in theology will almost certainly go nowhere.

Second, the debates related to the JDDJ have tended to elide the

8. E. Jüngel, *Justification, the Heart of the Christian Faith: A Theological Study with an Ecumenical Purpose*, trans. J. F. Cayzer (Edinburgh: T&T Clark, 2001), p. 13.

9. Jüngel, *Justification*, p. 11.

10. Cf. the comment on Schmoll in J. Ratzinger, "The Augsburg Concord on Justification: How Far Does It Take Us?" *International Journal for the Study of the Christian Church* 2 (2002): 7-8.

notions of a criterion, an axiom, and a hermeneutical key or principle. A criterion is simply something used to distinguish some specific thing from other things. A ruler is a criterion of length; it distinguishes that which is a certain length from that which is not. The canon of the Bible distinguishes books that are scriptural from books that are not. To say that the doctrine of justification is a criterion is simply to say that it serves to distinguish one thing from another, usually the gospel or what is in accord with the gospel from that which is not gospel or not in accord with the gospel. A criterion is quite different from an axiom, a statement or principle from which other statements or principles might be derived. Sometimes, even if not often, justification is said to be an axiom from which all of theology derives. (Eilert Herms of the University of Tübingen, for example, explicitly makes this claim, and Dorothea Wendebourg of the same university sometimes seems to.)[11] More often, a criterion is confused with a hermeneutical key, i.e., some principle or statement that constitutes an interpretive perspective through which some reality is interpreted.

Justification could be a criterion without being a hermeneutical key. If justification is an indispensable criterion, then the evaluation of the possible Christian status of any assertion or practice should include a test for the consistency of that assertion or practice with the doctrine of justification. A theology could meet that criterion, however, while giving justification no particular hermeneutical or interpretive role at all. We may decide that the theology of Gregory of Nyssa passes the test of being compatible with a true doctrine of justification. It would be odd, however, to say that the doctrine of justification was hermeneutically important to Gregory, and an interpretation of Gregory that used justification as a central interpretative concept may be

---

11. "Es ist darauf zu insistieren, dass alle Einzelsätze der reformatorischen Theologie sich analytisch als Implikate *eines* Grundsatzes müssen verstehen lassen" (E. Herms, "Stellungnahme zum dritten Teil des Lima-Dokumentes 'Amt,'" *Kerygma und Dogma* 31 [1985]: 69). In this essay, this one "Grundsatz" seems to directly concern the Word-character of revelation more than it does the acceptance of the sinner by the righteous God. On at least one occasion, Dorothea Wendebourg comes close to describing the doctrine of justification as a sort of axiom from which all other teaching must be derived (D. Wendebourg, "'Kirche und Rechtfertigung': Ein Erlebnisbericht zu einem neueren ökumenischen Dokument," *Zeitschrift für Theologie und Kirche* 93 [1996]: 90).

appropriate for certain purposes, but it would be using categories foreign to Gregory's own theology. Nor, conversely, need a hermeneutical key necessarily be used as a criterion. Criteriological and hermeneutical roles may be interrelated, but they are quite different. (I would argue that a theology that contradicts a rightly understood doctrine of justification is to be rejected; but a theology may or may not use justification as a hermeneutical key or organizing principle.)[12]

Third, rarely is it made clear what sort of criterion the doctrine of justification is meant to be. Criteria come in various logical sorts: e.g., necessary criteria, sufficient criteria, and necessary and sufficient criteria. A necessary but not sufficient criterion would be a criterion needed to identify some particular thing, but not adequate by itself to identify that thing. For example, in race walking, there are two criteria that must be met if a competitor is judged to be walking rather than running: the constant contact criterion (one foot must always be in contact with the ground) and the straight leg criterion (quoting International Amateur Athletic Federation Rule 230.1, "The advancing leg shall be straightened (i.e., not bent at the knee) from the moment of first contact with the ground until the vertical upright position." Both criteria are necessary, but neither is sufficient. A sufficient criterion would be sufficient by itself to identify some thing, but may be one of a number of such criteria, no one of which is necessary. For example, two criteria are now internationally recognized as defining the distance of one meter — 1,650,763.73 wavelengths of the orange-red radiation of krypton 86 in a vacuum, or the distance traveled by light in a vacuum in $1/299{,}792{,}458$ seconds. Each is sufficient, so neither is necessary. A necessary and sufficient criterion would meet both conditions. Is the doctrine of justification as a criterion necessary, sufficient, both, or of some other logical sort? A debate over whether justification is "a" or "the" criterion in theology without any further elaboration of what sort of criterion is meant is simply pointless.

I believe that once greater conceptual clarity is achieved about just what is being claimed, the more extreme Lutheran claims about justification as a criterion will dissolve. By extreme claims I mean such statements from Eberhard Jüngel as: "The doctrine of justification is

---

12. It should perhaps be noted that the JDDJ itself in §18 tends to conflate the ideas of criterion and hermeneutical principle.

the one and only criterion for all theological statements,"[13] or, again from Jüngel, "It is only when explained by means of that doctrine [of justification] that Christology becomes a materially appropriate [*sachgemäß*] Christology at all [*überhaupt*]."[14] These sorts of claims simply cannot stand up to sustained analysis (or they mean something rather different than they appear to mean). They certainly do not represent the way the Reformers themselves argued theologically. Here I can merely assert without much supporting evidence my belief that in the end we will come around to the far more balanced view put forward by Karl Barth in *Church Dogmatics* IV/1: "The *articulus stantis et cadentis ecclesiae* is not the doctrine of justification as such, but its basis and culmination: the confession of Jesus Christ, in whom are hid all the treasures of wisdom and knowledge (Col 2:3); the knowledge of his being and activity for us and to us and with us."[15] Barth wrote this in criticism of an essay by Ernst Wolf on the doctrine of justification as the center and limit of Reformation theology. Barth's brief discussion strikes me as still the best discussion of the subject. I think Barth shows that there is no significant reason for Lutheran-Catholic or Protestant-Catholic division over the criteriological issue. In fact, I see no reason to dissent from the statement in the original Vatican response of June 1998: "the message of justification, according to Scripture and already from the time of the Fathers, has to be organically integrated into the fundamental criterion of the *regula fidei*, that is, the confession of the one God in three persons, christologically centered and rooted in the living Church and its sacramental life."[16]

All this is not to say that there is no theological issue buried here beneath a great deal of confusing discourse. I believe there is, and I believe it points to a cause of repeated misunderstandings between Lutherans and Catholics.

In his Heidelberg Disputation of 1518, Luther famously con-

---

13. E. Jüngel, "On the Doctrine of Justification," *International Journal of Systematic Theology* 1 (1999): 51.

14. Jüngel, *Justification*, p. 29; translation altered.

15. K. Barth, *Church Dogmatics* (Edinburgh: T. & T. Clark, 1956-1975), IV/1, p. 527.

16. Clarifications, 2. The text of this reply is still (in February 2005) present on the Vatican website at: http://www.vatican.va/roman_curia/pontifical_councils/chrstuni/documents/rc_pc_chrstuni_doc_01081998_off-answer-catholic_en.html.

trasted the theologian of the cross who "understands the visible and manifest [or posterior] things of God seen through suffering and the cross" with the theologian of glory who "looks upon the invisible things of God as though they were clearly perceptible in those things which have actually happened" (WA 1, 354; LW 31, 40).[17] Without going into the background or details of Luther's contrast, one can say, at a rather general level and a bit anachronistically, that Luther is here contrasting two approaches to theology: on the one hand, an approach that clings closely to the situation of the self still in the situation of dying and rising with Christ in this life and that views God strictly from this perspective, and, on the other hand, an approach that seeks to transcend that situation for a more objective and comprehensive view.

This contrast, removed from its polemical setting in Luther's argument, bears at least some similarity to the contrast between Luther and Aquinas developed by Otto Hermann Pesch in the late 1960s. Pesch contrasted Luther as an existential theologian with Aquinas as a sapiential theologian. In this contrast, existential theology "seeks to make thematic our very existence in faith," while in sapiential theology, "the act of faith does not itself play an immediate thematic role." A sapiential theology seeks "the understanding of reality in terms of its ultimate causes, as we learn in faith the very thoughts of God himself."[18] While I would not take over Pesch's analysis entirely, he is getting at an important contrast. I would argue that Luther's theology and much (but not all) Lutheran theology has generally sought to stay close to the first- and second-person discourse of proclamation and response: "You are redeemed in Christ"; "I place my entire trust in Christ." Even when it speaks in the third person, Lutheran theology tends to remain in a first-person perspective. Lutheran theology is often analogous to what literary critics call "free indirect style" in the novel, i.e., a third-person narrative that tends to be permeated by a particular first-person language and outlook — usually of some char-

17. References to writings by Martin Luther will be to the original in the Weimar Ausgabe (*Werke: Kritische Gesamtausgabe* [Weimar: Hermann Böhlaus Nachfolger, 1883-1983]); and the English translation in the American Edition (*Luther's Works* [St. Louis: Concordia; Philadelphia: Fortress, 1955-86]).

18. O. H. Pesch, 1970. "Existential and Sapiential Theology — The Theological Confrontation between Luther and Thomas Aquinas," in *Catholic Scholars Dialogue with Luther*, ed. J. Wicks (Chicago: Loyola University Press, 1970), pp. 73-74.

acter in the story.[19] For Luther, a test of a third-person theological statement is how it relates to first-person discourse *coram deo*. For example, in Luther's *Against Latomus,* the central topic of discussion is Luther's assertion that even the good works of the saints are sins. At crucial points, his defense is in terms of what is to be said before God:

> Let us take St. Paul or Peter as they pray, preach, or do some other good work. If it is a good work without sin and entirely faultless, they could stand with appropriate humility before God and speak in this fashion: "Lord God, behold this good work which I have done through the help of Thy grace. There is in it neither fault nor any sin, nor does it need Thy forgiving mercy. I do not ask for this, as I want Thee to judge it with Thy strictest and truest judgments. . . ." Latomus, doesn't this make you shudder and sweat? And yet it is certain that all this could, indeed should, be said by so just a man, for it is especially before God that truth ought to be spoken, nor ought one to lie because of God. (WA 8, 79; LW 32, 190)

Latomus's assertion that the good works of the saints are not also sins is rejected because it cannot be said in the first-person coram deo. This first-person focus contributes to the forcefulness of Luther's theology; it accounts for much of the evangelical power that many find in his writings. It does also, however, limit its scope; one does not find the systematic sweep or comprehensive vision more typical of a theologian such as Aquinas, especially in his two Summas. As Pesch emphasizes, Aquinas's theology is not neutral in relation to the gospel or the self's reception of the gospel, but it does seek a "way of doing theology from outside one's self-actuation in the existence in faith, in the sense that in its doctrinal statements the faith and confession of the speaker is the enduring presupposition, but is not thematic within this theology."[20]

Existential and sapiential modes of theology do not form mutually exclusive opposites, but are ends of a spectrum. How far and in what way does the first-person perspective of the person *coram deo* bleed into the third-person perspective typical of reflective theology?

19. W. Martin, *Recent Theories of Narrative* (Ithaca, N.Y.: Cornell University Press, 1986), pp. 138-39.

20. Pesch, "Existential and Sapiential Theology," p. 76.

A variety of options are available. I see no reason to insist that theology must always follow one option. There are topics and contexts in which one approach is more appropriate; others that may dictate a different approach. For example, Luther's theology is rhetorically powerful to a significant degree because of the skill with which a first-person perspective enters into third-person discourse. But at least some of the perennial problems of Lutheran theology are attributable to the difficulties that can arise from shifting perspectives. Lutheran theology often has some difficulty stating the role of faith in the justification of the self. Objectively, Lutherans have usually stated that the reception of grace, a faith that depends on God's gracious act in Christ and on the Spirit who now makes Christ present to us, is intrinsic to our justification. But in the first person, faith shows its utter dependence by saying nothing about itself but focusing on Christ. A reference in the first person by faith to itself runs the danger of saying I depend on grace and on my faith for my justification. No, faith is the form in which I depend entirely on God's grace. A faith that depends on itself is not true faith. In the first person, the role of faith is shown rather than asserted, while in a third-person description that role needs to be explicitly stated and described. When a shift from the first- to the third-person perspective occurs, the language must change.

If we are to move beyond the JDDJ's argument about the role of justification in theology, we need to develop a more binocular vision, an ability to look at the realities upon which theology is based from more than one perspective. The insistence of some Lutherans on the unique role of the doctrine of justification is related, I believe, to a sense that theology must never lose touch with its soteriological center in the death and resurrection of Jesus Christ. We relate to this soteriological center not just objectively as a matter for description. Even as theologians, we speak as persons who are dying and rising with Christ and who cannot simply transcend that situation. A greater attention to the ways third- and first-person discourse interrelate will, I believe, contribute to Catholic-Lutheran understanding.

Let me give an example. The *Catechism of the Catholic Church* has a series of paragraphs on justification, grace, and merit (1987-2011) that I would describe as giving a rather Augustinian reading of Trent. Because they are so close to the language of Trent, they often give my Lutheran students trouble. Strikingly, the section closes with the assertion that "the saints have always had a lively awareness that their merits were pure grace," and as illustration of this attitude, gives the following quotation from the Act of Oblation to Merciful Love of St. Thérèse of Lisieux, in which she addresses God:

> After earth's exile, I hope to go and enjoy you in the fatherland, but I do not want to lay up merits for heaven. I want to work for your *love alone*. . . . In the evening of this life, I shall appear before you with empty hands, for I do not ask you, Lord, to count my works. All our justice is blemished in your eyes. I wish, then, to be clothed in your own *justice* and to receive from your love the eternal possession of *yourself*.[21]

It is difficult to imagine a statement closer to a Lutheran outlook. One way of understanding a Lutheran theology of justification is that it is an attempt to state in a third-person form an understanding of our status before God that clings as closely as possible to the perspective expressed in a first-person statement such as that of Thérèse of Lisieux. One of the various ways forward beyond the JDDJ on the discussion of the role of the doctrine of justification in theology leads through a more careful consideration of how different modes of theology interrelate.

Simul Iustus et Peccator

It is, in one respect, not surprising that the question of the ongoing sinfulness of the justified person became a center of the debate surrounding the JDDJ. Lutherans and Catholics each find the language of the other simply perplexing. For Lutherans, it is simply strange to hear that Catholics would insist that a Christian at any time in this life ceases to be a sinner, a person who can stand before the righteous God only by appealing to the merit and mercy of Christ. For Catholics, it is strange to hear Lutherans say that a small infant, immediately after its baptism, is yet a sinner. On the technical issue involved in this question, whether concupiscence (or, as Lutherans might prefer to say, the ongoing resistance within the self to the grace of God, the old Adam

21. *Catechism of the Catholic Church*, 2nd ed. (Rome: Libreria Editrice Vaticana, 2000), para. 2011.

and Eve within each of us) is still sin within the justified person, the Lutheran and Catholic official documents seem to give diametrically opposed answers to precisely the same question and to solemnize their answers with condemnations.

In another respect, however, it is surprising that the *simul* proved so difficult. The earlier U.S. Lutheran-Catholic dialogue on *Justification by Faith* registered Catholic-Lutheran differences in this area, rooted in different concerns, but also noted that the traditional mutual accusations made on the basis of these differences are hard to sustain.[22] The German Catholic-Protestant (mostly Lutheran) study of *The Condemnations of the Reformation Era* also registered differences of language and concern here, but saw no fundamental difficulties.[23] When I talked with Wayne Stumme about my topic for this conference, I did not know that the German Ecumenical Study Group that produced the condemnations study had, following the debate over the JDDJ, taken up precisely the question of the *simul*. Their study, published at the end of 2001, is by far the most voluminous study of the question in recent history. Again, they note clear differences of language and concern between Lutheran and Catholic theology, but find that, under closer examination, these differences are far less fundamental than meet the eye. They assert, in line with the JDDJ, a differentiated consensus on the *simul* sufficient for church fellowship, should other obstacles be overcome. As the Study Group rhetorically asks: "How great is the actual difference between a conception in which the concupiscence present in the baptized is really sin, but does not separate one from Christ, so long as one does not let sin rule, and a conception in which concupiscence, *because* it does not separate the baptized from Christ, is *only* a tendency to sin and only becomes really sin, i.e., only separates from Christ, when one consents to it?"[24] Any argument that the question of the ongoing sinfulness or non-sinfulness of the justi-

22. *Justification by Faith*, ed. H. G. Anderson, T. A. Murphy, and J. Burgess, Lutherans and Catholics in Dialogue, vol. 7 (Minneapolis: Augsburg, 1985), pp. 51-52.

23. K. Lehmann and W. Pannenberg, eds., *The Condemnations of the Reformation Era: Do They Still Divide?* trans. M. Kohl (Minneapolis: Fortress, 1989), pp. 44-46.

24. T. Schneider and G. Wenz, eds., *Gerecht und Sünder zugleich? Ökumenische Klärungen*, Dialog der Kirchen, vol. 11 (Freiburg: Herder, 2001), p. 439.

fied person represents a serious theological obstacle will need to deal with the scholarship and conclusions of this study.

As the Catholic response of June 1998 makes clear, the decisive problem in this area is the paradoxical sound of the Lutheran claim. What does it mean to say that the justified person is simultaneously a sinner and yet justified? Is the efficacy of baptism being denied? Is justification being reduced to a mere counterfactual, "as if" reality? I believe many problems can be solved by returning to the text in which Luther discussed the *simul* in the most detail, his *Against Latomus* of 1521. This work should be the touchstone, I believe, of a Lutheran understanding of the sense in which the justified person is and is not a sinner. Jacob Latomus, of the University of Louvain, had attacked Luther for asserting that even the good works of the saints are sins. Luther's defense is thorough (in the way that only Luther could be thorough).

Crucial to Luther's explanation is the distinction between grace and gift, a distinction he draws as early as the Romans commentary of 1515-16 and as late as the Licentiate Examination of Heinrich Schmedenstede in 1542. (Lutheran theology has been weakened by its lack of systematic attention to this distinction.) As sin leads to a double evil, the wrath of God externally and the corruption of the self internally, so justification, Luther says in 1542, has two "parts" (WA 39, 202; LW 34, 320): grace, which is "an outward good, God's favor, the opposite of wrath," and gift, which "heals the corruption of nature" (WA 8, 106; LW 32, 227). Sometimes Luther refers to Christ or the Holy Spirit as themselves the gift, in that they are given to us so that they come and dwell in us. On other occasions, he refers to faith, the human act that grasps Christ and the Spirit even while being moved by Christ and the Spirit, as the gift. (Thus, the grace/gift distinction is not identical to the created/uncreated grace distinction.) Justification involves both the favor or grace of God as a reality in God, forgiving me my sins, and the gift of Christ and the Spirit, received in faith, mediating that favor of God. In *Against Latomus,* Luther interrelates grace and gift in complex ways. Usually, he stresses the priority of grace to gift, of the divine favor to our reception and transformation. Nevertheless, he can also say that "a person neither pleases nor has grace, except on account of the gift which labors in this way to cleanse from sin" (WA 8, 107; LW 32, 229).

In relation to the grace/gift distinction, Luther elaborates two different senses of the *simul.* The grace of God, like the wrath of God, relates to the total person. "He who is under wrath is wholly under the whole of wrath, while he who is under grace is wholly under the whole of grace, because wrath and grace have to do with persons" (WA 8, 107; LW 32, 228). If I am justified and under God's favor, then I must be totally under that favor. There is no other possibility. In relation to God's grace and wrath, one is either wholly justified or not justified at all.

Internally, I am not wholly transformed but am, Luther says, using a standard Augustinian simile, like the injured man in Jesus' parable of the Good Samaritan, who has been lifted up but is still in need of healing. "This man was not healed all at once, but was raised up all at once in order to be cured. . . . So also John [13:10], 'He who is bathed is clean all over,' namely, through grace; and yet it is through active faith that the feet, that is, the remaining sins, are cleansed" (WA 8, 109; LW 32, 232). While externally, in relation to God's judgment, the justified person is wholly justified, internally, the self is still divided between the new self, constituted by faith and the indwelling Christ, and the old self, still resisting. These two realities are not related statically or equally; even internally the justified is not equally just and a sinner. While sin earlier ruled the self, it is now ruled by the new self: "So also we, having been called into the kingdom of faith by the grace of baptism, gain the rule over sin, for all its powers are smitten. Now only grumbling remnants, possessing the nature and character of what was destroyed, remain in the members" (WA 8, 89; LW 32, 203). Nevertheless, Luther insists, both on biblical grounds and pastoral grounds, that which remains is sin. Sin is what is opposed to God's law. God's law is that I am to love God with all my heart, mind, and strength. If I struggle with the remains of sin within me, even if I struggle successfully, then I am of a divided heart, mind, and strength and so do not fulfill the law of God. "The rigor of the divine law can demand that this conflict not be in us, for as the wise man says, God did not in the beginning create us thus: 'God made man upright, but they have sought out many devices' [Eccles. 7:29]. We are hampered by evil so that we are not wholly within his law, and a part of us which fights against us is opposed to his law" (WA 8, 95; LW 32, 212). Thus, to the degree that the old self is not extinguished and may be present in all of my actions, all of my actions are partially just, in that they are shaped by faith and partially sinful, in that they are shaped by the old self. Internally, anthropologically, I am partially just and partially a sinner.

But note: if sin infects all of my actions, even those works that Luther is willing to celebrate as truly good works, works in which the remaining sin in the self is dominated by faith and Christ, then it follows that were it not for the grace of God in Christ by which I am wholly justified, I would be wholly damned, judged by God as a whole person to be a sinner, for the law demands an undivided heart, mind, and strength and I do not fulfill that law. I am totally, as a whole, justified in Christ, but would be totally, as a whole, judged a sinner outside of Christ. The sense in which I am, internally, partially just and partially a sinner closely interrelates with the sense in which I am, externally, in relation to God's judgment, totally justified and totally a sinner. Note, however, that what is hypothetical, ultimately counterfactual, in relation to God is not the "totally justified," which is real in Christ and the Spirit, but the "totally sinner." The sinner would be judged sinful as whole were it not the case that the sinner is justified in Christ. In *Against Latomus,* the *simul,* in both its total and partial versions, is tilted toward the "justified" side of the pair.[25]

The *simul* as presented in *Against Latomus* avoids the problems that have concerned many Catholic (and Reformed) critics of Lutheranism. The *simul* here is not a static dialectic, in which the new righteousness and the old self simply sit side by side. As Karl Barth (and, for that matter, Eberhard Jüngel) emphasizes, we are always moving away from sin and toward our justification in Christ. The remaining ecumenical difficulty is simply whether the term "sin" is or is not rightly applied to the resistance of the self to grace and gift even in the justified.

Let me make two comments on this issue. First, it is difficult to imagine how this rather technical, terminological difference can be church-dividing or communion-hindering. As the Catholic Luther scholar Erwin Iserloh said in an excellent study of Luther's *Against*

---

25. My analysis here is close to the excellent recent essay by David Yeago ("Martin Luther on Renewal and Sanctification: Simul Iustus et Peccator Revisited," in *Sapere teologico e unità della fede: Studi in onore del Prof. Jared Wicks,* ed. C. Aparicio Valls, C. Dotolo, and G. Pasquale [Rome: Editrice Pontificia Università Gregoriana, 2004], pp. 655-74), which I read only after my own essay was written. Yeago does not, however, stress the counterfactual character of the "totally sinful."

Latomus: "If we look away from the theological formulation and toward the intended subject matter, the controverted theological differences become in many ways insignificant and in any case far fewer than the impression given by the polemical language.[26]

Second, is the term "sin" a univocal term, with a single "true and proper sense," or is it an analogous term, with a variety of interrelated senses, some of which may be true and proper in some contexts, while others are more prominent and definitive in others? Luther does in fact assert at one point in *Against Latomus* that the term "'sin' is used in Scripture in a single very simple way, not in many different ones: "Sin is simply that which is not in accord with God's law" (WA 8, 83; LW 32, 195). As Iserloh notes, however, Luther goes on to make a variety of distinctions between kinds of sin (e.g., Luther explicitly affirms the distinction between mortal and venial sins; WA 8, 96; LW 32, 213) and makes sharp distinctions between sin ruling and ruled over. Sin ruled over is "sin without wrath, sin without the law, dead sin, harmless sin" (WA 8, 107; LW 32, 229). Luther is willing to say that, in a sense, the sin that remains in the justified is not really sin: "So also there is here genuine sin, even though the whole man is not destroyed, condemned and subject to wrath, for grace and the gift preserve a man so that he cannot sin, that is, he does not consent to sin and perish" (WA 8, 120; LW 32, 247). In one sentence, Luther combines his own typical position with that of Trent. Later he says more straightforwardly: "Because of grace and the gift, sin is no longer sin" (WA 8, 126; LW 32, 257).

In Scripture, the final source and norm of Christian theology, does sin have a single sense or a range or family of senses? If, as I suspect, the latter is true, then might Lutherans and Catholics achieve a richer understanding of the nature of the justified and their relation to sin by noting the varying senses in which concupiscence or the remaining resistance of the self to grace, Christ, and the Spirit is and is not sin?

26. E. Iserloh, "Gratia und Donum, Rechtfertigung und Heiligung nach Luthers Schrift 'Wider den Löwener Theologen Latomus' (1521)," *Catholica* 24 (1970): 83.

Conclusion

I have addressed only two topics and these all too briefly. There are other topics within the doctrine of justification that call for additional attention. I believe that Cardinal Dulles in his essay in this collection has put his finger on the most difficult topic: the nature of the self's involvement in its own conversion to grace. Does the self cooperate? Paragraphs 19-21 of the JDDJ, which address this question, are sufficient for their purpose, which is to show that a sufficient degree of consensus exists to declare the relevant condemnations inapplicable. Significant issues nevertheless remain.

In addressing the issue of the self's involvement in and cooperation or non-cooperation with its own conversion and justification, we should remember how difficult these issues have been internally for each of our traditions. Augustine and Aquinas are notoriously difficult on this topic and each significantly changed his mind during his career. In the century after the Reformation, Catholic theologians were bitterly divided by the *de auxiliis* controversy; the Luther Confessions moved away from Luther's position in his *Bondage of the Will*, but American Lutheranism was still divided in the nineteenth century by the debate over faith as the basis for or consequence of election;[27] and the Reformed have struggled with Arminianism and the heritage of the Synod of Dort. We must not demand more consensus with others than we have achieved within our own traditions.

On these issues — those that I have discussed and those such as that of cooperation — can we move beyond the JDDJ? Most importantly, I would ask, Can we move beyond thinking of these questions primarily as Lutheran or Catholic or Reformed theologians? Can we think simply as theologians, or at least as theologians of the Augustinian, Western tradition that has formulated the problems we are addressing, drawing both on the resources of our own sub-traditions and on the resources of others? Is it reasonable to seek an understanding of justification that is true to the deepest insights and convictions of both Luther and the Fathers of the Councils of Trent, both of John Calvin and Cardinal Cajetan? I believe that is now the only way forward, the

27. T. Tappert, *Lutheran Confessional Theology in America 1840-1880* (New York: Oxford University Press, 1972), pp. 139-226.

only path that will lead us to the center of the doctrines of grace, for-giveness, justification, and sanctification so that we may adequately and accurately proclaim the message these doctrines explicate. I don't deny that such a project would send the historical Luther, Calvin, and Cajetan spinning in their graves, but I hope it would find the support of Luther, Calvin, and Cajetan as they now rest together in glory.

The Divinity of God:
A Curse for Us

Michael E. Tassler

10 For all who rely on the works of the law are under a curse; for it is written, "Cursed is everyone who does not observe and obey all the things written in the book of the law." 11 Now it is evident that no one is justified before God by the law; for "The one who is righteous will live by faith." 12 But the law does not rest on faith; on the contrary, "Whoever does the works of the law will live by them." 13 Christ redeemed us from the curse of the law by becoming a curse for us — for it is written, "Cursed is everyone who hangs on a tree" — 14 in order that in Christ Jesus the blessing of Abraham might come to the Gentiles, so that we might receive the promise of the Spirit through faith.

GALATIANS 3:10-14

Grace unto you and peace from God our Father and the Lord Jesus Christ. Amen.

Dear friends in Christ, the theme of our Theology for Mission Conference, "The Gospel of Justification in Christ," could very well serve as a subtitle to Paul's letter to the Galatians, this most passionate and feisty of his epistles. For that indeed is Paul's theme, too: the good news that God, apart from the law, has chosen to justify sinners through Jesus Christ, and in that act create a whole new world, inaugurate a new age, and fashion a new humanity in which ethnic, social,

and gender distinctions no longer mean insider versus outsider, supe-
rior versus inferior, and privileged versus disadvantaged. In Galatians
Paul contends anew for the Torah-free gospel he proclaimed to the
churches of Galatia, and expresses astonishment that some have
turned so quickly to a pseudo-gospel which threatens to enslave them
to that from which they had been set free by and in Christ.

Paul's gospel in Galatians, as in Romans, is most certainly "apart
from the law." One of the most perplexing and complex features of
Galatians is Paul's teaching about the Mosaic Law. While he asserts in
Galatians that the law is not opposed to the purposes of God, one cannot help but sense the seemingly pejorative status Paul assigns to the
law. For example, he grants it a temporary role. The law, says Paul,
came four hundred thirty years after the promise and lasted until
Christ. Paul grants the law a largely suppressive role. The law served
as a jailor and guard until, as he says, "faith was revealed" (3:23). The
law functioned like a disciplinarian for children until Christ came
(3:24). By way of analogy Paul even connects the Mosaic Law with the
"elemental spirits" to which human beings were enslaved until Christ
came. Yet, on the other hand, says Paul, as a result of the coming of
Christ and of his death upon the cross, the law can now be summarized by the commandment, "You shall love your neighbor as yourself." Paul speaks of the meaning of the law for the Christian community in terms related to Christ, of bearing one another's burdens as
fulfilling the law of Christ.

It might appear, then, that with regard to the law, Paul is speaking out of both sides of his mouth. What's the deal with the law? In
point of fact, Paul argues that something crucial has happened in the
history of the law to change its status. And that something is what our
lesson announces: in order to redeem us, Christ has taken the curse of
the law upon himself. More than that, he himself *became* a curse for us.
There is no chance here that Paul is speaking out of both sides of his
mouth. Christ's becoming a curse for us originates from the very heart
of a faithfully true and consistent God. As God's Son, Christ has entered our situation, "born of a woman, born under the law," in order to
set us free from enslavement to the law. Because of sin, the law took on
this kind of disciplinary and distorted and nearly grotesque function
of accusing and cursing.

As an aside, I mentioned previously that Paul calls the law a "disciplinarian" for children. That term "disciplinarian" is a technical term in Paul's day for a family servant who had authority over a child, to lead and guide and guard a child. I know there are many people in this room who know exactly what this means, that the law functioned as a disciplinarian. For anyone who has spent even a little time teaching confirmation to seventh and eighth graders knows exactly what it's like to become accusing and cursing! You can't recognize yourself with these people!

But very seriously, in Christ's death for us, in his assuming the position of the accursed, the cursing voice of the law has been silenced. And most profoundly, the law has been fulfilled in his death as an act of divine, total, and self-giving love. With the curse removed, the law is restored to the function of being in accord with the promises of God.

Our lesson today is part of an argument in which Paul makes the claim that the true descendants of Abraham are people of faith, and not people defined by "works of the law." Why does Paul take up Abraham? It may be that he has in mind the agitators of the Galatians he opposes so vigorously. It may be that these teachers had drawn heavily upon the figure of Abraham in asserting their claim — and this is what infuriates Paul — that circumcision was necessary for Christians. According to Genesis 17:9-14, circumcision was established with Abraham. A terrible threat faced those who were not circumcised: "Any uncircumcised male who is not circumcised in the flesh of his foreskin shall be cut off from his people; he has broken my covenant" (17:14). This is the point the new teachers visiting Galatia insisted upon and against which Paul had to argue.

In the verses immediately preceding our section, Paul has initiated a scriptural counter-argument. He cites Genesis 15:6: "Abraham believed God, and it was reckoned to him as righteousness." The true children of Abraham, therefore, are people of faith — specifically, people of faith in Christ Jesus, people wrapped up in the faithfulness of Christ himself by believing in him. *These* are the fruits of the promise to Abraham, that in him "all the Gentiles shall be blessed."

But now Paul goes on the offensive. He asserts that those who rely upon the works of the law are under a curse. In alleged support of this, he cites Deuteronomy 27:26, which says, amazingly, "Cursed is everyone who *does not* observe and obey all the things written in the book of the law." Well, which is it? Cursed if you go the way of the law, according to Paul. Cursed if you don't, according to Deuteronomy! On the surface, this passage from Deuteronomy says the exact opposite of what Paul claims it says. All kinds of theories have been proposed in the history of biblical interpretation to explain what Paul is up to. A traditional one — at least in churches of the Reformation — is to emphasize the word "all" and provide the unstated assumption that the law is impossible to keep. And so the curse of the law falls upon those who do not keep the law in its entirety. Is this really what Paul is saying? It runs contrary to the fact that the law itself provided a means of forgiveness of transgressions, and it counters Paul's own claim in his letter to the Philippians that he was blameless in matters of the law.

No, not the transgression of the law, but the law itself, the way of the law, brings a curse. What Paul means when he says that those who rely upon the works of the law are under a curse has to do with material I mentioned before, namely Paul's description of the temporary, suppressive, and confining function of the law. It is *this* that makes the law an agent of cursing. The commentator Charles Cousar writes that what lay at the heart of the law in its suppressive capacity was the

> division of the world into law and not-law, into Jew and Gentile, into circumcision and uncircumcision. Thus the Gentiles did not escape the law's curse. They were not under the law in precisely the same way that Jews were; nevertheless, they were "under the curse" in that they were kept from the promises of God. They were excluded, isolated by the wall the law erected and victims of the antinomies it created."[1]

For Paul, the Mosaic Law is powerless to deliver the promise.

Paul now juxtaposes two more Old Testament texts that pose a contradiction for him. He cites Habakkuk 2:4: "The one who is righteous will live by faith." To Paul this is self-evident, given his belief in the priority of promise to the law. He wants to prove that the keeping of the law in no way rests on faith, so he calls upon another text that also promises life, but on the basis of keeping the law. Leviticus 18:5 reads, "Whoever does the works of the law shall live by them." For

1. Charles B. Cousar, *Galatians, Philippians, and 1 Thessalonians: A Literary and Theological Commentary* (Macon, Ga.: Smyth & Helwys, 2001), p. 60.

Paul, these two paths offering life simply oppose each other. Is there a contradiction in God? Is there a way out of this conundrum?

What indeed *does* deliver life, what renders the curse of the law void and null, is now stated: "Christ redeemed us from the curse of the law by becoming a curse for us." Paul cites yet another Old Testament text, Deuteronomy 21:23, by which he links the manner of Jesus' death on the cross with the law's condemnation of those hanged on a tree ("Cursed is anyone who hangs on a tree"). This, then, is the full force of the cursing law at work: the death of Jesus. It is the final proof that the law kills and does not give life.

Paul engages in all of this rather complex and to us unfamiliar scriptural interpretation in order to show that in the death of Jesus, God has remained true to himself, true to his original intention of giving the promise through faith. J. Louis Martyn has masterfully summarized the core of Paul's Galatians message:

> The promissory blessing of God that had been waiting in the wings met the curse of the Law for the first time at the cross. As Paul hears Deut 21:23 (Gal 3:13), it was the Law, not God, that pronounced its curse on the crucified one, and the one thus cursed by the Law was in fact God's Christ. It was in the cross that Paul came to see a momentous fact about the Law: its cursing voice is not the voice of God. But he saw also that that voice was robbed of its power when, approved by God in his Law-cursed death, Christ embodied the Law's curse, for in that embodiment Christ vanquished that curse, freeing the whole of humanity from its power.[2]

We might think it enough if Paul had merely said, "he bore the weight of the curse for us." But Paul goes further, saying the extraordinary: that Christ *became* a curse for us. This is, indeed, what theology has called the wonderful exchange. It's the same swap that Paul speaks of in 2 Corinthians: "For our sake [God] made him to be sin who knew no sin, so that in him we might become the righteousness of God" (5:21). He became like us in our cursedness so that we might become like him in his blessedness. He became sin so that we might become righteousness. This is the driving purpose of God in Jesus Christ.

2. J. Louis Martyn, *Galatians: A New Translation with Introduction and Commentary*, The Anchor Bible (New York: Doubleday, 1997).

In the death of Jesus Christ, in his becoming human and becoming a curse for us, we see the divinity of God in its clearest and most gracious expression.

Those of us who are leaders in the church, as teachers and pastors, and as those preparing for this vocation here in the seminary, are called to recognize and apply this divine clarity and grace in our preaching, teaching, and care of others. We are called to identify those areas in life in which the particular burdens of sin weigh down the people within the sphere of our care and concern. If you are a parish pastor as I am, then you know — I don't have to tell you — that we encounter people who, each and every day, live cursed lives. Just last week there came to me an immigrant, homeless couple, the woman a full thirty-nine weeks pregnant. They hoped to establish an apartment home in the community our church shares, a community in which ground is broken every day with new home construction, so that the man could use his skills as a roofer. They were able to find money from social agencies that would pay a full month's rent for an apartment, but not a single agency, religious or secular, would supply the fifty-dollar application fee for an apartment. That same day I met an elderly man from Jerusalem who had made a living in the United States as a professional oud player. But a stroke has left him unable to play his instrument. His whole left side is numb. Could you imagine a worse curse that could afflict an oud player? Since he and his wife are now estranged, he lives hand to mouth trying to afford a room in the expensive sphere of life that is the Washington, D.C. area. I think of the single mother I know whose six-year-old daughter has had thirteen surgeries, and who suffers from a degenerative disease that will soon completely deafen her, and in all likelihood, blind her by early adolescence. Because Medicaid pays for the literally hundreds of thousands of dollars these surgeries have cost, its strict requirements mean the mother cannot get a job that would pay a decent salary, let alone provide insurance for herself.

Some of the circumstances of people such as these simply reflect the dismal pathos of human life. Yet many of these life-stories manifest continuing injustice in and our all-too-easy tolerance of structures in our society that continue to rob human beings of the blessings of life. Too many of us in the church live with the unchecked assumption that nothing will change, nothing can happen to change the landscape of the lives of the most vulnerable among us.

Watching the news this morning in St. Paul showed me, as it reported a further decline in the overall value of the stock market, that the bewailing attitudes about this current phenomenon, which has so many scared, are not found only in Washington or Wall Street. Now, I'm not saying that the betrayal of the trust of investors by the leaders of corporations is a small thing, but how pathetic, frankly, that the cry of outrage in the social mainstream was sounded only when such losses were perceived to threaten *my* easy vision of an early and carefree retirement. Of course, these losses spell trouble for those counting on these earnings, but the real victims are the tens of thousands of employees who have suddenly lost jobs due to the lying and greed of the advantaged classes. But beyond even this are the countless many who never have and never will reap any benefit from an economic system that excludes them in the first place.

As our Theology for Mission director Wayne Stumme has recently written, "The God who mercifully justifies sinners calls people to respond to that grace by seeking justice for the weakest and most threatened of their neighbors."[3] As leaders, teachers, and pastors of the church, we can, as Paul did in his day, sound an alert and speak with critical passion and feistiness when we see forces at work in the lives of people that oppose the freedom and access to the rich blessings of God that have been won for them in Jesus Christ.

It was Paul's call and it is ours today to announce that human beings have been set free: free from the ruling and false power of sin, free from all enslaving forces, and free for one another in Christ Jesus. At the end of Galatians, Paul says that neither circumcision nor uncircumcision is anything, but a new creation is everything. We bear witness to this new creation of God. It is our joy to announce that Christ has borne our curses — no, he has *become* our curses! Because he has, a new future has dawned in him. A new becoming is available to us and to all people. A new and hopeful world has opened in the midst of our old world, granting new and real possibilities for human beings.

This is the goodness and the divinity of God: a curse for us. Thanks be to God! Amen.

---

3. Wayne C. Stumme, "Workplace Justice and the Church," *Currents in Theology and Mission* 29, no. 2 (April 2002): 99.

Fides Christo Formata: Luther, Barth, and the Joint Declaration

George Hunsinger

Ecumenical agreement seems to become more and more elusive precisely as it becomes more successful. At least that is the paradoxical conclusion that might be drawn from the 1999 Catholic-Lutheran Joint Declaration on the Doctrine of Justification. Gratitude to God must surely be expressed, in the words of the Declaration, "for this decisive step forward on the way to overcoming" past divisions and for seeking to reflect a more visible unity. At the same time, however, perplexity must also be expressed. For the more the Joint Declaration is pondered, the more uncertain it becomes whether the unity made visible is real or largely verbal.

Ecumenical agreement is notoriously difficult to achieve. The problems are not merely substantive. The dialogue partners may well mean different things by the very same words, and yet the same things by very different words. Matters that are taken up at a particular point by one theological tradition may be dealt with at a different point by another. The urgent desire for unity may inspire unstable compromise, while the fear of compromise may ruin achievable unity. These are only a few of the dilemmas that need to be handled in a sensitive way. From his experience in ecumenical dialogue, Hans Küng concluded: "All human truth stands in the shadow of error. All error contains at least a grain of truth. What a true statement says is true; what it fails to say may also be true. What a false statement says is false; what it means but does not say may be true."[1]

The doctrine of justification by faith has not always been seen as a doctrine that is thoroughly eschatological. The relative neglect of eschatology has arguably hindered ecumenical dialogue from achieving full clarity in its analysis of justification. This essay will therefore take the form of a thought experiment about eschatology. It will propose that any doctrine of justification is somehow located within an overall eschatology of salvation. Certain persisting ecumenical differences can therefore be traced to differences in eschatology.

For the Catholic, justification belongs to an eschatology of salvation in the present tense *(in nobis)*; for the Protestant, to an eschatology of salvation in the perfect tense *(extra nos)*. For the Catholic, justification initiates a saving spiritual formation; for the Protestant, a saving spiritual participation. For the Catholic, faith is formed by love *(fides caritate formata)*; for the Protestant, by Christ alone *(fides Christo formata)*. Whether these two eschatologies — the one an eschatology of formation, the other an eschatology of participation; the one focused on Christ in us, the other on us in Christ; the one more gradual, the other more dialectical — are finally compatible will be considered more fully in conclusion.

The Roman Catholic View:
Justification as a Process of Formation

In any eschatology, salvation has three tenses. Everything depends on how the occurrence of salvation is seen to involve them: the perfect tense, the present tense, and the future tense. By the "perfect tense" I mean what Christ is thought to *have accomplished* for our salvation once for all in his life, death, and resurrection; by the "present tense," the way in which his accomplishment is brought to bear upon us *here and now*; and by the "future tense," the way in which our salvation as accomplished and present is expected to assume *a final and definitive form* at the end of all things. These three tenses provide the eschatological framework of salvation within which justification occurs.

The definitive Roman Catholic statement on justification is found

---

1. Hans Küng, *The Church* (New York: Sheed and Ward, 1967), p. 442.

in the Decree on Justification issued by the Council of Trent in 1547. Although later authoritative statements use different language and thought-forms, Trent contributed the basic shape of justification as understood by the Roman Catholic Church right down to the present day. An understanding of Trent on justification is essential background for interpreting the Catholic-Lutheran Joint Declaration.

Our thought experiment about eschatology gives us a set of diagnostic questions to ask. Although in Trent's Decree such questions are not explicit, implicit answers are not difficult to tease out. What does Trent presume about the three tenses of salvation when discussing justification?

When the question is posed in this way, the striking aspect is Trent's concentration on the present tense. The *perfect* tense seems to function primarily as the precondition for the occurrence of salvation in the *present*, even as the *future* tense is then primarily the final consummation of this present-tense occurrence. Trent is interested above all in how salvation occurs *in nobis* here and now. Justification is discussed within the framework of an eschatology that focuses on the present tense.

When Trent thinks of the perfect tense — of what God has done for our sakes in Jesus Christ with respect to justification — it speaks about Christ's passion, and particularly, about the "merit of his passion." Prepositional phrases beginning with the word "through" are used repeatedly, as in "through the merit of his passion" (*per meritum passionis eius*) (e.g., Ch. 3).[2] Through the merit acquired by Christ's passion, grace is imparted to us here and now, and this grace is specified as the "grace of justification."

In Trent's fullest statement about the perfect tense, which appears in Ch. 7, Jesus Christ is called justification's "meritorious cause." "The meritorious cause," states Trent, "is [God's] most beloved only-begotten, our Lord Jesus Christ, who, when we were enemies, for the exceeding charity wherewith he loved us, merited justification for us, by His most holy passion on the wood of the cross, and made satisfaction for us unto God the Father" (Schaff, p. 95). The perfect tense thus

---

2. "The Canons and Decrees of the Council of Trent," "Sixth Session: On Justification," in *The Creeds of Christendom*, ed. Philip Schaff, vol. 2 (Grand Rapids: Baker, 1983, 6th ed.), pp. 89-118, on p. 90. Hereafter cited in the text as "Schaff."

becomes the prerequisite for what goes on to occur in the present. Christ, by virtue of his cross, has three closely related functions. He is the meritorious cause, the source, and the precondition for the grace of justification as imparted here and now.

What then occurs in the present tense is essentially a process of spiritual formation. Justification, the name for this process, has a beginning, a middle, and an end. The middle, moreover, has its ups and downs. The process is not necessarily a smooth one. But barring some very grave breach, the imparted state of grace is secure enough to contain any lapses into sin. Lapses may be recovered from through the sacrament of penance, and in general growth and progress in justification can be expected. One can increase in the justification one has received through grace, and so become "still further justified" (Ch. 10). Just as grace is a kind of transforming power that enables justification to increase, so justification is a kind of holistic condition that depends not just on faith but also on hope and love. Justification begins when grace is imparted in baptism, and culminates after death at the Last Judgment, when we must all stand before the throne of Christ and give an account of our life on earth.

Eternal life is the future toward which justification moves here and now. Just as the merits of Christ are the precondition, the cause, and the source of justification, so in turn is justification the precondition, the cause, and the source of eternal life. With respect to the eschatology of salvation, we might therefore say that, just as the perfect tense is the precondition, the cause, and the source of the present, so in turn is the present tense the precondition, the cause, and the source of the future. What it is crucial to see is that the present, which receives from the perfect tense, is decisive in determining the future. Although what happens in the present does not contribute to what Christ has merited by his cross, it does indeed contribute to what a person will merit at the Last Judgment.

The present tense is the site of cooperation between divine grace and human freedom. Whether a person will merit eternal life at the Last Judgment depends significantly on the exercise of human freedom in the present. Justification as received initially through baptism is not sufficient in itself for eternal life. It must be preserved, recovered if lost, and increased in the course of time by divine grace in conjunction with human freedom.

Good works as performed with the assistance of grace, or as performed through divine grace by human freedom, thus contribute to both the fact and the quality of one's justification. Since justification is the precondition, the cause, and the source of eternal life, and since justification is either lost or preserved, in part, by human works, good works contribute, necessarily, to the gaining of eternal life. Good works merit both an increase of grace and the attainment of eternal life itself. Eternal life at the Last Judgment is at once the gift of grace and yet also a human achievement on the basis of what transpires in the present.

In short, justification may initially be given by grace alone, but it is not preserved, recovered, or increased by grace alone. Nor is it preserved, recovered, or increased by faith alone. Nor is it by Christ alone. It is preserved, recovered, and increased only in conjunction with human freedom. Therefore, only in a qualified and restricted sense can it be said that we are justified by faith without works.

Faith alone is clearly not sufficient for post-baptismal justification. If justification is to be preserved and increased, rather than actually lost, faith must be supplemented by love. In other words, if faith is not supplemented by love (and, as need arises, by penance), justification can in fact be lost. Eternal life, therefore, can also be lost. The distinctive Catholic eschatology of salvation in the present tense — as it draws from the perfect tense and moves toward eternal life — is an eschatology of faith formed necessarily by love *(fides caritate formata)*.

The Reformation View:
Justification as a Process of Participation

When we turn to how the Reformation saw justification and ask about salvation's three tenses, a very different pattern emerges. For the Reformation, the accent falls not on the present but on the perfect tense. The perfect tense does not just function as a prerequisite for salvation's occurrence in the present. It defines the content and reality of salvation as an indivisible whole.

Everything that Christ has accomplished apart from us becomes present to us here and now through Word and Sacrament. Word and Sacrament are not just the sources of spiritual formation. They are secondary and dependent forms of the one salvation that Christ has perfectly accomplished, or better, of the one salvation that he himself perfectly is. Word and Sacrament at once attest and yet also mediate, mediate and yet also attest, Christ himself in the perfection of his saving significance. His person is in his work, and his work is in his person. All that he has accomplished for our salvation and who he is for us here and now are one.

As Luther never tired of urging, Christ and Christ alone is our righteousness and our life. Our righteousness is his before it is ever ours, and it becomes ours only as it remains his *(iustitia aliena)*. In the same way, our life is his life alone, and becomes ours only as eternally his *(vita aliena)*. He is not just the external cause of our righteousness and our life. Nor is he the source of any righteousness or life that is not identical with himself. His righteousness and life in all their perfection — as grounded in his passion for our sakes — really become ours here and now. We do not receive the one without receiving the other — his righteousness without his life, or his life without his righteousness. They both at once become ours as he imparts himself to faith and incorporates us by grace into himself, and therefore into his body, the church. The gift and the giver are one, and he makes us one with himself, even as by his passion he has already made himself one with us.

Through Word and Sacrament, we might therefore say, the perfect tense is mediated into the present, and attested in the present for what it is. Through Word and Sacrament, the present tense comes to participate in the perfect tense even as the perfect tense gives itself to be known and received here and now. The perfect tense makes itself present, without ceasing to be what it is, and draws the present tense into itself. The perfect tense is, so to speak, the site where we find the original and constitutive form of Jesus Christ in the full perfection of his righteousness and life. By making himself manifest here and now in Word and Sacrament, which are the secondary and dependent forms of his one saving reality, he imparts himself in his perfection to faith, and through faith binds us to himself.

The relationship of the perfect tense to the present tense can thus be looked at from three vantage points: Christ, grace, and faith. By virtue of his resurrection from the dead, Christ is our contemporary here and how. He is present to us through Word and Sacrament. Through them he comes to us in his saving significance as he enacted it there and then. That saving significance can be summed up as his righteousness and his life. They were fulfilled by his cross and validated by his resurrection.

By grace he imparts them to us precisely by imparting himself. In other words, he imparts the full fruit of his saving work, as perfected there and then, by imparting his person. In the proclamation of the gospel, and supremely in bread and wine, he gives himself to be received here and now, and so to be known in the perfection of who he is.

His perfect self-giving, in these kerygmatic and sacramental forms, is acknowledged, received, and partaken of by faith. Faith is the appointed means by which we enter into union and communion with Christ. It is the unique act of apprehension by which the perfect tense is received in the present, and by which the present tense participates in what is perfect, that is, in the Christ of the perfect tense. Faith is thus the means by which we participate in all that he has accomplished for us, apart from us, and against us. It is what gives us access to the risen Christ, and so to his life-history of perfect obedience as fulfilled in his passion for our sakes.

Faith as participation, I would suggest, is the very heartbeat of the Reformation. It is the key to the doctrine of justification by faith alone. Although this aspect has not always enjoyed the prominence it deserves, it can be discerned very clearly, I think, in both Luther and Barth. In Luther we can arguably detect a certain priority for wedding metaphors over courtroom metaphors. Christ's relationship to the church is primarily that of bridegroom to bride, and only secondarily that of a Judge who somehow acquits the guilty.

In the union of bridegroom and bride — Luther's great metaphor for *participatio Christi* — the great exchange takes place. Christ the bridegroom takes our sin and death completely to himself, even as he imparts to his bride, the church, his perfect righteousness and life. When Luther is read in this way, we are not righteous because we are declared righteous. On the contrary, just the reverse. Because we are truly righteous, we are declared righteous by Christ the Judge. We have been made righteous precisely by virtue of our participation in him, and so by grace through faith. Through our *participatio Christi*, he imputes to us his righteousness and grants us a share in his life. The proper sequence, logically speaking, runs from participation to imputation to declaration, not the reverse.

Barth says much the same as Luther, only differently. His concept of *participatio Christi* emphasizes, if possible, the perfect-tense aspect even more strongly than we find in Luther, for whom it is nonetheless often explicit and always presupposed.[3]

When Barth writes of our justification before God, that Christ's history is as such our history,[4] he is thinking of *participatio Christi.* He is thinking of how we participate, in the present tense, precisely in what Christ has done for us in the perfect tense. He is thinking of our real participation here and now in what Christ perfectly accomplished there and then. Exactly like Luther, he believes that when Christ died, we died; that when Christ was buried, we were buried; and that when Christ rose again from the dead, we rose with him. It is precisely because Christ's history is, as such, our history that our sin is judged in him, that our right is established in him, that our death is put to death and our life is born in him, that we can regard ourselves as justified in his righteousness because it is our own righteousness, and that our faith is thus a real apprehension of our real being in Christ (IV/1, 636).

When we turn from the perfect tense to the future tense, we do not turn to an uncertain goal. We turn to a new form of the one salvation that is ours in Christ through faith. As Luther and Barth of course affirm, the future of this salvation will be definitive. "It will be the goal," writes Barth, "beyond which there is no need of any further

---

3. As Luther once said of Christ: "He has accomplished everything" (*Sermons of Martin Luther,* vol. 8, ed. J. N. Lenker [Grand Rapids: Baker, 1989], p. 154, italics added). This statement nicely brings out how the *totus*-aspect rests on the perfect-tense aspect in Luther's doctrine of justification. (Works from this series are hereafter cited as SML.) Compare also the following: "Christ's sole effort in the whole Gospel is to draw us out of ourselves *into himself.* . . . Christ alone has favor with God. No one but he *has done* the will of God and merited eternal life. In view of the fact that he did it not for his own sake but for ours, all believers should be so perfectly one with Christ that all he *has done* for them will, through him and through his grace, be regarded as if the believer himself had accomplished it" (SML, vol. 6, 164, italics added). These sentences bring out how our union with Christ by faith makes us one with his righteousness as accomplished in the perfect tense. Our being *in Christ* by Christ is the sole basis on which his righteousness becomes ours, so that our partaking of his merit is then the sole basis on which we receive the gift of eternal life.

4. Karl Barth, *Church Dogmatics* IV/1 (Edinburgh: T&T Clark, 1956), p. 548 (hereafter cited in the text as IV/1).

movement" (IV/1, 603). It will be eternal life in communion with God. It will be participation, through the mediation of Christ, in the eternal communion of the Holy Trinity. It will be a life of worship, adoration, service and praise, perpetual yet ever new.

Considered from the standpoint of justification, our eternal life will consist precisely in unveiling the righteousness that is already ours in this present life. "It will be this temporal life itself," writes Barth, "in the newness which is already ascribed to it in the judgment and sentence of God" (IV/1, 603). Without our ceasing to be creatures, our eternal life with God will mean, Barth avers, a new "kinship of being" (IV/1, 599), or as Luther sometimes put it, our "divinization." Either way, what is meant is not the loss of created human nature, but the conferring upon that nature of a new and glorious form. Divinization or kinship of being will be the final form given to our justification as God's gracious and miraculous act (IV/1, 601).

When we turn finally to the present tense, justification has a peculiar eschatological status. As seen by Luther and Barth, our justification here and now is real, hidden, and yet to come. It is real here and now because, in Luther's words, "Christ is our principal, complete, and perfect righteousness,"[5] and we are one with him. It is hidden because it cannot be discerned for what it is. "Nothing is lacking to a perfect realization," writes Luther, " — except that the veil whereby it is hidden, so long as we are in mortal flesh and blood, is yet to be removed" (SML, vol. 7, p. 228 trans. rev.). Finally, notwithstanding its reality, it is also the object of hope. "In Christ," writes Barth, "it is our future that cannot become the past" (IV/1, 558 rev.). Since our righteousness depends entirely on what Christ has done apart from us (*iustitia passiva/extra nos*),[6] we may await its final unveiling in the assurance of faith that trusts in the promises of God.

---

5. Martin Luther, *Luther's Works* (American Edition), vol. 27 (St. Louis: Concordia, 1964), p. 71. (Works from this edition are hereafter cited in the text as LW.)

6. Luther's understanding of "passive righteousness" needs to be correlated with his understanding of the significance of the perfect tense. Great confusion results when this correlation is overlooked. Our righteousness in Christ is "passive" because it *has been* constituted apart from us, namely, by Christ's earthly obedience as fulfilled in the cross. We do not add anything to it when we receive it in the present. The word *passive* does not pertain to the mode by which we receive it (as if it were simply imposed upon us), but rather to our status as agents with respect to

Yet because sin still clings to us so closely, we are more perfectly in Christ than he is in us. In and of ourselves we are still sinners even as we are righteous in him. The Reformation makes no strong distinction between "venial" and "mortal" sin. As Luther insisted and Barth agreed, all sin is mortal sin. Any sin, in itself, deserves the wrath of God and corrupts our works of love. Although, in some sense, we are partially righteous in ourselves here and now, "partial righteousness," notes Luther, "does not justify" (LW 34, 127).

Even our best works must therefore be justified by faith. We can only turn to God again and again with empty hands. As Luther said in his last recorded words, "We are beggars. That is the truth." As those who remain sinners, even after baptism, we find no merit in ourselves, nor can we acquire any, nor do we need any of our own. We have the merit of Christ, which is sufficient for us. The good works that we may do by divine grace neither contribute to, nor in any way constitute, our justification. They simply manifest it. How could our good works contribute anything to the perfect righteousness of Christ, which comes to us each morning anew as a sheer gift?

Grace comes only to lost sinners, Luther urged, but to them it really does come. It comes not so much more and more as again and again. In the time between the times, we are sinners and justified at the same time, *simul iustus et peccator,* at once totally sinful and yet also totally righteous before God *(totus/totus).* Our being sinners is the real presence of that which is essentially past. It is the persistence of our old fallen nature that has been crucified with Christ. At the same time *(simul),* our being as persons justified and righteous before God is the real presence of that which is essentially future. It is the real presence of our new humanity as risen with Christ, and hid with Christ in God (Col. 3:3).

Our life here and now is a constant turning from this past to this future, from the old to the new, from what we are in ourselves to what we are in Christ. It is daily repentance. It is dying and rising with Christ each day. It is daily baptism until the end. Nor is the *simul* merely a matter of equilibrium, for in Christ the future has triumphed, and contin-

---

bringing it into being. Our righteousness is passive in the sense that we receive it and participate in it without contributing to it or constituting it. It comes to us as a sheer gift, i.e., as *having already been* constituted in its perfection by Christ alone.

ues to triumph in our lives, despite our persistence in sin. Sin no longer has dominion over us because of our union with Christ by faith.

Finally, as Luther and Barth both affirm, faith does not need to be formed by love in order to be saving faith. It does not need to be formed by love, or in any way formed by our cooperation with grace, because faith from the very outset is already formed by Christ. *Fides Christo formata* is the Reformation's answer to the *fides caritate formata* of Trent.[7]

Because Christ is faith's content, reality, and object, writes Barth, Christ is "the One who forms it" (IV/1, 637). Luther concurs. "It is Christ," he writes, "who is the form of faith" (LW 26, 130). Faith is not, therefore, deficient "until love comes along to make it alive" (LW 26, 129). Certainly, faith needs love in order to be genuine. But it does not need love to preserve, recover, or increase the justification it freely receives, nor does it need it to merit eternal life. On the contrary, writes Luther, "the Christ who is grasped by faith, and who lives in the heart, is the true Christian righteousness on account of which God counts us righteous and grants us eternal life" (LW 26, 130). We have no righteousness but Christ himself and Christ alone. The Christ who is "our only righteousness" (LW 27, 148) is more than sufficient.

Studied Ambiguities: The Joint Declaration

If this thought experiment has been valid, then the differences between Catholicism and the Reformation, when it comes to justification, are primarily eschatological. The differences are not, as some

---

7. In Trent's "Decree on Justification," the idea is anathematized that we are made formally righteous by the righteousness of Christ itself (Canon 10). Both Calvin and Chemnitz regarded this as central to the controversy. In recent discussion Pesch has argued, without being wholly convincing, that Can. 10 does not touch the Reformation. See John Calvin, "Canons and Decrees of the Council of Trent, with the Antidote," in *Selected Works of John Calvin: Tracts and Letters,* vol. 3, ed. Henry Beveridge (Edinburgh: Calvin Translation Society, 1851/Grand Rapids: Baker, 1983), pp. 108-62; on pp. 118-19. Martin Chemnitz, *Examination of the Council of Trent,* part I, trans. Fred Kramer (St. Louis: Concordia, 1971), pp. 457-544; on p. 468. Otto Hermann Pesch, "The Canons of the Tridentine Decree on Justification: To Whom Do They Apply?" in *Justification by Faith: Do the Sixteenth-Century Condemnations Still Apply?,* ed. K. Lehmann, M. Root, and W. G. Rusch (New York: Continuum, 1999), pp. 175-216; on pp. 183-84.

have suggested, primarily between a "sapiential" and an "existential" theology. Nor are they to be found between a more contemplative and a more confessional stance. It is not that Catholic theology speaks in the third person where the Reformation would speak in the first person. While such analyses are not without validity, they fail to go to the heart of the matter. Nor do the differences merely concern using diverse thought-forms or languages for the same basic content. The disagreements are structural. They are therefore substantive. They represent contrasting ways of understanding how the three tenses of salvation are essentially defined and related.

Where Catholicism sees justification as a process of formation in us, the Reformation sees it as our participation in Christ. Where Catholicism concentrates on the present tense, the Reformation concentrates on the perfect tense. Where Catholicism regards Christ as justification's essential cause, source, and prerequisite, the Reformation regards Christ as its essential reality and content. Where Catholicism holds that post-baptismal justification must be preserved, recovered, and increased by human freedom in cooperation with divine grace, the Reformation holds that justification in Christ is one and indivisible in itself so that it is either received, maintained, and partaken of by faith alone or not at all. Where Catholicism teaches that the gift of eternal life depends significantly on human merit, the Reformation teaches that it depends strictly on grace alone, and therefore not on any real or supposed merit that can be ascribed to works of love. Finally, where Catholicism teaches that faith is not effectual for salvation (defined as justification and eternal life) without being formed by love, the Reformation teaches that faith alone is effectual for salvation, precisely because from the very outset faith is formed by Christ.

In conclusion, it should be noted that the difference between Catholicism and the Reformation does not come down to a simple contrast between formation and participation. Catholicism has its own version of "participation" (as evident already at Trent), just as the Reformation has its own version of "formation." However, where Catholicism sees participation as leading to justification (defined by formation), the Reformation holds much the reverse, namely, that formation is a consequence of justification (defined by participation).

For Catholicism, participation is primarily a matter of *Christ in us*. Christ's participation in us functions as the *source* of justifying grace, and this grace, as *infused* into us, is the transforming power by which we become inherently righteous through our cooperation with it. Inherent righteousness, by divine grace, becomes ours through a process of formation in which we necessarily cooperate. As the essence of post-baptismal justification, the righteousness that takes form within us, by faith in conjunction with hope and love, is a necessary condition for the possibility of our *meriting* the gift of eternal life. Eternal life does not become ours without some sort of *synergism* between divine grace and human freedom.

For the Reformation, by contrast, participation is primarily a matter of *our being in Christ.* Our participation in Christ functions as the *reality* of our being made *one* with him, and so *completely* righteous by virtue of the great exchange. Through that exchange, Christ's perfect righteousness is *imputed* to us even as our sin is imputed to him.

The process of *formation* that *then* takes place in us, and by which we are brought increasingly into *conformity* with Christ, is seen strictly as a consequence of imputation. Formation (or "sanctification") *manifests* our justification in Christ but does not contribute to it. Eternal life is the *unmerited* reward of our having been made one with Christ, and so with the sufficient righteousness of Christ *alone,* as received by grace alone, through faith alone. Although we may subsequently *cooperate* with divine grace, that cooperation adds *nothing* to the righteousness by which we receive the gift of eternal life. As the perfect righteousness of Christ, it is ours essentially by participation, *not* by formation through some sort of *synergism.*[8]

If we place the Joint Declaration against this background, three things stand out above all.

---

8. If we let "formation" be represented by f, and "participation" by p, then by a kind of shorthand we can state the contrast as follows. It is not between 'f without p' and 'p *without f*.' It is rather between '$f > p$' (Catholicism) and '$p > f$' (the Reformation), where the symbol '>' means "takes precedence over." Again, the contrast is not so much between formation "in us" and participation "in Christ." Rather it is more nearly between "in us > in Christ" (Catholicism) and "in Christ > in us" (the Reformation). These distinctions rest in turn on different understandings of how the three tenses of salvation are defined and related. Especially regarding the condition for the possibility of eternal life, for Catholicism, "what occurs in the present tense" > "what has taken place in the perfect tense." For the Reformation, it is just the reverse.

First, the eschatological dimension of justification, or the relation among its three tenses, is seriously blurred. In general, the Declaration does not adequately set forth the perfect, the present, and the future tenses in their proper distinctions and interrelations. For example, when we read in paragraphs 17 and 25 of "God's saving action in Christ," just when is this saving action thought to occur, and of just what is it thought to consist? Too often the Declaration glosses over crucial matters by speaking vaguely in the present tense.[9]

Second, the decisive contrast between formation and participation fails to emerge with precision. Although neither idea is absent, other ideas like declaration or impartation or imputation or renewal or whatnot surround them without any clear and distinct ordering of the concepts. Without more clarity here, ecumenical progress seems hampered. Might not Catholicism find a new or better way of incorporating the Reformation concern about *participatio Christi* and righteousness *extra nos* into its own understanding of justification? And might not the Reformation find a new or better way of incorporating the Catholic concern about formation? In the Declaration, to be sure, the formation question seems to have been dealt with more satisfactorily, on both sides, than the participation question. In the end, however, intractable differences seem likely to remain, since for Catholicism, formation finally allows room for meriting eternal life in a way that, for the Reformation, participation does not.[10]

Finally, the Declaration too often seems to be an exercise in studied ambiguities. Virtually all of the common affirmations are so worded that they can be read in two very different ways. They are ambiguous enough to allow for either justification as formation, or else as participation, depending on how they are interpreted. For example, in

9. See The Lutheran World Federation and The Roman Catholic Church, *Joint Declaration on the Doctrine of Justification* (Grand Rapids: Eerdmans, 2000).

10. Trent's teaching that we can merit eternal life (Ch. 16; cf. Can. 32) is clearly echoed by the new *Catechism of the Catholic Church*: "Moved by the Holy Spirit and by charity, we can then merit for ourselves and for others the graces needed for our sanctification, for the increase of grace and charity, and for the attainment of eternal life" (2010). (See *Catechism of the Catholic Church*, trans. United States Catholic Conference, Inc. [The Vatican: Libreria Editrice Vaticana, 1994], p. 487.) The Reformation, of course, was (and remains) largely a struggle against the doctrine of merit.

paragraph 10, we find two sentences juxtaposed to one another: "In Christ he makes it our righteousness (2 Cor. 5:21). Justification becomes ours through Christ Jesus. . . ." Here the difference between the phrases "in Christ" and "through Christ" arguably splits the difference between participation and formation. The first sentence, tilting toward participation, could just as easily be read in light of the second sentence, tilting toward formation, as the reverse.

Again, in paragraph 15, perhaps the heart of the Declaration, we find two more sentences in juxtaposition: "The foundation and presupposition of justification is the incarnation, death and resurrection of Christ. Justification thus means that Christ himself is our righteousness, in which we share through the Holy Spirit. . . ." Here the first sentence tilts toward the Catholic emphasis (Christ as the foundation or prerequisite to a process in which we cooperate), while the second sentence sounds like the Reformation (Christ as our righteousness, in whom we participate). If we read the second sentence in light of the first, we get a Catholic outcome, and many Catholics will no doubt insist on reading it that way. If we reverse the order, and read the first sentence in light of the second, we get a Reformation outcome instead.

Above all, the term "justification" itself (or its cognates) is often used ambiguously, so that it could mean either something essentially one and indivisible (with the Reformation) or else (with Catholicism) something that, while it lacks our cooperation initially, then requires it subsequently, namely, after baptism. This fatal ambiguity runs through at least ten of the thirty-two substantive (as opposed to explanatory) paragraphs (paras. 10, 11, 15, 17, 20, 24, 25, 27, 37, 38).[11] It is far from clear that ambiguous formulations add up a solid consensus.

Nonetheless, it would be wrong to conclude that the Joint Declaration does not represent a real milestone. Whatever its shortcomings, progress has undoubtedly been made. The spirit of goodwill that so

---

11. This ambiguity also pertains to the important statement in Annex 2C, where we read: "Justification takes place 'by grace alone' . . . , by faith alone; the person is justified 'apart from works.'" Despite affirming the *sola fide,* this statement could still pertain *either* solely to the initial phase of justification as a process of formation in which we subsequently cooperate (with Catholicism) *or else* (with the Reformation) to justification as an indivisible whole as received through *participatio Christi,* in which we do not cooperate in constituting the righteousness we receive.

obviously pervades the document is salutary and should not be taken for granted. On the positive side of the ledger we may note the following points of substance. Justification is commonly described as the "chief" way that the New Testament sees the gift of salvation (para. 9). It is also lifted up as "an indispensable criterion" for doctrine (para. 18). In the common affirmations, on four different occasions, Christ is explicitly affirmed as our righteousness (paras. 10 [2x], 15, and 22). In the common paragraphs, the theme of union with Christ is also prominent (though not always without ambiguities; e.g., para. 23). All persons are said to depend "completely on the grace of God for their salvation" (para. 19). A significant basis would seem to be established for advancing toward the unity we seek.

In conclusion, it might be useful to turn the tables a bit. As noted, it has sometimes been said that Luther's doctrine of justification is closer to first-person or devotional discourse, while the Catholic doctrine is more detached and descriptive. From a Reformation perspective, we might think it is sometimes the reverse. Consider this beautiful prayer from St. Thérèse of Lisieux as included in the new *Catechism of the Catholic Church* (2011):[12]

> After earth's exile, I hope to go and enjoy you in the fatherland, but I do not want to lay up merits in heaven. I want to work for your love alone. . . . In the evening of this life, I shall appear before you with empty hands, for I do not ask you, Lord, to count my works. All our justice is blemished in your eyes. I wish, then, to be clothed in your own justice and to receive from your love the eternal possession of yourself.

Forced to decide between a proper Reformation doctrine of justification and this kind of Catholic piety, it would not be too difficult to choose.

---

12. *Catechism of the Catholic Church*, p. 487.

Social Gospels:
Justification, Social Salvation,
and Modern Theology

Gary J. Dorrien

My subject is the doctrine of justification and salvation in the theologies of the social gospel and Niebuhrian realism, and on first impression one might expect that the first part of this lecture will be very brief. The social gospelers almost never used the word *justification,* and even when they wrote dogmatics, they gave short shrift to this category. But the social gospel was nothing if not a theology of salvation, and many of us still get our bearings by negotiating between the social gospel and Niebuhr's Christian realism.

At the height of their influence in the late nineteenth and early twentieth centuries, the movements for liberal theology and the social gospel were not exactly the same thing: there were liberal theologians who were not social gospelers, such as Theodore Munger and Borden Parker Bowne, and social gospelers who were not theologically liberal, such as Josiah Strong and Charles H. Parkhurst. But for the most part the liberal theology and social gospel movements were deeply intertwined. The founding dogmatic texts of the American liberal theology movement were written by social gospelers: William Newton Clarke's *An Outline of Christian Theology* (1898), William Adams Brown's *Christian Theology in Outline* (1906), Washington Gladden's *Present Day Theology* (1913), and Walter Rauschenbusch's *A Theology for the Social Gospel* (1918). Against an aggressively modernizing tide in the movement, which came to be centered at the University of Chicago Divinity School, these theologians insisted that the "new theology" was gospel-centered and historically continuous with classical Christianity; yet even for them, the gospel did not include what they called "the legalistic machinery" of the theology of justification.

Liberal theology is the product of two streams of thought and experience, which may be called (with some problems on both sides) the "evangelical" and "Enlightenment-modernist" traditions. During the social gospel era, the evangelical heritage of liberal theology showed through in its affirmation of the authority of Christian experience, the divinity and sovereignty of Christ, the need of personal salvation, and the importance of Christian missions. From its Enlightenment-modernist heritage, liberal theology affirmed the authority of modern knowledge, the continuity between reason and revelation, and the values of tolerance, humanistic individualism, and democracy. From 1900 to 1930, while theological liberalism dominated the field of theology, the form of liberalism that prevailed featured a balance between the movement's evangelical and Enlightenment-modernist traditions. Gladden, Clarke, Rauschenbusch, and Brown took it for granted that their movement needed to affirm the reality of a personal God who possesses power over non-being and whose being is both immanent within, and transcendent to, history and the natural order. They opposed the aggressively naturalistic version of liberal theology advocated by the Chicago school, which swept away the transcendental apriories of Kant, Hegel, and Schleiermacher, replaced gospel norms with an empirical-pragmatic worldview, emphasized the differences between pre-modern thinking and modern scientific consciousness, rejected the spirit/nature dualism of evangelical and romanticist liberalism, and conceived divine reality not as transhistorical spirit, but merely as the concrete reality of historical process.

The gospel-centered liberals countered that one can be fully modern and liberal without giving up the transcendent-personal divinity of God and the spiritual divinity of Christ. Modern theology marked an advance upon theologies of the past, they affirmed: it was based on reason and experience, not external authority; therefore it accepted the verdicts of modern science and historical criticism; and its ethical spirit was informed by the values of modern democracy and humanism. At the same time they insisted that their movement marked a development within, not a break from, historic Christianity. Liberal theology had made its peace with historical criticism, Rauschenbusch explained, and by doing so it had recovered the very gospel and spirit of Jesus: "The more our historical investigations are laying bare the roots of Catholic dogma, the more do we see them running back into alien Greek thought, and not into the substance of Christ's message nor into the Hebrew faith. We shall not get away again from the central proposition of Harnack's *History of Dogma,* that the development of Catholic dogma was the process of the Hellenization of Christianity; in other words, that alien influences streamed into the religion of Jesus Christ and created a theology which he never taught nor intended." By embracing higher-critical scholarship, Rauschenbusch claimed, liberal theology had recovered the religion of Jesus and made historical criticism its friend. The Protestant Reformation had begun this process by recovering the emancipating Pauline idea of "justification by faith," but modern theology and the social gospel completed the Reformation by recovering the kingdom religion of Jesus.[1]

The early theologians of American social gospel liberalism said the same thing, though less vividly. The movement's first dogmatist, Colgate theologian William Newton Clarke, gave unusual attention to the doctrine of justification — nearly three pages. Explaining Paul's theology, Clarke observed: "Paul evidently thinks of justification as a divine act that affects man's standing in the sight of God. A justified man, with him, is an accepted man, whom God regards as sustaining toward himself the relation that men ought to sustain. Justification, in the thought of Paul, is the act of such acceptance on God's part, and the state of such acceptance on man's part." Clarke cautioned that Paul did not conceive justification as acquittal, for acquittal declares a lack of wrongdoing: "Justification is rather the acceptance of a man by God, although he has done wrong."[2]

Clarke replied that this cannot be right. God is moral and truthful, and does not entertain fictions, he reasoned. It cannot be that God accepts any given person as sustaining to Godself the right relation if such

1. Walter Rauschenbusch, *A Theology for the Social Gospel* (New York: Macmillan, 1918), pp. 23-30, quote, p. 25; see Gary Dorrien, *The Making of American Liberal Theology: Imagining Progressive Religion, 1805-1900* (Louisville: Westminster/John Knox, 2001); Dorrien, *The Making of American Liberal Theology: Making Christianity Modern, 1900-1955* (Louisville: Westminster/John Knox, 2003).

2. William Newton Clarke, *An Outline of Christian Theology* (New York: Charles Scribner's Sons, 1898), p. 406.

a relation does not exist. If justification is the act by which God affirms the right relation between any person and God, justification must imply the actual existence of this relation. Therefore, though Paul does not say this, the act of justification must rest upon and assume the beginning of the new divine life in the person who is justified. Though none of the early social gospelers used this precise language, all of them asserted, in effect, that justification is not real or even conceivable if it is not closely related to, or simultaneous with, the experience of sanctification. Clarke put it this way: "The renewing touch of the Holy Spirit is put forth upon the soul; the soul commits itself in trustful faith to the saving grace of God. When these two acts have been performed, one divine and the other human, the man does occupy the position before God that is right for a man to occupy. He has accepted the divine influence for his salvation, and is doing toward God exactly what every sinful soul ought to do, for he is trusting God and welcoming his gracious help."[3]

The justified person is a new creature who has come by God's grace to be in right relation to God. Clarke allowed that "we may say with Paul that we are justified by faith," as long as we recognize that this is a partial expression of the human experience of trusting in God's grace. It is better to say that justification is the first fruit of spiritual regeneration, he argued: "Acceptance with God is the natural lot of the new creature that the Holy Spirit has made." From the human perspective, justification may be described as the first fruit of faith, but from the divine perspective, justification is necessarily the fruit of a prior and Spirit-caused spiritual regeneration. Justification is an outcome or result of new life, not its precondition. It never means acceptance "on false or unreal grounds," Clarke cautioned, anymore than it means acceptance by merit on legalistic grounds. The gift of new life and divine justification is a "real and solid gift of holy character." As for the theologies of justification formulated by the Reformers and Protestant orthodoxy, Clarke advised: "We must also make it plain that there is no need of forcing Christian experience into forms that do not possess reality in our time. We must allow the utmost largeness and liberty to the renewing Spirit, who works in each age according to the life of each age."[4]

3. Clarke, *An Outline of Christian Theology,* pp. 406-7.
4. Clarke, *An Outline of Christian Theology,* pp. 407-9.

Clarke was a Baptist who wrote with a warmly Pietist spirit; his Presbyterian friend, Union theologian William Adams Brown, modeled his influential textbook closely on Clarke's, while toning down the Pietism. Brown distinguished more clearly than Clarke between justification and sanctification, he did not struggle with Paul's meaning, and he quickly dispatched the entire subject. "The doctrine of justification by faith is the reassertion, in theological language, of the truth put more simply by Jesus in his teaching concerning the childlike spirit," he asserted. Justification is about the "substitution of the attitude of personal trust" for the legalistic relationships of contract, merit, and reward. Essentially it is the conviction that moral effort is not the way to assurance and peace, and the best analogy for it is the trusting attitude of a child for its parent. With a nod to the Westminster Confession, Brown maintained that justification, while closely related to sanctification, is prior to and separate from it: "When a man abandons all hope of self-righteousness, and turns to God in penitence and trust, to find in grateful dependence upon him the spring and power of a new life, then, and not until then, is he conscious of the moral renewal whose full outworking will involve the complete transformation of the character into the likeness of Jesus Christ. This is the truth for which the reformers contended in their distinction of justification and sanctification."[5]

Christian salvation is essentially "the substitution of the outgoing for the self-centered life," Brown explained. In personal religion, salvation consists of the renunciation of self-righteousness and the acceptance of trust, which is the meaning of justification by faith; in ethical religion, salvation is the renunciation of the individualistic principle of self-love and the acceptance of the social principle of love to others, which is the meaning of sanctification; in social religion, salvation is the process by which the divine ideal, the kingdom of God, is realized in society. The process of kingdom-building consists of the "progressive revelation" of God's will to individuals and the "progressive realization" of God's will in society. Brown explained: "In both cases it is made possible through the appearance of exceptional individuals, who, as teachers and preachers, proclaim God's will to man, and by

---

5. William Adams Brown, *Christian Theology in Outline* (New York: Charles Scribner's Sons, 1906), pp. 314-15.

their character and example set in motion the influences by which it is ultimately to be realized." For Christians, he added, one figure epitomizes the moral and spiritual ideal. Jesus was the prophet of God's kingdom and a uniquely God-conscious exemplar of the divine will.[6]

This way of construing the meaning of Christianity was pioneered in the United States by Congregationalist pastor Washington Gladden, the father of the social gospel, whose theology of social salvation I shall describe in a moment. In the 1880s, Gladden formulated the idea of social salvation; by 1910, the movement for "applied Christianity," as he called it, had a name, "the social gospel"; in 1913, near the end of his life, Gladden explained his rendering of the idea of justification. "Instead of saying 'believe in Christ' or 'believe on Him,' or 'believe something about him,' which suggests theological formularies not easy of comprehension, I would begin by saying, 'Believe him,'" Gladden wrote. "Believe what he tells you about the meaning of life. Believe what he has said in the Sermon on the Mount. Believe that the Golden Rule is the right rule to live by every day and everywhere." To be saved is to be released from the bondage of selfishness; for Gladden, doctrine and theology were part of the problem if they obscured this central matter. Justification is a practical matter, and to believe in Christ is to believe that the way of Christ is practical. In Gladden's words, "The very beginning of salvation, I say, is the change of mind by which you come to see and realize that the way of Christ, which is the way of unselfishness, is the right way for you to live."[7]

As usual, Rauschenbusch provided the most vivid social gospel rendering of this subject. Like Clarke, Brown, Gladden, and most of the movement, he was deeply gospel-centered. "The doctrines of sin and salvation are the starting-point and goal of Christian theology," he declared. Theology is inherently prescriptive, it is ruled by gospel norms, and its central matters are the problems of sin and salvation. More deeply than Clarke, Brown, and Gladden, however, who fixated on the social agency of inspired individuals, Rauschenbusch worked social ideas into his theology of salvation. He observed: "If every individual had to work out his idea of God on the basis of his own experi-

---

6. Brown, *Christian Theology in Outline*, pp. 315-16.

7. Washington Gladden, *Present Day Theology* (Columbus, Ohio: McClelland & Company, 1913), pp. 84-85.

ences and intuitions only, it would be a groping quest, and most of us would see only the occasional flitting of a distant light. By the end of our life we might have arrived at the stage of voodooism or necromancy." To acquire an understanding of God as personal, loving, infinite spirit is a social achievement and a social endowment, Rauschenbusch argued. It is like entering a public park or a public art-gallery and sharing in the wealth of common goods. He explained: "When we learn from the gospels, for instance, that God is on the side of the poor, and that he proposes to view anything done or not done to them as having been done or not done to him, such a revelation of solidarity and humanity comes with a regenerating shock to our selfish minds. Anyone studying life as it is on the basis of real estate and bank clearings would come to the conclusion that God is on the side of the rich. It takes a revelation to see it the other way." This revelation has been given to us through Jesus and the prophets, Rauschenbusch argued, but on the whole, the church has not been a good steward of it.[8]

Medieval Christianity pictured God as a feudal lord, "holding his tenants in a grip from which there was no escape." Rauschenbusch observed that to most Christians, God was not the great Comforter but the great Terror, and "the main concern in religion was to escape from his hands." Martin Luther's motivating question was how he might find a gracious God, and Rauschenbusch noted that Luther trembled with fear when he walked in a Corpus Christi procession. Jesus severed the idea of God from the predatory state and transferred it to the realm of family life, which is the realm of solidarity, intimacy, and love, Rauschenbusch argued. By contrast: "The worst form of leaving the naked unclothed, the hungry unfed, and the prisoners uncomforted, is to leave men under a despotic conception of God and the universe; and what will the Son of Man do to us theologians when we gather at the Day of Doom?" Heretofore Christianity has classified theology as either Greek or Latin, or as Catholic or Protestant, Rauschenbusch observed; modern Christianity needs to be more modern and more Christian than that, for the fundamental divide is between the spirit of despotism and the spirit of democracy.[9]

8. Walter Rauschenbusch, *A Theology for the Social Gospel* (New York: Macmillan, 1917), pp. 167-68.
9. Rauschenbusch, *A Theology for the Social Gospel*, pp. 173-75.

This was the ruling idea that Rauschenbusch applied to the theology of justification. It was Luther's great achievement to remove the idea of merit from theology, Rauschenbusch believed. For Luther, Christ alone had merit, and by his sacrifice on the cross, the entire debt of humankind was paid. Human beings did not earn merit and did not need to try; in Rauschenbusch's phrase, Luther ended "the contract labor system in religion." God was appeased and ready to forgive, and "the sinner need only believe and accept the great transaction made on his behalf." But Rauschenbusch judged that Luther and Calvin recovered only a small piece of the Christian conception of God. Despotic government prevailed in the sixteenth century, Luther and Calvin did not support democracy, and the age of absolutism was still to come. Christianity remained a religion of fear, buttressed by the old monarchical conceptions of God and rationalized by the forensic language of scholastic theology.[10]

The spirit of legalism and the genuinely Christian idea of salvation are not compatible, Rauschenbusch observed, but "as long as religion borrows its terms from the procedure of law-courts, the spirit of coercion and terror leaks in." His chief example was the language of justification. "The idea of 'justification' did not come to us from Jesus and it does not blend well with his way of thinking," Rauschenbusch asserted. "For Paul and Luther 'justification by faith' was an emancipating idea; it stood for an immense simplification and sweetening of the process of salvation. They used the terminology of legalism to deny its spirit. To us, who are not under the consciousness of Jewish or Roman Catholic legality, 'justification' does not convey the same sense of liberation, but the phrase is now a vehicle by which legal and often despotic ideas come back to plague us." For Rauschenbusch and the social gospelers, "salvation" was a precious word, but "atonement" smacked too much of the ancient sacrificial system, and "justification" evoked an autocratic concept of God. "The reformatory and democratizing influence of the social gospel is not against religion but for it," Rauschenbusch explained. "The worst thing that could happen to God would be to remain an autocrat while the world is moving toward democracy."[11]

10. Rauschenbusch, *A Theology for the Social Gospel*, pp. 176-77.
11. Rauschenbusch, *A Theology for the Social Gospel*, pp. 177-78.

It followed that modern Christianity needed to substitute the reconciliatory language of moral-influence theory for the legalistic language of substitutionary atonement, and speak of deliverance from selfishness instead of the justification of sinners, and worship a God who belonged to the social struggle for justice, freedom, and the kingdom of God. Rauschenbusch exhorted: "A God who strives within our striving, who kindles his flame in our intellect, sends the impact of his energy to make our will restless for righteousness, floods our subconscious mind with dreams and longings, and always urges the race on toward a higher combination of freedom and solidarity — that would be a God with whom democratic and religious men could hold converse as their chief fellow-worker, the source of their energies, the ground of their hopes."[12]

Rauschenbusch insisted that the social gospel was "neither alien nor novel," but he protested too much; the social gospel was something new. Essentially it was the theology of social salvation and its idea that Christianity has a mission to transform the structures of society. In 1893, with no glimmer whatsoever of how dated his language would become, Gladden described this idea in the form of a liberal twist on postmillennialism. "The end of Christianity is twofold, a perfect man in a perfect society," he declared. "These purposes are never separated; they cannot be separated. No man can be redeemed and saved alone; no community can be reformed and elevated save as the individuals of which it is composed are regenerated." The gospel is addressed to individuals, he allowed, but the gospel addresses each individual as a member of a social organism, which creates the medium through which individuals respond to the message: "This vital and necessary relation of the individual to society lies at the basis of the Christian conception of life. Christianity would create a perfect society, and to this end it must produce perfect men; it would bring forth perfect men, and to this end it must construct a perfect society." The themes of the social gospel were the themes of Christ, by Gladden's reckoning: repentance, regeneration, and the presence of the kingdom. Jesus told his followers to be perfect as God is perfect (Matthew 5:48) and to "repent, for the kingdom of heaven has come near" (Matthew 4:17). Repentance is intrinsically connected to the presence of the king-

---

12. Rauschenbusch, *A Theology for the Social Gospel*, p. 179.

dom: "The opportunity, the motive, the condition of repentance is the presence of a divine society, of which the penitent, by virtue of his penitence, at once becomes a member."[13]

The social gospelers were reformers and idealists, not radical utopians; Rauschenbusch allowed that perfection was not within reach. Persistently he urged that we cannot learn how much of the kingdom ideal is attainable if we do not struggle to attain it. "We shall never have a perfect life, yet we must seek it with faith," he declared. "At best there is always but an approximation to a perfect social order. The Kingdom of God is always but coming. But every approximation to it is worthwhile."[14]

Taken together, the liberal theology and social gospel movements were remarkably successful. They changed the language and culture of American Protestantism, captured the major chairs of America's elite divinity schools and seminaries, and rewrote the curriculum of religious and theological education. All of the social gospel theologians can be quoted on their surprise that so much of American Protestantism could be changed so quickly. Liberal personalist theologian Albert Knudson is a telling example of the transforming impact of the social gospel movement, well after the movement had gone into eclipse. Knudson was very short on social gospel feeling. Intellectually he was devoted to the personalist metaphysical idealism and ethical individualism of his teacher, Borden Parker Bowne, who spurned the social gospel; politically, Knudson was a moderate (for his time) who had little concern for racial justice and often lectured that there is such a thing as good imperialism. Yet the impact of the social gospel was so strong in Knudson's generation that he not only made his peace with it in social ethics, but recast his theology in its light.

John Wesley and the Wesleyan tradition taught that justification and sanctification are closely related, or even simultaneous, and that full salvation is attainable in this life. Knudson's theological teacher at Boston University, Olin Curtis, taught that this doctrine had nearly the same significance for the doctrine of holiness that Luther's theology

---

13. Washington Gladden, *Tools and the Man: Property and Industry under the Christian Law* (Boston: Houghton Mifflin, 1893), pp. 1-2.

14. Walter Rauschenbusch, *Christianity and the Social Crisis* (New York: Macmillan, 1907), pp. 420-21.

had for the doctrine of justification by faith and that Athanasius's theology had for the doctrine of the incarnation. In 1933, Knudson countered that the social gospel had permanently redefined the Christian message on this point. The idea of sanctification was still needed in Christianity, he assured, but it could not mean the same thing to modern people that it meant to Wesley: "Today the whole subject is viewed in a different light." Modern Christianity believed in ethical sanctification, not mystical sanctification, he explained. It spoke the kingdom-building language of the social gospel, not the individualistic soul-language of Protestant Pietism.[15] Modern Christianity placed its hope on the transformation of society by the persuasive power of the Christian spirit. The Christian message was that individuals *and* society must be saved from sin, regenerated, and made new. Knudson declared: "The conversion of individuals here and there will not suffice. Society itself must be converted, inwardly and outwardly transformed, so that it may be a fit home for the children of God. Nothing short of this will satisfy either the secular or the religious mood of the day."[16] This was what it meant to speak of sanctification in the age that made Christianity modern.

Shortly after Knudson described the social gospel as an epochal transformation of Christian thought, it was blasted for a litany of illusions. Beginning with Reinhold Niebuhr's icy proto-Marxist assault of 1932, *Moral Man and Immoral Society,* the social gospelers were ridiculed for their middle-class moralism, sentimentality, pacifism, and liberal idealism. They had revered a liberal Jesus who reflected their own middle-class idealism; they had preached that love is the answer to social problems; they had put aside their antiwar convictions to embrace Woodrow Wilson's pledge to make the world safe for democracy; after that they had repented of war and equated the gospel with pacifist idealism. Many of us first learned of the social gospel through Niebuhr's blistering criticism of its faults. Today the trend is to emphasize other faults, especially the movement's sexism and Anglo-Saxonist chauvinism.[17]

15. Albert C. Knudson, *The Doctrine of Redemption* (New York: Abingdon-Cokesbury Press, 1933), pp. 412-13.

16. Albert C. Knudson, "The Social Gospel and Theology," *The Personalist* 5 (April 1924): 109.

17. See Christopher H. Evans, ed., *The Social Gospel Today* (Louisville: Westminster/John Knox, 2001).

With all of its faults, however, the social gospel was more creative and constructive, and contributed more to the progressive legacy of modern Christianity, than any of the movements that have followed it. Christian realism inspired no hymns and created very few ministries or lasting institutions; liberation theology has opened the institutions and language of the church to the perspectives of previously excluded people, but it has created few enduring structures. It was the social gospel movement of the Progressive Era that created the ecumenical institutions, peace fellowships, and social justice ministries that remain the heart of modern social Christianity. It changed Christianity in ways that influence all of us gathered here today; we would not think of holding a conference like this one without saying something about the relation of its topic to social issues.

Theologically the legacy of the social gospel is more dismal than its legacy in ecumenical affairs, social ethics, and social justice ministry. The social gospelers contributed greatly to the denigration and trivialization of theology that characterize so much of contemporary American Christianity. They prized the practical and relevant; their anti-intellectualism was usually just below the surface; they encouraged the popular impression that abstract arguments about the Trinity and Christology are a waste of time; and they gave little thought to the question of how Christian life and theology might be sustained over the long term. Think of the thousands who read Rauschenbusch's dismissal of Luther and then never gave another thought to Reformation theology.

On the doctrine of justification, instead of setting Jesus against Paul and dismissing justification as a legalistic relic of a law-court approach to religion, the social gospelers would have done better to emphasize the close relation between the New Testament terms for "justify" and "justification" (*dikaioō* and *dikaiōsis*) and the word for "righteous" (*dikaios*). Many of the social gospelers were quite clear that they opposed the interpretation of justification as the treatment of a sinful person as righteous (an acquittal), but for nearly all of them, Christianity centered on the *making* of righteousness. Christianity was fundamentally about the conversion of sinners into righteousness and the making of a good society. Had they held out for the doctrine of justification in at least the sense of *making* righteous, they might have made more effective theological use of their persistent admonition that there are things that a sinner must do to be saved, such as repenting, believing, sustaining faith, and caring for the afflicted. The social gospelers sometimes teased that the Synoptic gospels are remarkably Pelagian, but their own emphasis on the social mission of the gospel might have been strengthened had they emphasized equally, with Paul, that we are totally dependent on God's creative action and for-giving love, that our very existence depends on God's grace, and that after all our efforts to change the world are finished, it is God who will make something new out of our strivings for justice and peace.

More importantly, the social gospelers wrongly moralized the gift of forgiveness. They rejected the Pauline idea that the righteous-ness of Christ is imputed to the repentant sinner, who does not possess righteousness except by faith. In *The Nature and Destiny of Man*, Niebuhr aptly replied: "This doctrine of the 'imputation of righteous-ness' has always been offensive to moralistic interpreters of Christian faith. They have made much of the non-moral character of such impu-tation. But forgiveness, as a form of love which is beyond good and evil, is bound to be offensive to pure moralists. The Pauline doctrine really contains the whole Christian conception of God's relation to hu-man history. It recognizes the sinful corruption in human life on every level of goodness. It knows that the pride of sin is greatest when men claim to have conquered sin completely." Wrongly construed, Niebuhr allowed, the idea of justification by faith supports a legalistic approach to religion, but rightly apprehended, it "strikes man in the very center of his spiritual being."[18]

Niebuhr's larger themes built upon this one. The essential princi-ple of liberal theology is that religious claims must be based on reason and experience, not external authority. Even in its romanticist forms, liberal theology prized its claim to rational credibility and coherence, and from Washington Gladden to Albert Knudson to Gordon Kaufman, liberal theology has preached that rationality is an instru-ment of redemption. Through the training and exercise of reason, hu-man beings are liberated from ignorance, backwardness, selfishness, provincialism, and aggression. In the late 1920s, however, Niebuhr be-gan to question the exalted status of reason in modern theology, cau-

18. Reinhold Niebuhr, *The Nature and Destiny of Man*, one-volume edition (New York: Charles Scribner's Sons, 1949), vol. 2, p. 104.

tioning that reason is not necessarily good or objective. In 1932, *Moral Man and Immoral Society* featured this argument. The thesis of his title, that groups are inevitably selfish and hypocritical, kindled an immediate controversy in American liberal Protestantism, but the book's more important argument was that reason is inherently ambiguous.

On the one hand, Niebuhr argued, reason is the principle and means of creativity in human life; people grasp the existence of a good that is larger than their private interests through the exercise of reason. On the other hand, reason is the principle and means by which people rationalize and defend their selfish interests; reason is the servant of interest. Liberal theology taught that power is inherently corrupt and that rational goodwill is the answer to society's problems. Niebuhr countered that people do not cease to be dishonest after their dishonesty has been self-discovered or revealed by others: "Whenever men hold unequal power in society, they will strive to maintain it. They will use whatever means are convenient to that end and will seek to justify them by the most plausible arguments they are able to devise." On this theme, *Moral Man and Immoral Society* coined one of Niebuhr's most famous epigrams: "The will to power uses reason as kings use courtiers and chaplains, to add grace to their enterprise." Unrelentingly, Niebuhr admonished that reason rationalizes and expands the predatory impulses of nature. Far from delivering humankind from the smallness and immorality of selfish ends, reason defends the gains of individuals and their groups, it creates more advanced means of destruction, and it rationalizes the use of advanced weaponry. The predatory instincts of animals are sated by a full stomach, but human lusts are refueled by the imaginative capacities of reason: "He will not be satisfied until the universal objectives which the imagination envisages are attained."[19]

This chastening message was very hard, though not impossible, for liberals to swallow; their favorite counter-charge was that Niebuhr was a pessimist. Just as liberals exaggerated the connection between Niebuhrian pessimism and conservative reaction, Niebuhr exagger-

19. Reinhold Niebuhr, *Moral Man and Immoral Society: A Study in Ethics and Politics* (New York: Charles Scribner's Sons, 1932), pp. 34, 44. See Gary J. Dorrien, *The Making of American Liberal Theology: Idealism, Realism, and Modernity, 1900-1950* (Louisville: Westminster/John Knox, 2003), pp. 435-83.

ated the perfectionistic idealism of liberal theology; hardly any liberal theologians matched the picture of moralistic sentimentality and naïveté that Niebuhr repeatedly ridiculed in his writings. There were no prominent liberal theologians who did not believe in sin or interpreted sin merely as ignorance, though Niebuhr implied that they were legion. Yet Niebuhr's powerful doctrine of sin and his emphasis upon it cut against the grain of even the most realistic liberal theologies. Among leading liberal theologians, Rauschenbusch came closest to Niebuhr's understanding of the inevitability of personal and social evil and the limitations of middle-class idealism. Rauschenbusch's *Theology for the Social Gospel* devoted separate chapters to the consciousness of sin, the fall of humanity, the nature of sin, the transmission of sin, the super-personal forces of evil, and the kingdom of evil. His concept of the kingdom of evil presented a stronger sense of the organic socio-historical inheritance of evil than Niebuhr's existential interpretation of original sin, and his various writings on the class struggle could have been written by Niebuhr during his Marxist phase. Rauschenbusch admonished that "we must not blink the fact that idealists alone have never carried through any great social change." The struggle for any great truth "must depend on the class which makes that truth its own and fights for it." On these issues, Rauschenbusch was closer to Niebuhr than to the moralistic liberal idealism that Niebuhr blasted.[20]

But even Rauschenbusch was typically liberal in conceiving the social gospel as a struggle between the "forces of righteousness" and the forces of ignorance and sin. Though he emphasized the nihilating power of the kingdom of evil, Rauschenbusch never doubted that the kingdom of God is a stronger force not only beyond, but also within history. Though he emphasized that the kingdom of evil is solidaristic and accumulative, and though he recognized that the kingdom of evil afflicts all human hearts and all social orders, he persisted, like his movement, in a straightforward ethical dualism. To his understanding, the divine kingdom was prefigured in the life of the church as the body of Christ and as a sign of true community. Rauschenbusch assumed that the reign of God will never be fully realized in history; at

---

20. Rauschenbusch, *A Theology for the Social Gospel*, pp. 31-94; Rauschenbusch, *Christianity and the Social Crisis*, pp. 400-401.

the same time he assumed that the church's vocation is to work at building the divine kingdom. The church will never build a perfect social order, he allowed, yet the church is obliged to strive for as much of the kingdom ideal as is attainable. The only way to find out how much of the ideal is attainable is to struggle for the whole thing in faith. The kingdom will never be fully disclosed in history, "but every approximation to it is worthwhile."[21]

That was the ethics, politics, and theology of the social gospel in a nutshell. Like all the social gospelers, Rauschenbusch conceived evil as an enemy that can be impeded and even defeated by the good. The social imperative of the social gospel was that Christians are to regenerate the social order through moral, political, and spiritual efforts that diminish the force of evil in the world. Rauschenbusch straightforwardly identified certain social structures as regenerate and others as unregenerate. He described the struggle for social justice as a fight between the "forces of righteousness" and the "forces of evil," and he urged that regenerated social institutions can have redeeming effects on individuals.

This was precisely the mind-set that Niebuhr attacked. The problem was not merely that liberals had a weak sense of evil or they were naïve about politics; sometimes they had a strong sense of evil and a fairly realistic grasp of politics. In either case, the problem was their simplistic ethical dualism. *Moral Man and Immoral Society* launched a ferocious attack on the social gospel faith that democratized collectivities can have redeeming effects on individuals; later Niebuhr decided that the notion of "moral man" was a social gospel illusion, too. His alternative was a dialectic of sin. Good and evil are not merely opposing forces, Niebuhr reasoned; they are inevitably mixed together in human nature and history.

Sigmund Freud helped Niebuhr find the root of his realism. Niebuhr judged that the popularity of Freudian psychology owed much to its conception of a death instinct that competes with eros for control over self and society. To disillusioned intellectuals who no longer believed in the Enlightenment myth of human progress, Freud's

---

21. Rauschenbusch, *Christianity and the Social Crisis*, pp. 420-21; this section adapts material from Gary Dorrien, *Soul in Society: The Making and Renewal of Social Christianity* (Minneapolis: Fortress, 1995), pp. 148-50.

account of the struggle between eros and death marked a compelling advance over rationalistic psychologies. Freud envisioned the work of eros as binding together "single individuals, then families, then tribes, races, nations, into one great unity, that of humanity." In his view, culture and civilization were products of the work of eros, which competes in every individual, group, and society with the death instinct, the nihilating power that destroys culture and civilization. To Freud, this struggle of the human species for existence was the essential clue to the meaning and evolution of culture; it explained, for example, the meaning of religion: "And it is this battle of Titans that our nurses and governesses try to compose with their lullaby song of Heaven."[22]

Niebuhr appreciated Freud's realism about the tragic aspects of human nature and society. He allowed that Freudian psychology marked an advance in the modern secular attempt to confront the reality of evil. He remarked that Freudian psychology had the virtue "of calling attention to the dynamic character of evil in the world." But he gave short shrift to Freud's understanding of evil: "These supposedly profound words, which pretentiously offer a clue to the meaning of 'the evolution of culture,' throw little light on the actual human situation." Freud posited an inner conflict between a distinct death impulse and a distinct life impulse, but Niebuhr countered that only psychopaths act out of a pure love of destruction. For most people, and for all animals, the death instinct serves the life impulse. People attack and kill to save their own lives and the lives of their loved ones, and to protect the communities and social orders created by eros. The death instinct is real, Niebuhr reasoned, but not Freud's dualistic understanding of it.[23]

Freudian psychology and the Rauschenbuschian social gospel had the same problem; they viewed the forces of creativity and destruction as distinct. Niebuhr admonished that the death instinct is more than a nihilating power that competes with and struggles against the life impulse, for the powers of creativity and destruction are inextricably bound up with each other. Morally, evil is always constitutive in the good. No human act, no matter how loving, altruistic, or seemingly in-

---

22. Sigmund Freud, *Civilization and Its Discontents*, trans. James Strachey (1930; reprint, New York: W. W. Norton, 1961), pp. 102-3; Reinhold Niebuhr, *An Interpretation of Christian Ethics* (New York: Charles Scribner's Sons, 1935), p. 59.

23. Niebuhr, *An Interpretation of Christian Ethics*, pp. 59-60.

nocent, is devoid of egotism. Purity of any kind is an illusion. It is not enough to see that evil is real or that evil competes in every soul and society with the good. A truly realistic dialectic must view the powers of creativity and destruction not as forces held in tension, but as a dialectic of interpenetration. Good and evil are always part of each other.

Niebuhr conceded that his view of the interpenetration of good and evil was bound to seem "morbidly pessimistic to moderns." The chief implication of his view for politics was that any gain toward a good end simultaneously engenders new opportunities for evil. Every movement that creates greater democracy, equality, freedom, or community also creates new opportunities for tyranny, squalor, or anarchy, and every effort to make the public sphere more humane heightens the possibility of producing unintended evil consequences. Democratic gains increase the possibilities for greater numbers of people to do evil things. It followed for Niebuhr that reformist and revolutionary movements are most dangerous when they are oblivious to the harmful possibilities they create. He knew very well how this advice sounded to his progressive friends: "The conclusion most abhorrent to the modern mood is that the possibilities of evil grow with the possibilities of good, and that human history is therefore not so much a chronicle of the progressive victory of the good over evil, of cosmos over chaos, as the story of an ever-increasing cosmos, creating ever-increasing possibilities of chaos."[24]

Niebuhr's theological deficiencies were numerous.[25] He ignored basic questions about theological method, hermeneutics, language, and exegesis; he failed to define his key terms; his scholarship was often sloppy and tendentious; he was very short on theological analysis of the divinity of Christ, the Holy Spirit, or the Trinity; his theology of resurrection rested on a vague theory of the dialectical relation of body and soul; he had a merely sociological understanding of the church; and he conceived the kingdom merely as a transcendental ideal standing in judgment over history. He also abstracted one type of self-transcendence (egocentric will-to-power) and minimized the redeeming power of mutuality, love, and solidarity in human life (though his later writings pressed harder on the relation of love and justice). He overgeneralized a

24. Niebuhr, *An Interpretation of Christian Ethics,* p. 60.
25. See Dorrien, *Soul in Society,* pp. 143-61.

decidedly pre-feminist model of the self and held out no hope of re-demption within history, which is not biblical. For Niebuhr, love and the work of the Holy Spirit had no regenerative power except as symbols of transcendence and God's grace beyond history.

Yet his brilliant thematization of sin and realism justify his stand-ing among the giants of modern theology. Niebuhr rightly, propheti-cally insisted that all human behavior is infected with self-interest; that reason is the servant of interest; that groups are synergistically more self-regarding than individuals; and that the experience of redemption does not lift human beings out of their bondage as sinners.

Persistently he admonished that realism about sin is socially pro-gressive. It is the truth-telling virtue that makes genuine gains toward justice possible and that copes with the unanticipated consequences of reform movements. The life-giving impulse within human beings makes democracy possible; the life-destroying impulse within human beings makes democracy necessary. Democracy is most valuable and important as the best political brake that we possess on human greed, will-to-power, and destructiveness, Niebuhr taught, including the de-structiveness that inheres in the life impulse.

This message was too morbid and depressing for liberal theolo-gians and secular progressives alike, as Niebuhr keenly understood. In later life, even as he was making his peace with liberal theology and his place within it, Niebuhr recalled that for many years he was "falsely accused of being a reactionary" by secular critics who sneered at his Christian faith. It was instructive to him that the Deweyan liber-als and socialists who mocked his "reactionary" commitment to Chris-tianity never derided the Christianity of the social gospelers: "But it must be remembered that the proponents of the Social Gospel were not under suspicion, because they did not believe in 'sin'; and they had in any case a faith which did not differ too grievously from the main outlines of the 'American dream.'" Niebuhr carried that bitter re-membrance to the end of his days. One reason that he attacked liberal Protestantism so stridently was that the social gospelers got exemp-tions from secular criticism that were not granted to him.[26]

26. Reinhold Niebuhr, "Intellectual Autobiography of Reinhold Niebuhr," in *Reinhold Niebuhr: His Religious, Social, and Political Thought*, ed. Charles W. Kegley and Robert W. Bretall (New York: Macmillan, 1956), p. 13.

The Augustinian Imperfection:
Faith, Christ, and Imputation
and Its Role in the Ecumenical
Discussion of Justification

Steven D. Paulson

If I were speaking today of *love*, which bears all things, I could perhaps say that the Joint Declaration (and its confusion of law and gospel) "is being economical with the truth." But since I am speaking of *faith*, and faith rejects all suitors who would wed it to their favorite virtue with a simple conjunction ("and"), here we can yield nothing. I suggest that we do not adopt the growing ecumenical practice of double entendre that reads each assertion of faith as a partial grasp of truth, as if each church had a blind hold on some part of the same elephant, or that all were looking at the same scenery, just "elocuting" differently. Down that road the church and its own authority becomes theology's preoccupation. Such a preoccupation presently indicates a problem with the most significant theological proposal concerning justification of the last generation: justification is a "meta-linguistic proposal of doctrine."[1] That is, justification would function like rules of grammar for proclamation. Unfortunately, that encouraged ecumenical dialogues to treat differences on justification as interpretations, models, or different levels of communication of what, after all, was assumed to be the same content of faith.

But justification functions as the criterion even on the ground

---

1. Most clearly in Eric W. Gritsch and Robert W. Jenson, *Lutheranism: The Theological Movement and Its Confessional Writings* (Minneapolis: Fortress, 1976), pp. 2-15.

level, so to speak, in a difference in the words and content, even the telling of the story, especially in what the Reformers called *"particulae exclusivae"* ("none," "all," "only," and "alone") that distinguish law and gospel.[2] It is time for ecumenists to come out of the clouds of the "meta-level," where they act as if they stood in a monarchical position from which to censor church history and confessional assertions as applying or not, and reinterpreting where necessary.[3] One of the ways of refusing radical otherness in one's self, the church, and even God is to exercise a theological version of reason's will to rule. It comes out in the form of a determination to establish unity as identity that does not die. Identity identical with itself is presumed to be uninterrupted by the ravages of history, if not on the personal or local level, then on what is taken as a universal, "meta," level of church communion. So I suggest practicing a little laughter and forgetting, then publicly confessing again, the faith created in us by God's word, Jesus Christ alone. Lutherans confess that "apart from this human being there is no God"; and his cross, we might say, is an interruption in our drive for personal, ecclesial, and cosmic continuity.[4] Even new theories of church as communing in the triune being of God will not overcome this disjunction by transcendental, romantic, or Hegelian dialectical means.[5] So the purpose of taking up justification is to help identify the gospel amid confused religious talk in order to give that very gospel to God's active opponents.

A modern British humorist once quipped: "The marvelous thing about a joke with a double meaning is that it can mean only one thing."[6] The ecumenical method of allowing each "agreed" statement to mean two different things that are nevertheless not "church-dividing" is already an abandonment of Scripture's clarity on the cen-

---

2. For example, Formula of Concord III, 7 and 36, in *The Book of Concord: The Confessions of the Evangelical Lutheran Church*, ed. Robert Kolb and Timothy J. Wengert (Minneapolis: Fortress, 2000), pp. 563 and 568.

3. See the related argument in Inge Lonning, "Lifting the Condemnations: Does It Make Sense?" *dialog* 36 (Spring 1997): 143-47.

4. Solid Declaration VIII, *Book of Concord*, 631.81.

5. Oswald Bayer has an important essay on the philosophical and theological drive for unity in "The Being of Christ in Faith," *Lutheran Quarterly* 10, no. 2 (1996): 135-50.

6. Ronnie Barker, *Daddies Sauce*, 1977.

tral matter of justification as it occurs in preaching. Thus, we get statements that can mean only one thing. The JDDJ gives us a weak form of the old warhorse "double justification." In fact, it is more likely a simple reiteration of Trent's "one formal cause" (Decrees, chapter 7), i.e., not God's justness by which God alone is just, but that "by which he makes us just," apportioned by the Spirit "in view of each one's dispositions and co-operation."[7] It falsely represents one of the versions of justification identified by the American Lutheran/Roman Catholic dialogue as the *one* "agreed" use. Since that double doctrine dreamed up by sixteenth-century ecumenists has been singularly unsuccessful over the years, I anticipate that it will prove no more fruitful today. True ecumenism depends on justification by faith alone apart from works of the law. It is the most ecumenical, but for all that, the least-used "doctrine" in the church. We will better serve the true church already united in Christ by expressing this chief article clearly. Let's try to actually use it! The pleas offered for the Joint Declaration's usefulness, that this is not a systematic theology but an ecclesiastical negotiation, or that it is a first step with a long journey ahead, are no excuse for bad theology, especially when Christ is being buried and the Holy Spirit nudged out in favor of the fiction of the eternal free will. I choose to spend our time considering the long-standing problem beneath such a statement and what we can do to stop it for the sake of true ecumenism.

To do that, we should not deal with a "pacified Luther without horns and teeth,"[8] but be willing to engage in dialogue with the *heretic* Luther and the heretical Lutherans.[9] Let the condemnations fly rather

---

7. *Decrees of the Ecumenical Councils,* vol. 2, ed. Norman P. Tanner (Washington, D.C.: Sheed & Ward and Georgetown University Press, 1990), p. 673: *"unicas formalis causa"* (Chapter VII of the Decrees of the Council of Trent, Session 6).

8. Gottfried Maron: "Is not that an inadmissible blunting of Luther, a way of neutralizing him, such that essential matters go missing and we are left only with a pacified Luther without horns and teeth?" *Die Katholische Lutherbild der Gegenwart: Anmerkungen und Anfragen* (Göttingen: Vandenhoeck & Ruprecht, 1982), p. 28. Quoted and translated in Daphne Hampson, *Christian Contradictions* (Cambridge: Cambridge University Press, 2001), p. 116.

9. Speaking of the attempt of the dean of Catholic Luther interpreters, Joseph Lortz, to make Luther usable to Roman Catholics, Peter Manns states: "This means in consequence that, in dialogue with Luther, a conversation with the heretic is theologically impossible and one can, naturally, learn nothing at all from him." John

than consider it epoch-making to reach agreements that only condemn the straw man Pelagius. That means coming to grips with the Luther and Lutherans who say things like this: "It is a marvelous thing and unknown to the world to teach Christians to ignore the Law and to live before God as though there were no Law whatever." And this: "Then do we do nothing and work nothing in order to obtain this righteousness? I reply: Nothing at all." And this: "For between these two kinds of righteousness, the active righteousness of the Law and the passive righteousness of Christ there is no middle ground."[10] And this: ". . . that Christ became a curse for us to set us free from the curse of the Law — of this the sophists deprive us when they segregate Christ from sins and from sinners and set Him forth to us only as an example to be imitated."[11] Or this: "Paul . . . said . . . 'I have died, etc.' Here a malicious person could easily cavil and say: 'What are you saying, Paul? Are you dead? . . . He replies: . . . Paul, living in himself, is utterly dead through the Law but living in Christ or rather with Christ living in him, he lives an alien life. . . . do not be offended but make the proper distinction."[12]

Let's take *that* Lutheranism, rather than the Annex that says, "The working of God's grace does not exclude human action. . . ." Despite the intended double meaning of such a statement, it can only mean one thing.[13]

The Problem with the Ecumenical Dialogues

In the *Apology* to the Augsburg Confession, Philipp Melanchthon identified the basic problem of ecumenical dialogues from the time of the rejection of the Augsburg Confession in 1530 up to the present:

Paul II added this suggestion on his trip to Norway as quoted in Gregory Sobolewski, *Martin Luther: Roman Catholic Prophet* (Marquette, Wisc.: Marquette University Press, 2001), p. 131: "What we need today most of all is a joint new evaluation of many questions which were raised by Luther and his preaching."

10. LW 26, 6-9.
11. LW 26, 278.
12. LW 26, 170-71.
13. *Annex to the Official Common Statement* 2.C.

All Scripture should be divided into these two main topics: the law and the promises. . . . Of these two topics, the opponents single out the law . . . and through the law they seek the forgiveness of sins and justification.[14]

The law, until Christ (Gal. 3:24), says Paul: "When He came, Moses and the Law stopped." There is no middle ground here. Whether you like it or not (and those busily justifying themselves decidedly don't like it), "Anyone in Christ is a new creation; the old has passed away, behold, the new has come. All this is from God . . ." (2 Cor. 5:17-18a).

The problem with Christ is that righteousness is only "in this one Person." Moreover, his is a person who was killed by those making themselves righteous by the law. That spells an end to our own best things, including religion, law, and the free choices of the will before God — even, finally, an end to the church and faith. A will described as free in relation to the law, doing works of love, comes up short here. It arrives at its end as a claim before God. Only Christ stands at the last, and him crucified, with sinners given into his hand by the Father. That is why Luther insisted that we need a "third" word to hold to faith *alone*, and Christ *alone*, and that word is "imputation" — our sins are on Christ, completely and without remainder, and there they not only kill him, but he kills them.[15] Then a new thing happens, a new creation, which ontological language of "participation" or *"koinonia"* always misses, bound as it is to single out the law as God's own righteousness.

Luther's Warning

One of Luther's most famous writings is his autobiographical introduction to his Latin works. It has been rubbed and polished by scholars and antagonists alike until it shines like St. Peter's bronze foot. Often

14. Apology 4, *Book of Concord*, 121:5-8.
15. "Here it is to be noted that these three things are joined together: faith, Christ, and acceptance or imputation" (LW 26, 132). Luther's language is even stronger than the standard translation on this matter: *"Est et hic notandum, quod ista tria, Fides, Christus, Acceptio vel Reputation, coniuncta sunt"* (WA XL, 233.16-7). Word, not ontological being, is the matter.

the little autobiography is read as revealing Luther's breakthrough, or heresy, as you like. Actually, the little piece was written at the end of his life when Luther was surrounded by "Lutherans," so-called, and schismatics of every kind already befouling the heart of the matter, i.e., "We have no other God than this man Jesus," and so justification is "by faith alone." It is a tricky business to assume that what the old man Luther recollected about his exegetical discovery properly reflected the young teacher of Scripture, but it is not such a leap to understand Luther speaking to his contemporaries, especially Philipp Melanchthon, in order to give them a tune-up on the central matter of justification by faith alone through a *Rückblick* — a look back at the whole thing.

Lutherans, after all, have had the hardest time of any dealing with this live electric wire in their midst, both in the person of Luther and especially in the "chief article," justification apart from works of the law. The JDDJ appears to be of little consequence for the Roman Catholic magisterium. The agreement has already been generously ignored in subsequent statements from the Vatican, since it can be read as a valid interpretation of Trent via Augustine. But the document *will* be used as vindication by one group of Lutherans to silence another. Those Lutherans who have been troubled by the radical article of justification from the very beginning because of one enthusiasm or another have found a way to press their advantage by means of the canard of *visible church unity.*

Many times Luther himself had to observe the magnetic draw of the law alone as our righteousness. He observed the timidity of colleague after colleague on this matter, including his dear Melanchthon. So Luther used the opportunity of the printing of his "greatest hits," late in his life, not just to reminisce, but to warn and *confess* once again, putting the ongoing problem of dealing with justification, in his own *bon mot,* as *Augustine's imperfection:*

> And I extolled my sweetest word with a love as great as the hatred with which I had before hated the word "righteousness of God." Thus that place in Paul was for me truly the gate to paradise.

Then Luther paused for the key comment about the catholicity of this teaching, and at the same moment the false catholicity of its diminution:

Later I read Augustine's *The Spirit and the Letter,* where contrary to hope I found that he, too, interpreted God's righteousness in a similar way, as the righteousness with which God clothes us when he justifies us. *Although this was heretofore said imperfectly and he did not explain all things concerning imputation clearly,* it nevertheless was pleasing that God's righteousness with which we are justified was taught.[16]

Luther ended this little reminder with a prayer he wanted his colleagues to hear: "But may God confirm in us what he has accomplished and *perfect* his work which he began in us, to his glory, Amen." That perfection is decidedly not filling up a partial imputation!

What Luther saw in Augustine, *after* seeing it in Paul and the Psalms, was that *God* is right in making the *ungodly* right. The righteousness of God is not a self-possessed attribute or habit of God's *being,* but an act of God doing what God alone does: create anew merely by speaking. To that extent, Luther was pleased beyond his own hope that Augustine taught the same — that *God's* righteousness is that by which *we* are justified. God's own reason for being is for the likes of you. So righteousness is relational, not distributive. God seeks not to *be* God (to speak foolishly) in *himself* (even as a triune *perichoresis*) — but to be right *among us ungodly.* In his *words* no less. As Paul exclaimed: "Let God be true though every human being be false, as it is written: 'That thou mayest be justified in thy words, and prevail when thou art judged'" (Rom. 3:4). Amazing! God justifying the anti-godly makes God right in a *new* and *final* way. God in words among sinners is not slumming it for a day, or giving gifts to the deserving, but identifying and determining who God is in the midst of the rebellion. God is Spirit, as John's letter put it — "a creator of the new," not just "being there."

Now, were we fighting Pelagians, this in itself would be "pleasing" though imperfect. Rediscovering Augustine is always salutary against a series of out-and-out Pelagianisms such as "do what is within you," or even those that taught faith as a "form," needing love to make it righteous. But even during Luther's own day, while he wrote his au-

---

16. LW 34, 337-38. See R. Staats, "Augustins *De spiritu et lettera* in Luthers reformatischer Erkenntnis," *Zeitschrift für Kirchen Geschichte* 98, no. 1 (1987): 28-47.

tobiographical fragment, rediscovering Augustine was not salutary when it came to *imputation*. It is certainly not the case for us. Selling justification as an anti-Pelagian codicil is not only not *enough*, it is in fact more dangerous than a teaching that is open about its confusion over law and gospel.[17] At this point in church history we have such a well-worn path *away* from faith alone, Christ alone, the word alone, and grace alone via one enthusiasm or another (believing in our own belief), that the convergence recorded in such a document will simply exacerbate the problem. When law and gospel are no longer distinguished in the chief article of justification, another center and heart of the Christian faith takes the place of Christ and the Holy Spirit, who kill and make alive; in our case it is the doctrine of church. When the *church* and its ordering become the doctrine by which the church stands or falls, then of course there can be no agreement on justification.[18]

That is why the very narrow conclusion of the *Official Common Statement*, that within the confines of the text's own interpretation condemnations don't apply, means very little indeed. Though a few of the condemnations of Trent miss the point of justification by faith alone as a resurrection from the dead, most of them continue to apply handily. At least occasionally they hit the nail on the head, as in Canon 9: "If anyone says that the sinner is justified by faith alone, meaning thereby that no other co-operation is required for him to obtain the grace of justification, and that in no sense is it necessary for him to make preparation and be disposed by a movement of his own will: let him be

17. The fifth article of the Formula of Concord identified this as a key problem for Lutherans and all Christians: "Therefore the true and proper distinction between law and gospel must be advocated and maintained most diligently, and anything that might give rise to *confusio inter legem et evangelium* (that is, through which the two teachings, law and gospel, would be confused and mixed together into one teaching) must be diligently prevented." *Book of Concord*, 586.27.

18. See Gregory Sobolewski's summary of the Pontifical Council for Promoting Christian Unity's evaluation of the study on *Condemnations*: "Thus Luther's emphasis on forensic justification through the sole efficacy of Christ provides difficulties for Catholicism that emphasizes the mediatorial role of the church, particularly through the sacraments, especially baptism. . . . Correspondingly, Luther's restrictions on human lawmaking bump frequently into the Catholic understanding of ecclesial polity with its restricted but clear appreciation of canon law and laws of the church. . . ." In *Martin Luther: Roman Catholic Prophet* (Marquette, Wisc.: Marquette University Press, 2001), p. 145.

anathema."[19] Of course I take it that they hold no water at God's eternal throne, but they are *salutary warnings,* as the ecumenical language goes, that something is not right.

Augustine's Imperfection

So we take up the Augustinian *imperfection,* which when repeated becomes the burial ground for Christ and the Holy Spirit under the church floor, as it were. Luther himself was pleased to see that what he heard in Scripture was already there in Augustine — *God's* own righteousness is none other than God making *us* righteous. But then an equivocation entered, an imperfection, an imprecision in Augustine, who was assiduously trying to deflect two frightening conclusions that come from God making himself right among God haters.

First, that God has so identified with sinners that God's own law counts Christ a curse (Gal. 3:13), and so it conspires with sinners to destroy this God. God has become a sinner, we must conclude, since we have no other God than this man Jesus, who dies under God's distributive wrath. That is, after all, a great deal to swallow, especially for one who considers God "good" or "love" in the old Greek way. How do you really get God as the subject of a sentence with the verb "died," and an attribution like "sinner"? That would be the end of the law and the pagan ontology of goodness. It would also bring to an end one of the scarlet threads of Augustine's imperfection running through the center of Christian theology ever since, as we find it classically in Anselm's *Cur Deus Homo:* "But a sinful man can by no means do this, for a sinner cannot justify a sinner."[20] God's righteousness means that God became a sinner, and the wages of sin is death according to the law.

The second conclusion that Augustine immediately avoided may make more sense to reason, but it is many times more uncomfortable for our own consciences. Justification for sinners means *death* to them, not metaphorically but literally. The ministry of Moses and the law serves up death for all, since "no human being will be justified in his

---

19. *Decrees of the Ecumenical Councils,* II, 679.
20. Anselm, *Cur Deus Homo* (New York: Open Court), p. 246.

sight by works of the law" (Rom. 3:20a). Moses leaves no other loophole in the law than to die to it, and that is not an appealing loophole.

Justification, it turns out, is a metaphor in Scripture with *two* roots not one, as is commonly assumed. The obvious origin for the term comes from the image of the public court, with judge, defendant, prosecutor, and witnesses. The other, hidden beneath false assumptions of imputation, is the image of the cemetery where the dead lie silent in their tombs and the living ask in fear: Is that all there is? These two together make what we call the biblical description of justification, with God's own distinction between law and gospel: the legal, *moral* one concerning God's wrath and judgment, and the *mortal* one concerning the old human question: Can these bones live?[21] The silly notion we keep hearing about the Bible being full of metaphors and therefore we ought not confine ourselves to "justification" never realizes that the reality being grasped in such a proclamation "for you" is final, ultimate, the end of the line, where the buck stops. It is not one more piece of the big puzzle of God's mystery. It marks the point at which humans shut up as generators of words by analogy, and come to speak God's own final word in proclamation. In justification God is going public about God's real identity, and what is being done with creatures. In the same vein we have the attempt to suggest that Christianity's *rule of faith* is full of a hierarchy of doctrines that are prior to justification, like Trinity and Chalcedon's two natures and one person.[22] *Only* one who already has abandoned God speaking a new gospel word can come to such a conclusion — thinking, as Melanchthon put it, by singling out the law.

Augustine's equivocation, even within the great *On the Letter and*

---

21. Here a reading of Gerhard Forde's *Justification: A Matter of Death and Life* (Minneapolis: Fortress, 1982) is most helpful.

22. See the amazingly confused expression (especially for a Lutheran bishop): "Even if the doctrine of justification is the center of the Lutheran tradition, it does not stand alone but always in relationship to the totality of the faith. The organic relation of the doctrine of justification to the whole of the Christian faith is also clearly expressed by the Augsburg Confession. In fact, the structure of the Augustana makes it clear that the doctrine of justification belongs together with the other articles of faith. It is the fourth of the articles of the Confession. It is preceded by the doctrines of God, original sin and that of the Son of God." Eero Huovinen, "How Do We Continue?" *Pro Ecclesia* 11, no. 2 (Spring 2002): 170.

the Spirit, was understandable and lamentable at the same time. Augustine wanted to protect God from the slander of "change" (death being a big change), and preserve humans as God's good creation by removing the will from death. So, though beginning well, he pulled back by producing a justification without the killing of the law. Once having broached justification as God's own way of making himself right, Augustine stepped out of Scripture for a sheer theoretical abstraction in order to protect God and the free will. He proposed that God has a being that is righteous in itself (infinitely) and so is distinct from God making sinners right. God could make himself just only if he had a reservoir from which to pour and a smaller, creaturely cistern into which to pour it.[23]

This notion of *God's being* apart from justification of sinners is a pure speculation, an abstraction. It opens up a great ditch between God's own justification and the divine justification among sinners in words. In doing so, Augustine missed the *particulae exclusivae* in which Scripture publicizes the mystery of God's righteousness: all have sinned; the final judgment for works is already rendered; justification is faith *alone.* Actually Augustine doesn't so much miss them as *dismiss* them in order to keep a God who doesn't change, and a free will that *can* change as measured by God's eternal law. Thus, the train once heading in the right direction with God made righteous in his words — among the anti-godly — gets turned around in order to keep God and those being made righteous from real sin and its sting, death.

The Problem with Getting "Imputation" Wrong

The confusion of law and gospel kept justification as a *moral* matter alone rather than a *mortal* one, both for God and sinners. Augustine's imperfection kept the law, God's own order, as the only form of righteousness so that love became a form of distribution. Consequently, he kept free will as an active agent, however small, in being made right

---

23. See J. Burnaby's description of Augustine and Bernard of God's love poured into those being made righteous: "The cistern flows over because it is full." *Amor Dei: A Study of the Religion of St. Augustine* (London: Hodder & Stoughton, 1938), p. 262.

by God. Thus neither free will nor God is liable to the "letter," but is included ontologically under "spirit." They do not undergo the ministry of death. But that is exactly what Luther discovered was the bondage of the will, being unable to distinguish the right given to a neighbor and that given to the sinner by God. The terror of death is too great. A series of problems emerged from this "imperfection."

Christ remained judge, not sinner — and so could not be the sin of sin. God had to be conceived as "one" before triune in order to secure a reservoir of grace. Holy Spirit became "gift" in distinction from grace as a source (the Father). Indwelling or participation protected, healed, cleansed, or enlivened the will's love, making righteousness for sinners a partial reality until the full goal was reached. Eschatology itself became a journey of perfection in the parts becoming whole. Augustine, and the church subsequently, got stuck on another question than God's own righteousness among the ungodly: How does God's act become *mine?* Mine in reality, not as a fiction or mere wish! Or put another way, God is already righteous by definition; now how do I get some of that substance as my own? Or more "relationally," how does *it* participate in *me* or *I* in *it?* With a sleight-of-hand, the question of justification became *my* righteousness or the *church's* righteousness as something that can be counted or tallied in relation to law. The result is that the church as the *somewhat righteous*, participating in God's grace, takes over the central matter of theology from God's justifying of himself by coming, eating, suffering, and dying for sinners. The doctrine of the church consequently became who is *in* and who is *out* of its righteous fellowship, rather than "the law, until Christ!"[24] Schism is then the only real heresy. Ecumenism on that basis is then in the business, especially for Lutherans, of deciding whether one likes more the ecclesial enthusiasm of Protestants or that of Rome. But as Luther observed:

24. Anders Nygren once identified the difference as that between a human-centered or God-centered theology, but this was slightly to the side of the mark, as history has shown. Augustine's imperfection leads to the constant refrain, "The church, the church!" while justification by faith alone leads to the declaration: "I have no God but this man Jesus Christ, the sinner, the dead, the risen." This is why, when the church takes over everything in terms of its authorization of true eucharist by the external, hierarchical communion of church order, Luther keeps appearing "individualistic" and breaking true *communio*, as, e.g., in Joseph Ratzinger, "Luther and the Unity of the Churches," *Communio* 11:220-26.

... [W]e have the innate fault that we show great respect for the position ... of men and pay more attention to it than to the Word. God, however, wants us to cling and be attached only to the Word itself. He wants us to choose the kernel rather than the shell, to care for the householder more than for the house. He does not want us to admire and adore the apostolate [apostolic office] in the persons of Peter and Paul, but the Christ who speaks in them and the Word of God itself that proceeds from their mouth.[25]

Augustine remained an ontologist instead of following the biblical eschatology. He was interested in the distinction and relation between God's substance and our own, unable to entertain "the new" for any length of time. But *we* don't need to stay locked into that box. An ontologist, a speculator concerning the nature of being and grace, gets bollixed up concerning how, in the radical act of justification, God does not change and humans do. However, when righteousness refers for its meaning to Christ and his cross, it means not *law* and God's wrath. It means the particular becoming-right that is God's *own* unthwartable destination to make the ungodly "right," apart from all works of the law, only in the Son. This comes as a final pronouncement working both the death of the old Adam/Eve and the resurrection of the new creature in faith itself. Therein lies the true distinction of letter and Holy Spirit. Augustine stopped short of the real effect of justification on sinners.[26] Instead of death and resurrection, i.e., law and gospel applied to sinners, Augustine used a misreading of Romans 5:5 that came to distinguish *gratia* and *donum* (grace and gift).

Augustine had explicitly taken the idea of God making or declaring the sinner righteous — "that wherewith he clothes man, when he justifies the ungodly ..." — as clearly distinct from God's own personal being righteous. Therein he did not get "imputation" right. Augustine says that the biblical references to "righteousness of God" are "not that by which he is righteous but that by which we are made so by

---

25. LW 26, 94.

26. The Spirit and the Letter: "For there is no doubt that, without His assisting grace, the law is 'the letter which killeth'; but when the life-giving spirit is present, the law causes that to be loved as written within, which it once caused to be feared as written without." NPNF series 1, 5, pp. 321-22.

him."[27] Used badly, as it has been by Lutherans in particular, this became a distinction between forensic and essential righteousness, something declared from the outside *ad extra* (that really belongs only to God), and something that actually is or becomes right inside a person. It becomes an individualizing salvation in a most condemnable way. It also tears the Trinity apart, giving the Holy Spirit a false job description of completing or perfecting what was begun in Christ. But God does not make himself righteous by enforcing the law or enabling those under it to survive. When grace and gift are distinguished badly, as two species of righteousness under God's eternal law, controversies constantly spring up about Christ's indwelling, the inherent righteousness of the person, preservation of grace, certainty, and the current darling of this crowd: our *participation* or communion in God's triune being.

The Current Problem: Participation

The arrangement for using Augustine today is not a simple repetition of his ontology. It is to shift the "gift" and "grace" distinction into the relational notion of a creature "participating" in God's being. Augustine's doctrine of the Trinity has come under a withering attack for its substantialism. That certainly has been a problem, and a Roman Catholic theology that seeks to use a relational ontology shows signs of openness to the Lutheran confession but misses widely the far more important apocalyptic context of law and gospel. Karl Rahner thus identified the basic difference between Lutheran and Roman Catholic this way: ". . . the very thing which distinguishes the Catholic theology of grace [is] (that grace is not only pardon for the poor sinner but 'sharing in the divine nature'). . . ."[28] This follows a rather long line of Roman misinterpretation of Lutheranism. It suggests that Catholicism is interested in real, ontic things and Lutheranism expresses itself "existentially" in something like an individual "I-Thou" encounter.[29] Partic-

27. *On the Spirit and the Letter,* c. 9, LCC, vol. 8, 205.
28. Karl Rahner, *Nature and Grace and Other Essays,* trans. Dinah Wharton (London: Sheed & Ward, 1963), p. 24.
29. For a recounting of this, especially in the recent work of O. Pesch, see Daphne Hampson, *Christian Contradictions,* pp. 97-142.

ipation is thought to receive God's being by using God's gifts of love. Augustine's imperfection is thus repeated, this time writ large so that God and our selves are saved from death and for the law, which is now described as a real "sharing in the divine nature."

None of this understands imputation and how the external word creates an alien existence, being glued to or baked into one cake with Christ's very righteousness, a righteousness that never ceases to be Christ's own, and so is hidden and alien to us whenever we consider our own persons. True imputation goes so far as to assert that our sin is hidden from the Father himself! So Luther says: ". . . our sins are covered, and . . . God will not impute them unto us (Rom 4:7ff.). Not as though sin were not to be found. . . . On the contrary, sin is actually present and the pious know of it, but *God* does not know of it." Righteousness is always about God — even the God who hides sin from God for the sake of sinners, since what God does not know is simply not living. But faith, then, is not reciting an inner experience, or even participating in the being of God. Faith means death and resurrection. It means an end of the old life and the creation of a new life in such a way that as long as this old world continues our flesh clings to, but does not determine, our hope. So *simul iustus et peccator* becomes the biblical assertion, with death and resurrection the actual result, rather than the participation of the soul in God's righteous being.

Though Augustine's doctrine of the Trinity has come under a withering attack for a generation now, Augustine's doctrine of the church, as a body with a somewhat absent head, Christ, will no doubt come back with the adoption of the language of "participation" in God's being. That means that one can get a "relational" doctrine that avoids the grosser crises of substance categories, yet the participation this envisions cannot handle God's *own* being made just among the ungodly or the real death of real sinners. God's being as a thing in which participation occurs must be uninterrupted when imputation is imperfectly understood. Humans by inclusion in God's speculative being are the righteous — those becoming like God, not the ungodly. Furthermore, the two natures of Christ are constantly pulled apart in this theology, building on the aged Nestorian drift of Roman theology at least since the Tome of Leo. Jesus Christ's indwelling is understood in terms of his divine nature, as in the famous Lutheran case of Osiander. After all, how does one "participate" in the human nature, unless this has been made properly mystical and only temporarily present by a special otherworldly power?

Shifting from substance to relational ontology is a helpful theological discussion, but Luther's concern with Augustine's imputation remains. The matter of justification in Augustine was "heretofore said imperfectly," and continues to be so. If God imputes righteousness, there must be some reservoir of righteousness in God's being (before and outside, making sinners right). Then there must be an empty or open vessel into which it is poured — something there that God created good. Even if empty, the cup is still a cup. Not everything dies, not everything falls under the curse, or we would be Manichaean, no? This is imputation without distinguishing law and gospel.[30] The same holds for those who, "thinking relationally," would have the Spirit uphold God's being during the difficult time of Christ's death. Or that because our very being is relational to a good God, only the sinful "parts" die, leaving the necessary free will to respond to God's grace. By this means the Scripture's *particulae exclusivae,* "There is none that does good," and, "You have died" (Ps. 53 and Rom. 7), are modified. And when an exclusive particle is modified it is simply no longer exclusive. Theoretically the sting of sin is avoided, at least for a graced will. Death for sinners becomes a metaphor for humility or obedience.

When imputation goes wrong, it is as if we are trying to turn back history's clock. Our theology becomes an "as if" theology — as if the crime of the cross had not already been committed *by all* and the judgment already leveled for this crime of killing the Christ. It is as if the execution already applied to you as a sinner in baptism was only an initiation into God's church of the righteous. This is what the Reformers meant when they repeatedly observed that the opponents in this matter "buried Christ."[31] In the imperfect imputation God gives the law, then a

30. Stephan Pfürtner was correct in noting, "Anyone who affirms the message of justification, and hence the distinction between law and gospel, cannot make what is a matter of law a matter of gospel. . . . It is just this fundamental differentiation which Catholicism finds so difficult." In "The Paradigms of Thomas Aquinas and Martin Luther: Did Luther's Message of Justification Mean a Paradigm Change?" in H. Küng and D. Tracy, eds., *Paradigm Change in Theology: A Symposium for the Future* (Edinburgh: T. & T. Clark, 1989), p. 156.

31. For example, Melanchthon in *Apology* IV of the *Book of Concord,* 123.18 and 133.81.

free will responds because of God's power of grace. The law is singled out as the form of righteousness. Christ himself then becomes extrinsic. Thus, when Lutherans are charged with extrinsicism for not granting an actual change of being for the sinner, it falls on a deaf ear since they are busy considering the prior, extraordinary, and deadly extrinsic assumption that makes Christ superfluous to justification.

God's Participation

By justifying on account of Christ, apart from the law, the Trinity is not out to preserve God's own righteous being or even to include us in them relationally who have somehow gotten outside. Everything God does with us, all of Scripture, is revealing God's coming to us in order to be righteous *in His words* — there alone, in the promises that have their "yes" in Christ, the Father seeks to be declared *right*. All that matters is not how *we* are going to participate in his being through the church, but how God has set the final divine destination and already reached it by Christ's participation among sinners. Christ ate with sinners, *sponte,* freely, willingly, precisely to signify to the world that this was no mere appearance. God became a sinner, the greatest of sinners, even sin itself, so that sin and its sting would be defeated. The end of sin and death is therefore not theoretical, or a new possibility, but has already arrived where sin really exists — that is, in those actively opposing God's way of becoming right. Participation is not what we do in God's being, but is what God has already done in his Son Jesus Christ, who is the word who came to dwell among his rebellious creatures. Christ completely undoes Plato here. He came and won't be ignored, though the creatures "knew him not" (John 1). It is Christ's very participation via the cross that self-righteous protectors of the law sought to end by giving Christ no room in this world. "Foxes have holes and birds of the air their nests, but the Son of Man has nowhere to lay his head" (Matt. 8:20). Sinners give Christ no place in God's creation organized by law. Those seeking to participate in God's being as the means of becoming right are the very ones who tried to limit and end God's participation among the ungodly, finally, as chief of sinners and sin itself. Participation without the cross makes the *church* its own chief article, removing it from true sin, and buries Christ and his Spirit.

God's is an alien participation, outside himself and among the ungodly, apart from the righteousness of the law and God's judging wrath. The rupture of Christ's cross will not be overcome in a greater unity of identities, whether cosmic, churchly, or individual.

Precisely there lies Augustine's imperfection. First, that God's *own* righteousness is not finally the same as his *declaring* sinners righteous. But the second is even more important, since Augustine misses imputation. There the missing matter is the direction and the discontinuity — it is not that God's being is where the real justification lies, and we have to get in there. God wants to be right outside, in the publicized words in Christ, and only there. So we must reject an imagined righteousness that occurs only when we make our journey back to love of God via the church. Instead, we find it in God's journey outward, to be declared right in that which is demonstrably not right in itself. God is true Holy Spirit who creates out of nothing by speaking.

God's being is "being used up," so to speak, in a senseless act of outpouring mercy in such a way as to have what is due the divine only in praise of this act. Outside of that, God simply remains the self-referential being of the right in the form of wrath at the unjust. There is nothing left of God who justifies God's self among the god-haters in giving the forgiveness of sins, in giving life and salvation. There *is* no more "being" in which to participate since he dwells among us. There just isn't anywhere else to go now that the Son of righteousness has arrived. "God died" is then the proper expression of justification as a pure negative, in a shameful crime. But apart from the law, in the vindicated Christ raised from the dead there is life and salvation, a new creation that is truly a communion.

The Function of the *Particulae Exclusivae*

Eschewing the Augustinian imperfection, Luther recalled to his colleagues and preachers what it means when Scripture distinguishes law from promises. Suddenly what sticks out as the very words of death and life are the *particulae exclusivae* from which Augustine was defending himself and the church. The Apostle Paul presupposed the Old Testament witness concerning righteousness, especially that God is faithful to promises, then sharpened his preaching according to the extraordinary gospel he received, that is, according to the *distinction* of law and gospel. That makes God's righteousness an entirely new and surprising matter. The Reformers noted the gospel's sharpening in the *particulae exclusivae*. They are:

1. "*none* is righteous, *all* have sinned"
2. "apart from the law," χωρὶς νόμου
3. "the one man Jesus Christ" (Rom. 5:15) is righteousness
4. "through faith," διὰ πίστεως
5. And the means by which faith comes: "How are they to hear without a preacher?" (Rom. 10:14).

Put together they read this way. Under the law, *none* is righteous. Apart from the law, and so through faith alone, *only* on account of Christ, God rightly makes *us* right while in ourselves ungodly — that is, faith *alone*. And how does faith come? Only by hearing. "God and the law are mutually exclusive in the matter of righteousness."[32] The righteousness of God is that righteousness created by God anew, an "authored genitive."

What is this righteousness of God, then? God, who is right in wrath at our sin before the law, makes the divine destination something other than wrath and judgment: righteous mercy to the actual ungodly. This distinction between wrath and mercy is given to us by two revelations or works of God: law and gospel. Paul's surprise was that God's own righteousness is revealed *only in the gospel;* the *law* brings only *wrath* (Rom. 4:15). This was "new." A surprise. A shock. As Luther once put it: "The law of God, the most salutary doctrine of life, cannot advance humans on their way to righteousness, but rather hinders them."[33] Apart from Christ, who could know?

---

32. Though the argument is my own, here I follow in part the summary of Eberhard Jüngel, *Justification: The Heart of the Christian Faith* (Edinburgh: T&T Clark, 2001), pp. 62ff.

33. It is no coincidence that Luther, in this first of the Heidelberg Disputation theses, exactly takes up Augustine's *On the Spirit and the Letter* concerning the fearless conclusion that this means the whole law, including the Decalogue — and that not reduced to ceremonial law alone. But the terror of the law and its real death remained imperfect for Augustine because of the problem with imputation. LW 31, 42-43.

By normal human reason, God's wrath alone would be the exercising of God's own righteousness. That righteousness according to the law is active and distributive, and so concerns merit and debt. But we hear from Paul's preaching of Christ crucified that God's wrath, using the law, is the opposite of God's righteousness. God's righteousness then is also the direct opposite of "my own righteousness" (what I produce or what is my essence), as in Romans 10:3. So, there is therefore no boasting in my own righteousness, based *on works of the law* (Rom. 3:27). Wrath itself needs to be revealed, as sinners do not fathom its extent. *None* is righteous; *all* have sinned and fallen short of the glory of God. Wrath truly does show the cosmic extent of God's *care* (as Heidegger might put it). But what wrath is, is God pushing forth the wills freely choosing their own righteousness over God's — singling out the law as God's game. In that sense, God hardened Pharaoh's heart, imprisoning him in his own will, thereby showing that the end of the notion of *merit* is a complete disaster for self and world — a catastrophe, we could call it, of biblical proportions. This is a willing "bondage," being bound and determined to avoid sin and its sting, death. When God unleashes wrath, it is the final judgment on human righteousness. But *wrath is not God's own righteousness*. The Father has more than wrath and law, for Christ and you.

Our righteousness under the law is announced as destruction. This is not a Manichaean speculation about the *source* of evil, but is God's own judgment about the *end* or *telos* of the free will. That which God intended for good, humans used for evil. One doesn't exempt parts of oneself, especially a mythical "free will" dreamed up by the frightened in order to escape God's right judgment. But though this wrath at sin is real, and active, it is not God's *own proper* righteousness. It is not the very heart of God. This must also be preached to those living a theological lie. Surprisingly, for anyone schooled in something like Aristotle's notion of distributive justice, God's way of being right is simply not according to the law. Paul announced this with his "but now." The revelation of God's righteousness *presupposes* the working of God's wrath, but is also its limit. Wrath is not infinite for those given into Christ's hand. The place where God's own self is given, God's heart, is "the gospel" (Rom. 1:16-17) — preaching! In word and sacrament! An external, public, humanly mediated declaration of the forgiveness of sins to actual sinners — i.e., to those who actually committed the crime of killing God's Son, the man Jesus Christ. Astonishing!

God's righteousness is given *only* in the gospel, apart from the law; and this decides, trumps, and determines any other meaning of the "righteousness of God" — only through faith for faith (Rom. 1:17). There is the *particula exclusiva* of the gospel — *only* or *alone.* Grace alone, Christ alone, word alone, faith alone. The exclusive particles are meant to keep the Augustinian imperfection from reworking gospel into a form of law — all in order to keep death from God and God's somewhat "righteous" sinners.

In particular in our present context this must be stressed in regard to "faith." Modern Americans get "imputation" very wrong. Where does faith come from? Not from a divine emanation found in the remaining righteousness of the person's free will. Not in participation in God's being through the church. Not in freedom as access to the public square. Those are legal versions of faith. Faith comes from the preaching of the gospel (Rom. 10:17), i.e., precisely not faith's legal meaning. But this utterly changes the notion of authority, ministry, sacrament, and church, which are always the visible fighting ground between Lutherans and Roman Catholics. The word makes a new priesthood of believers who see to it that a recognized, public call goes forth so that God's office of preaching word and sacraments remains to the end of the world. Such a public promise is the only and certain means of God justifying the ungodly. A great disjunction exists right in the middle of the sinner's existence where the law ends — a death and resurrection. It also exists in the church and cosmos. Christ alone, that particular person beside whom we have no other God, rules by way of promise. His kingdom is made up of those raised from the dead. What kind of God would do that and actually be right, unflinching, determined, and unthwartable in his will to love the unlovely? At the risk of breaking into a hymn: "O the depth of the riches and wisdom and knowledge of God! How unsearchable are his judgments and how inscrutable his ways! For who has been his counselor? Or who has given a gift to him that he might be repaid? For from him and through him and to him are all things. To him be the glory for ever. Amen" (Rom. 11:33-36). So, no other God for us than this very one, Jesus Christ given by the Father, and their Spirit who creates from nothing by speaking promise.

Justification and the Unity
of the Church

Avery Cardinal Dulles, S.J.

The signing of the Joint Declaration (JD) at Augsburg on October 31, 1999, was in many respects a celebration of the results of three decades of dialogue. The place, Augsburg, and the date, October 31, were symbolic, since they recalled the date when Luther launched his protest (October 31, 1517) and the place where the division became intractable (Augsburg, 1530). The ceremony therefore marked a certain healing of memories. The two chief culprits for splitting Western Christendom were going back to the very roots of their discord. They now claim to have reached consensus on what was originally considered the most divisive issue.

Value of the JD for Lutherans and Catholics

The heart of the JD undoubtedly consists in what it calls "a consensus on basic truths concerning the doctrine of justification" (JD 13), and especially in the crucial sentence: "Together we confess: By grace alone, in faith in Christ's saving work and not because of any merit on our part, we are accepted by God and receive the Holy Spirit, who renews our hearts while equipping and calling us to good works" (JD 15).

The JD is not, of course, a full reconciliation between the churches. There are many other issues concerning subjects such as sacraments, ministry, sources of doctrine, Mary, the saints, and papal primacy. But it is hoped that these other issues, approached in the light of an agreed doctrine of justification, can prove to be manageable. To the extent that the JD stands up under criticism, it marks an important stage in the progress toward that full communion between our churches which is the ultimate aim of the ecumenical movement. While falling short of the goal of full visible unity, it enables our churches to strengthen the partial communion they now enjoy and thereby contributes to Christian unity.

The first issue to be tackled is, I suppose, the authority of the JD itself. Although the text is certainly a public document, and not the mere work of private theologians, it makes no claim to be a binding doctrinal pronouncement. It states that its purpose is "to take stock of the results of the dialogues on justification so that our churches may be informed about the overall results of this dialogue with the necessary accuracy and brevity, and thereby be enabled to make binding decisions" (JD 4). On the Lutheran side, the Lutheran World Federation (LWF) is not empowered to establish doctrine for its member churches, though the synods can, according to their statutes, enact binding doctrine for their own members.

A similar problem of authority arises from the Catholic side. Granting that Cardinal Cassidy was authorized to sign, Catholics still wonder whether the Pontifical Council for Promoting Christian Unity can make binding pronouncements about matters of doctrine and whether it did so in this case. Can the JD be properly regarded as a statement of the Catholic magisterium? The JD, after all, does not simply state Catholic doctrine but also describes what it regards as Lutheran positions. Can the magisterium bind Catholics to hold certain views about what Lutherans teach? And conversely, can the LWF authoritatively instruct Lutherans about what Catholics teach?

From both the Lutheran and Catholic sides, the JD has evoked a measure of dissent. Reputable theologians have found that it exaggerates the consensus. A year and a half before the signing, the Pontifical Council, in collaboration with the Congregation for the Doctrine of the Faith, published a very critical assessment of the JD.[1] Is it not licit for

---

1. "Official Catholic Response to Joint Declaration," *Origins* 28 (July 16, 1998): 130-32.

Catholics today to raise similar questions and objections?[2] And conversely, is there any reason why Lutherans who are members of signing churches cannot agree with the 251 German Protestant university professors, who denied that consensus on the key issues had yet been achieved?[3]

The JD acknowledges that differences continue to exist between Lutherans and Catholics on seven doctrinal issues connected with justification. But it classifies these not as truly doctrinal differences but rather differences "of language, theological elaboration, and emphasis" and goes on to state that the differences are "acceptable" rather than worthy of condemnation.

I personally regard the term "acceptable" as poorly chosen. I would prefer to say "tolerable."[4] By this I mean that I would not want to expel from the Catholic Church anyone who held the Lutheran positions on justification as described in the JD. But if I were in a position to do so, I would prohibit these Lutheran positions from being preached in Catholic pulpits or taught in Catholic seminaries and catechisms. And conversely, I suppose that many Lutherans who subscribe to the JD consider the Catholic positions described in that document misleading and even false.

Even if the JD is correct, it fails to show why the respective positions are not matters of doctrine and why they are not mutually contradictory, as they were thought to be in the sixteenth century and for centuries thereafter. If Lutherans hold that the justified person remains always and inevitably a sinner, sinning in every act, and worthy of condemnation in the sight of God, while Catholics hold that justified

2. See, for instance, Ansgar Santogrossi, "Un accord oecuménique en faux-semblant," *Catholica* 66 (Winter 1999-2000): 51-69 and Christopher J. Malloy, "The Nature of Justifying Grace: A Lacuna in the *Joint Declaration*," *The Thomist* 65 (2001): 93-120. I have myself expressed some reservations in "Justification: The Joint Declaration," *Josephinum Journal of Theology* 9 (2002): 108-19.

3. The statement of the professors of theology is available in the *EKD Bulletin*, published from Hamburg. The numbers of signers are variously reported. I take the figure given by Aidan Nichols in "The Lutheran-Catholic Agreement on Justification: Botch or Breakthrough?" *New Blackfriars* 87 (September 2001): 375-86.

4. I am informed that at this point the English text differs from the German, which uses the word "tragbar" (tolerable) rather than "annehmbar" (acceptable). If the German text is the official one, this criticism of mine is directed only against the translation.

persons have been cleansed of all sin and can by their good works truly merit the crown of eternal life, are the two parties not truly opposed to each other?

However enthusiastic one may be about the JD, it cannot be denied that there is more work to be done between Lutherans and Catholics. At the time of the signing in Augsburg, the parties issued an Official Common Statement acknowledging this need. They stated:

> Based on the consensus reached, continued dialogue is required specifically on the issues mentioned especially in the Joint Declaration itself (JD no. 43) as requiring further clarification in order to reach full church communion, a unity in diversity, in which remaining differences would be "reconciled" and no longer have a divisive force.[5]

The JD does not intend to break new ground. Its aim is to summarize the results of dialogues on justification that have been going on between Lutherans and Catholics for some thirty years. Because so much work has already been done, it is difficult to see how new conversations between the same partners will materially alter the picture. But new approaches and ways of speaking could perhaps be injected by broadening the conversation to include other interested Christian parties. By listening to these voices we Lutherans and Catholics may be able to find a way beyond our present impasses and at the same time contribute to the larger cause of unity among all Christians.

Broader Ecumenical Interest in the Topic

The issue of justification, so ardently discussed between Lutherans and Catholics, has always been part of a broader ecumenical conversation. While central in Lutheran-Catholic discussions, the same theme has frequently surfaced when either Catholics or Lutherans have entered into dialogue with other Christians: Reformed, Anglican, Methodist, and Evangelical. For example, Lutherans and Methodists in 1984 produced a joint statement on "The Church: Community of Grace" with a section

5. "Official Common Statement," in *Joint Declaration on the Doctrine of Justification* (Grand Rapids: Eerdmans, 2000), pp. 41-42.

of about two pages on "salvation by grace through faith."[6] Methodists and Catholics treated the questions of justification and regeneration in their "Honolulu Report" of 1981[7] and, more briefly, in their Report "The Word of Life" completed at Baar, Switzerland, in 1995.[8] Lutherans and Reformed in the United States in 1984 published a "Joint Statement on Justification,"[9] which closely followed the lines taken in the 1973 European Leuenberg Agreement. The Reformed-Catholic bilateral dialogue issued in 1990 the report "Towards a Common Understanding of the Church," including a "common confession of faith" on what it called "justification by grace, through faith."[10] In 1986 the Anglican–Roman Catholic International Commission (ARCIC II) released a consensus statement on "Salvation and the Church,"[11] which dealt with justification as its major theme and registered a broad though somewhat vague consensus. Finally, in 1997, an unofficial group based in New York with the title "Evangelicals and Catholics Together" published a statement, "The Gift of Salvation." This group, which included some Southern Baptists, was able to report an agreement that justification is in some sense brought about by faith alone. While affirming that justification both declares and makes us righteous, the statement acknowledged that important questions such as baptismal regeneration still required further exploration.[12]

The JD has fed into these ecumenical conversations. In Novem-

---

6. Jeffrey Gros, Harding Meyer, and William G. Rusch, eds., *Growth in Agreement II* (Grand Rapids: Eerdmans, 2000), pp. 200-218, esp. 205-6.

7. Methodist–Roman Catholic Conversation, "Honolulu Report, 1981," in Harding Meyer and Lukas Vischer, eds., *Growth in Agreement* (New York: Paulist, 1984), pp. 367-87, at 370-72.

8. Methodist–Roman Catholic Dialogue, "The Word of Life: A Statement on Revelation and Faith. Sixth Series (1991-1996)," *Growth in Agreement II*, pp. 618-46, esp. 635.

9. "Joint Statement on Justification," in "An Invitation to Action," in Joseph A. Burgess, ed., *Growing Consensus: Ecumenical Documents 5* (New York: Paulist, 1995), pp. 141-69, at 148-51.

10. Reformed–Roman Catholic Dialogue, "Towards a Common Understanding of the Church," *Growth in Agreement II*, pp. 780-818, esp. 798-99.

11. Anglican–Roman Catholic Dialogue, "Salvation and the Church," *Growth in Agreement II*, pp. 315-25.

12. Evangelicals and Catholics Together, "The Gift of Salvation," *First Things* 79 (January 1998): 20-23.

ber 2001 it was the theme of a quadrilateral world-level consultation held at Columbus, Ohio, in which Lutheran and Catholic representatives met with Methodists and Reformed theologians. I have not seen any publication emanating from this consultation, but the literature on the conference indicates a basically favorable reception of the JD, together with a desire to enrich it. The Methodists wished to add greater emphasis on personal holiness and the fruits of the Holy Spirit in human lives. The Reformed as a group wanted to say more about justified persons being called to obedience in good works, while Reformed participants from the southern hemisphere wanted to emphasize the obligation of Christians to promote justice in the world.[13]

The example of the Columbus meeting, together with several other events, convinces me that we may now be entering a new stage in the dialogues on justification.[14] We are perhaps passing, at least for the moment, from the bilateral to the multilateral phase. This kind of transition is not unprecedented. Under the auspices of the Faith and Order Commission, efforts were made in the 1970s and early 1980s to gather up the fruits of several decades of dialogue on sacraments and ministry in the Church. In so doing, the Commission produced the famous paper on Baptism, Eucharist, and Ministry (BEM) unanimously adopted in Lima, Peru, in 1982. That paper showed how far faithful members of different churches — Catholic, Orthodox, Lutheran, Anglican, and Reformed — could go toward affirming a common doctrine on matters of church order. It did not of course claim to have established a full consensus, but it forged a common body of teaching that solidified the achievements of the dialogues of the preceding decades. It may be time for something similar to be done with regard to justification.

In order for this multilateral encounter to be fruitful, we shall need an openness to hear new voices. Catholics and Lutherans, having become quite familiar with each other's positions, can profitably listen together to Reformed Christians in the tradition of John Calvin, Angli-

---

13. See the account in Jared Wicks, "Lights and Shadows over Catholic Ecumenism," *Centro pro Unione Semi-Annual Bulletin* 61 (Spring 2002): 11-17, esp. 13.

14. My thoughts on this matter have been stimulated by a paper that Professor Gabriel Fackre delivered for the American Theological Society at a meeting on April 20, 2002, on the subject, "The Ecumenical Import of the Joint Declaration on the Doctrine of Justification." I had the honor to be a respondent to this paper.

cans in the tradition of Thomas Cranmer, Methodists in the tradition of John Wesley, and Orthodox in the Greek patristic tradition. By attentively listening to these other voices, Catholics and Lutherans may be able to gain new perspectives and discover new terminology that has emerged, like their own, from biblical revelation prayerfully lived out over the centuries. My supposition is that "what any large group of Christian believers have confidently held over a considerable period of time should be accepted unless one has serious reasons for questioning it. Even if one comes to the conclusion that the tenet was false, one should at least make the effort to unveil the positive reason that made people accept error and thus to disclose the truth at the heart of the heresy."[15]

Reformed Perspectives

In February 2000 Yale Divinity School held a conference on the JD at which Professor Gabriel Fackre presented a Reformed perspective, discussing the positions of John Calvin, Karl Barth, and others.[16] Calvin, he pointed out, took up Luther's essential teaching on justification by faith alone and set it in the framework of his broad theocentric vision. More interested in the glory of God alone *(soli Deo gloria)* than in Luther's faith alone *(sola fide),* Calvin kept his eyes fixed on the divine sovereignty. He emphasized what we may call the objective side of justification rather than its subjective reception through faith. His was a Trinitarian view including the Father, who freely chooses the objects of his love; the Son, who purchased righteousness for us through his obedience on the cross; and the Holy Spirit, who enlightens our minds so that we may adhere to Christ in faith.

Although Calvin, following Melanchthon, made a sharp distinction between justification and sanctification, Fackre, as a Reformed theologian, rejoices in the JD's inclusive understanding of justification as inseparable from interior renewal or regeneration. He is able to

15. Avery Dulles, *Models of the Church,* expanded edition (New York: Doubleday, 2002), p. 185.

16. To the best of my knowledge, this paper has not yet been published. Professor Fackre relies principally on the treatise on justification in Calvin's *Institutes of the Christian Religion,* Book III, chapters 11-18.

quote Calvin to the effect that justifying faith is union with Christ, who dwells in us and communicates his blessings.[17]

In the spirit of Calvin, Karl Barth slightly modified the Lutheran thesis that the doctrine of justification is the article by which the Church stands or falls. In a reformulation that I find helpful, Barth wrote:

> The *articulus stantis et cadentis ecclesiae* is not the doctrine of justification as such, but its basis and culmination: the confession of Jesus Christ, in whom are hid all the treasures of wisdom and knowledge (Col 2:3); the knowledge of His being and activity for us and to us and with us. It could probably be shown that this was also the opinion of Luther. If here, as everywhere, we allow Christ to be the centre, the starting point and the finishing point, we have no reason to fear that there will be any lack of unity and cohesion. . . .[18]

If Lutherans could recognize this as the true position of Luther and adopt it as their own, a major stumbling block in the Catholic-Lutheran dialogue would be removed.

Calvinism, it is true, has its shadow side. Preoccupied as it is with God's sovereignty, it tends to diminish the importance of ecclesial mediation and human freedom. Calvinists are reluctant to speak of the efficacy of sacraments in the style of the New Testament and of early Christian tradition. Many of them deny baptismal regeneration, which is crucially important for sacramental churches.

Minimizing human freedom, Calvinist theologians sometimes project a rather tyrannical picture of God, whom they depict as acting arbitrarily in choosing certain persons for election and others for damnation without regard for their merits. The doctrine of double predestination, which Fackre regards as hyper-Calvinistic, is hard to avoid. In an effort to extricate himself from this dilemma, Karl Barth came close to universalism, holding paradoxically that every individual, including Jesus Christ, is both reprobate and elect. Fackre himself rejects Barth's solution, partly on the ground that it removes faith from its role as a graced medium by which baptized believers are jus-

---

17. Fackre, "The Ecumenical Import" (manuscript), p. 17, with references to Calvin's *Institutes,* especially Book III, ch. 1, no. 1, and ch. 2, no. 24.

18. Karl Barth, *Church Dogmatics* IV/1 (New York: Charles Scribner's Sons, 1956), pp. 527-28.

tified.[19] Members of other Christian communions can perhaps assist Calvinists to show a greater appreciation of the mystery whereby God accomplishes his sovereign will by means of our free response to the grace of Christ.

Anglican Perspectives

The Anglican tradition is a broad stream with many runlets. Thomas Cranmer, in his Edwardian Homilies, adhered to the Protestant formula of justification by faith, but he was careful to add that faith, to be justifying, must be "lively," in the sense of being accompanied by true repentance, by hope and trust in God, and by love of God and neighbor. Such living faith, he said, brings forth good works, which lead to the blessed life to come.

The Elizabethan settlement is classically reflected in the theology of Richard Hooker, who speaks in terms similar to those of Calvin. In his treatment of justification Hooker proposes something like the theory of "double justification" formulated by the Colloquy of Regensburg in 1541. "We participate in Christ," he writes, "partly by imputation, as when those things which he did and suffered for us are imputed unto us for righteousness; partly by habitual and real infusion, as when grace is inwardly bestowed while we are on earth, and afterwards more fully both our souls and bodies made like unto his in glory."[20] Hooker's depiction of justification as consisting essentially in the personal presence of Christ, who dwells in the believer through the Holy Spirit, resembles that of Calvin. On the ground that faith is a work of the Holy Spirit within the believer, Hooker regards faith as both the prerequisite and the consequence of justification.[21]

19. Gabriel Fackre, "The Ecumenical Import" (manuscript), p. 14. Alister McGrath likewise writes: "It must be noted that Barth's doctrine of election is rejected by most Reformed theologians and thus ought not to be taken as typical of Reformed theology in general." See A. E. McGrath, "Barth, Trent and Küng," *Scottish Journal of Theology* 34 (1981): 517-29, at 524.

20. *Laws of Ecclesiastical Polity*, Book V, ch. 56, no. 11, in *The Works of Richard Hooker*, vol. 2 (Cambridge, Mass.: Belknap, 1977), p. 243 (spelling modernized). Cf. "Salvation and the Church," n. 2.

21. Alister E. McGrath, *Iustitia Dei,* 2nd edition (Cambridge: Cambridge University Press, 1998), p. 292.

John Henry Newman in his Anglican years at Oxford delivered his great *Lectures on the Doctrine of Justification,* seeking a middle path between what he viewed as Lutheran and Roman errors. In these Lectures he sought to recover the patristic theology of justification, which had previously appealed to George Bull, Jeremy Taylor, and other great Caroline divines of the seventeenth century. Newman's *Lectures,* although they no doubt depict Luther in too negative a light, set forth a positive theory that could have great ecumenical importance. By the sacrament of baptism, Newman holds, the Christian is made a member of the Body of Christ and a temple of the Spirit of Christ. While justification consists essentially in the indwelling of the Holy Spirit, it is received by faith, which in turn lives in works of love and obedience. Although Newman departs in some ways from the formulations of the Council of Trent, his doctrine of justification is, I believe, orthodox by Catholic standards. When Newman reissued the work as a Catholic, he felt no need to make any substantive changes.

Perhaps because Newman spoke rather harshly about Protestant authors, the ecumenical value of his *Lectures* has been neglected. But recent scholarship is correcting this oversight. The Anglican Evangelical Alister McGrath, for example, finds that Luther's doctrine of the real presence of Christ in the believer comes "remarkably close to Newman's own position." McGrath likewise takes note of "remarkable similarities" between Newman and Calvin on the nature of justification.[22]

Methodist Perspectives

While listening to the voices of the Reformed and the Anglicans, we would do well to attend also to those of the Methodists, especially John Wesley. In a very important article Geoffrey Wainwright has summarized Wesley's positions on the seven points of friction between Lutherans and Catholics noted in the JD.[23] Following Wainwright's account, I shall briefly address each of the seven questions.

22. McGrath, *Iustitia Dei,* pp. 313, 317.
23. Geoffrey Wainwright, "The Lutheran-Roman Catholic Agreement on Justification: Its Ecumenical Significance from a Methodist Point of View," *Journal of Ecumenical Studies* 38 (2001): 20-42. The same article may be found in *One in Christ*

On the first, whether human beings are powerless in relation to justification, Wesley, like the Catholics, speaks of the liberating power of God's prevenient grace in such a way that God's causality operates through human freedom. Here he seems to come close to the Catholic position without contradicting the moderate Lutheran view expressed in the JD and the Annex to the Official Common Statement.[24]

On the nature of justification, Wesley, like Calvin and the Anglicans, and unlike the Council of Trent, makes a sharp conceptual distinction between justification and sanctification, but he insists that neither can be present without the other. Since all who are justified are also interiorly renewed, righteousness is both imputed and imparted. "They to whom the righteousness of Christ is imputed," he writes, "are made righteous by the Spirit of Christ, are renewed in the image of God 'after the likeness wherein they were created, in righteousness and true holiness' [cf. Eph. 4:24]."[25]

On the question whether we are justified by faith alone, Wesley takes a mediating position similar to that of Cranmer. "We are justified by faith alone, and yet by such a faith as is not alone."[26] Justifying faith for Wesley necessarily brings with it repentance, hope, love, fear of God, and good works. Justification ordinarily comes from sacramental regeneration, but since those who have been born again through baptism repeatedly fall, they must regain righteousness through new acts of faith and repentance.

On the question whether concupiscence is sin, Wesley deftly carves out a position intermediate between that of Luther and the Council of Trent. In his Sermon 13, "On Sin in Believers," he declares:

---

37 (2002): 3-31. See also his "Rechtfertigung: lutherisch oder katholisch?" in *Kerygma und Dogma* 45 (July-September 1999): 186-206.

24. "Lutherans do not deny that a person can reject the working of grace. When they emphasize that a person can only receive *(mere passive)* justification, they mean thereby to exclude any possibility of contributing to one's own justification, but do not deny that believers are fully involved personally in their faith, which is effected by God's Word" (JD 21; cf. Annex 2C).

25. Sermon 20 ("The Lord Our Righteousness"), in *The Works of John Wesley*, vol. 1 (Nashville: Abingdon, 1984), pp. 449-65, at 459.

26. Letter of March 10, 1762, to George Horne, in John Telford, ed., *The Letters of John Wesley* (London: Epworth Press, 1971), 4:175; cited in Wainwright, "Agreement on Justification," *Journal of Ecumenical Studies* 38 (2001): 20-42; *One in Christ*, p. 12.

"*Having sin* does not forfeit the favour of God, *giving way to sin* does."[27] This terminology seems to me rich in ecumenical promise.

On the question of law and gospel, Wesley agrees with the JD that the law is not merely for the sake of accusing and punishing sinners, as some Lutherans have held. God's commandments retain their validity as directives for the justified, as the JD itself expressly states (JD 31).

On the question of "assurance of faith," Wesley's famous description of his conversion experience, when his heart was "strangely warmed," expresses his conviction of being fully assured that Christ had taken away his sins.[28] But Wesley does not hold that an assurance of this kind gives a guarantee of final salvation. According to Wainwright, he is on guard against what the Council of Trent called a "rash presumption of predestination" (DS 1540).

Finally, Wesley would agree with the JD and the Annex that the justified are obliged to perform good works, cooperating with the grace of God, who gives us the ability, as Paul says in his letter to the Philippians, both to will and to accomplish the work of our salvation (Phil. 2:12-13). Wesley frequently speaks of our cooperation with God in working out our own salvation. He teaches that our good works are crowned with heavenly rewards, but apparently refrains from stating that the rewards are merited.

Orthodox Perspectives

The theology of justification in Western Christianity, whether Protestant or Catholic, has been powerfully influenced by St. Augustine's anti-Pelagian writings and by Luther's critique of the medieval penitential system. But Western Christianity holds no monopoly on the theme of justification. All Christians are concerned with being rightly related to God in order that they may glorify him and be saved by him. Beginning with Origen, Church Fathers in the East wrote commentaries on the letters of Paul, in which the term "justification" holds an important place. It should be of interest, therefore, to inquire how the

27. John Wesley, Sermon 13, "On Sin in Believers," *Works,* 1:317-34, at 332.
28. John Wesley, *Journal* (New York: Philosophical Library, 1951), p. 51.

Eastern churches, which were only slightly influenced by Augustine and Luther, dealt with our question. The voice of Eastern Orthodoxy on the subject of justification has scarcely been heard in the West since the Patriarch Jeremiah II of Constantinople sent three lengthy letters responding to Lutheran theologians at Tübingen in the years 1573 to 1581.[29] Among the sharpest disagreements were those pertaining to justification.

The anthropology of the Eastern theologians is firmly based on the concept that man is created in the image and likeness of God. This implies among other things that human beings have free will. The theology of grace, therefore, must not be allowed to infringe on human freedom, as has sometimes happened, the Orthodox believe, especially among Calvinists. They quote the words of John Chrysostom: "God never draws anyone to Himself by force and violence. He wishes all men to be saved, but forces no one."[30] In the same spirit Cyril of Jerusalem writes: "It is for God to grant His grace; your task is to accept that grace and guard it."[31] In this sense we cooperate in our own salvation.

Although the Eastern Fathers hold the doctrine of original sin, according to which all of Adam's descendants have passed under the domination of sin, they take a more moderate view of the effects of the Fall than has been customary in the West, where the polemical writings of Augustine against the Pelagians have been determinative. Eastern theologians deny that the image of God was lost, that human nature became utterly depraved, and that free will was destroyed. In the words of Patriarch Dositheus of Jerusalem they say that God "takes not away from man the power to will — to will to obey or not to obey him."[32]

Patriarch Jeremiah accumulates a long series of texts from the Old and New Testaments to prove that even after the Fall man retained the power to choose good as well as evil. To achieve the good and be

---

29. George Mastrantonis, *Augsburg and Constantinople: The Correspondence between the Tübingen Theologians and Patriarch Jeremiah II of Constantinople on the Augsburg Confession* (Brighton, Mass.: Holy Cross Orthodox Press, 1982).

30. John Chrysostom, "Sermon on the Words 'Saul, Saul . . . ,'" 6 (PG 51:144).

31. Cyril of Jerusalem, *Catechetical Orations*, 1:4 (NPNF, 2nd ser., 7:7).

32. Dositheus, *Confession*, Decree 3. I take this reference from Timothy Ware, *The Orthodox Church* (London: Penguin Books, 1991), p. 229.

saved, however, we need help from God, without which we can accomplish nothing.[33]

Claims for the sufficiency of faith, according to the Eastern theologians, should not allow the sacraments or the other virtues to be discounted. Life in Christ, they assert, begins with the sacraments of initiation. Baptism causes the sinner to die with Christ and rise in the power of his resurrection. The justified Christian, furthermore, must possess not only the virtue of faith but the other two theological virtues: hope and love, without which it is impossible to be saved.

Jeremiah II also rejects the view of the Tübingen theologians that faith without works suffices for the remission of sins. The Church, he writes, "demands a living faith, which is made evident by good works; for as James says, faith without works is dead [Jas. 2:17]."[34] He then goes on to quote St. Basil to the effect that faith given from above by grace is of no value without human endeavor coming from below. At another point he inserts a long quotation from St. John Chrysostom on the absolute necessity of good works for salvation.[35] In his own words, Jeremiah writes:

> And just as the memory of the flame does not warm the body, in the same manner faith without love does not effect the light of knowledge in the soul. Indeed, it is impossible for love to be found without hope. Hence, the Holy Fathers say one thing is permanent: the hope in God. All other things are not in reality, but merely thought. He who has fastened his heart on the power of faith has nothing without works.[36]

On the basis of my limited familiarity with their tradition, I see no reason why Orthodox theologians could not subscribe to the basic consensus affirmed in paragraph 15 of the JD: "Together we confess: By grace alone, in faith in Christ's saving work and not because of any merit on our part, we are accepted by God and receive the Holy Spirit, who renews our hearts while equipping and calling us to good

---

33. Jeremiah II in *Augsburg and Constantinople*, pp. 304-5.

34. Jeremiah II in *Augsburg and Constantinople*, p. 37.

35. Jeremiah II in *Augsburg and Constantinople*, pp. 184-86; citing John Chrysostom, *On Genesis*, Homilies 4 and 5 (PG 53:47-50).

36. Jeremiah II in *Augsburg and Constantinople*, p. 182.

works." On most of the seven disputed questions, the Orthodox would seem to be in agreement with the Catholic positions, except that they might be more hesitant to speak of merit, which would strike them as too juridical a category. Lutherans and Catholics, for their part, would probably find the Orthodox positions no more objectionable than they find each other's. Thus the idea of a Joint Declaration including the Orthodox seems theologically possible.

The point of including the Orthodox in the conversation, I believe, would not be simply to gain more adherents to the consensus. The Orthodox would be able to offer a new soteriological framework, which is in many ways very biblical and attractive. For them salvation is not primarily a delivery from guilt but rather a matter of enlightenment, healing, and union with God, who bestows eternal life. Above all, it is a matter of perfecting the image of God within us so that we are renewed in God's likeness and in that sense divinized.

As William Rusch has shown in a valuable article on the Eastern Fathers, divinization (or *theosis*) is the key concept in Eastern soteriology.[37] This notion, although partly derived from Plato and Plotinus, is supported by numerous biblical passages in the Psalms (Ps. 82:6), in the Gospel of John (10:34), and in the second letter of Peter (2 Peter 1:4). It closely resembles the Pauline concept of adoptive sonship.

Theosis as understood in Eastern theology is not an achievement of human effort but a gift of grace. Athanasius speaks for the whole Eastern tradition when he writes that God "became man in order that we might become gods."[38] Only God can divinize, and the primary means by which he chooses to do so is the Incarnation. *Theosis* does not of course mean that we become creators. We retain our creaturely status but are truly made like our Creator and receive his life by participation. Through this wonderful union we are purified, illuminated, and delivered from corruption.

The Eastern theology of the indwelling of the divine persons has helped Western theologians to recover the doctrine of uncreated grace, so neglected by the Scholastics after the time of Peter Lombard.[39]

---

37. William G. Rusch, "How the Eastern Fathers Understood What the Western Church Meant by Justification," in *Justification by Faith: Lutherans and Catholics in Dialogue VII* (Minneapolis: Augsburg, 1985), pp. 131-42.

38. Athanasius, *On the Incarnation of the Word*, 54 (PG 25:192).

39. According to the United States Lutheran-Catholic Dialogue on Justifica-

Taken in combination with the insights of Luther, Calvin, and Newman on the real inhabitation of Christ through the Holy Spirit in the justified Christian, this Eastern contribution can help to offset the distortions introduced by the excessive preoccupation of Protestants with sin and guilt and of Catholics with the mechanics of created grace.

Hopes for a Multilateral Approach

My suggestion is, then, that Lutherans and Catholics can draw closer to each other by seeing what they can appropriate from the soteriologies of other Christian groups, especially Reformed, Anglican, Methodist, and Orthodox. By affirming together what they find authentic in these other traditions, the two parties may find it possible to perhaps transcend their previously limited perspectives and get beyond the impasses that have thus far prevented the dialogue from achieving full success. The Lutheran-Catholic consensus on justification, thus far incomplete and limited to two major communions, still needs to be deepened and placed in service of the broader cause of Christian unity.

I offer this proposal without full assurance that it will succeed. It needs to be tested by the actual experience of multilateral dialogue. Because the full results of such a dialogue cannot be calculated in advance, the venture is particularly exciting.

---

tion: "A few Catholic theologians in the seventeenth century (e.g., Lessius, Petavius, Thomassinus), assisted by their studies in the Greek patristic tradition, expanded on Trent's teaching regarding the divinizing presence of the Holy Spirit in justification. In general, however, Catholic theology concentrated on the nature and causes of created grace." See *Justification by Faith*, Common Statement, no. 66, p. 39.

Justification — Learning Its Meaning Amidst the Religions

Paul Varo Martinson

Introduction

In this chapter I understand justification as God's free action that makes sinners right with God, transforming a broken and false relationship that disrupted the trust and faith intended in creation. This action of God, which becomes effective for us in faith, conveys to us all the riches of Jesus' life, death, and resurrection, including forgiveness, the fullness of Jesus' own righteousness, and rebirth into a new life, a new life of community with God. It is the "joyous exchange" in which we give God our worst and God gives us God's best. To expound on this, one would have to talk about the *propter Christum,* the several *solas,* and much more. It is rightly described in these words: "We . . . become righteous before God by grace, for Christ's sake, through faith."[1] There is no growth beyond this, only into it.

I have been asked to say something about justification and the religions. Obviously this is only a small foray into the subject. I will do so in three parts. First I will initiate a proposal for a Universal Declaration on Justification by the religions. Second, I will briefly explore distinctive religious understandings. Third, I will ponder some implications.

---

1. Augsburg IV ("Homines gratis justificatiantur propter Christum per fidem").

Toward a Universal Declaration on Justification

Do we meet a similar teaching in other religions? Yes, there are look-alikes.

It is well known that in the Jodo Shinshu form of Pure Land Buddhism in Japan there is a striking similarity to many of Luther's, if not Paul's, formulations. This reform movement in Japanese Pure Land was sparked by Shinran, who lived some three centuries earlier than Luther (1173-1262). He, like Luther, met with an existential crisis that erupted into his radical reform. He lived, he believed, in the latter days of spiritual degeneration. Moreover, in Pure Land Buddhism there was the belief in an Amida Buddha who from time immemorial had attained a saving body of mercy that could be made efficacious for people simply by calling upon his name. For Shinran, however, oppressed by his own sense of bondage to evil in heart and life, this diligent calling was an insurmountable obstacle, for how could one know the calling was genuine? In his breakthrough he discovered that the mercy of the Amida Buddha was incalculable, and that in this time of evil, his mercy was granted freely, without any prior requirement. Indeed, it was those who least merited mercy that were its rightful recipients. Calling upon the Amida Buddha was not a means to gain or merit mercy, but a call of gratitude for a mercy already extended.

The above example comes from the Buddhist experience in Japan. One might also think of one of the Vaisnava Schools of piety within Hinduism in India (the Southern or Tengali School) where another striking look-alike to justification emerges. But we must press on. So far as I know, these two offer the most striking resemblance to the Reformation doctrine of justification by faith.

Nevertheless, I think we need to cast our net a bit further, to embrace at least Judaism and Islam in our conversation. With Judaism we have what has been described as "covenantal nomism." It has been defined as: "the view that one's place in God's plan is established on the basis of the covenant and that the covenant requires as the proper response of man his obedience to its commandments, while providing means of atonement for transgression."[2] This Torah view is similar,

2. See Martien E. Brinkman, *Justification in Ecumenical Dialogue: Central Aspects of Christian Soteriology in Debate* (Utrecht: Interuniversity Institute for Missi-

though not identical, to a Muslim understanding of God's gracious giving of divine guidance for life in the Qur'an and the divine gift of forgiveness of sins whenever and wherever God freely chooses.[3]

In this broadening of the conversation I take my cue from a statement by the biblical scholar James Dunn. Having discussed Paul's teaching of justification, which he sums up as "God justifies (accepts) people through faith and not by virtue of works of the law,"[4] he comments:

> . . . we need to rediscover Paul's original teaching on the subject. God accepts all who believe and trust in him: Gentile as well as Jew, . . . Roman Catholic and Protestant, Orthodox and Muslim."[5]

I take it that Hindus and Buddhists qualify as gentiles in the intent of this quotation and for the purposes of our discussion.

Since there is this much agreement, let us propose a Universal Declaration on Justification that articulates what we as Jews, Christians, Muslims, Hindus, and Buddhists hold in common. Now, of course, there are some gigantic cultural and linguistic differences that must be bridged in such an enterprise, but if the substance of our affirmations is the same, that should not provide an impassable barrier. Of course, we don't want to attempt a complete statement here, but only a starting effort to see what it might look like. I will try to be as faithful as I can to what little I understand of the respective indigenous traditions and keep the principle of strategic naïveté in play, necessary for all ecumenical agreements. So let us make a go at it.

> While we, as Jews, Christians, Muslims, Hindus, and Buddhists, come from widely different linguistic, experiential, and conceptual backgrounds, for the larger well-being of our common world, we wish to take this occasion to make known that which fundamen-

---

ology and Ecumenical Research, 1996), pp. 58f. n. 93 and E. P. Sanders, *Paul and Palestinian Judaism: A Comparison of Patterns of Religion* (Minneapolis: Augsburg Fortress, 1977), p. 75.

3. For one prayer of forgiveness see the concluding section of the second Surah of the Qur'an.

4. James D. G. Dunn and Alan M. Suggate, *Justice of God: A Fresh Look at the Old Doctrine of Justification by Faith* (Grand Rapids: Eerdmans, 1993), p. 27.

5. Dunn and Suggate, *Justice of God*, pp. 28f.

tally unites us all and to set aside any and all mutual antagonisms and acts of injustice that have shaped our past histories separately and together. It is hoped that this common affirmation can provide the basis for a deeper mutual exploration of our varied faiths, for fuller mutual sharing with one another, and for growth together in our mutual service to each other and the world.

While we do have our own authoritative texts, we believe that they allow a full concurrence in the following matters. *First,* this world is not of our own making, but has its source in that just and good power that we all variously name. *Second,* we confess together that this world which is now ours by right of birth we have corrupted. As humans we have fallen away from that just and good source that we all affirm. Indeed, we confess that, insofar as it obtains within us, we are unable to right our own estranged circumstance. *Third,* for this reason we are happy to join in mutual confession that our only hope is for a freeing power that comes from beyond us. It comes in covenant (Jew), it comes in incarnation (Christian), it comes in revealed guidance (Muslim), it comes in divine accessibility (Hindu), it comes in a saving vow (Buddhist). Here alone do we find any hope for the right-wising of our estranged circumstance. This restoration we can only receive by faith in that which comes in grace and mercy to us. *Fourth,* together we affirm that this restoration by grace through faith empowers us to live out this new life before one another and all the world.

Well, how does that sound? Pretty good for a first try?

There are some problems, however. In my effort to try to be faithful to everyone, I had to pretty much drop out that which was not simply distinctive, but central to each. The common affirmations all turn out to be a consensus on a general kind of anthropology. These common elements include a sense of finitude, a sense of failure and powerlessness in that failure, a sense that help must come beyond the empirical self (thus *extra nos*), an attitude of entrusting to another, fuller reality that brings that help, and through all this to experience a fresh empowerment to live life in conformity with the new sense of renewal. All these affirmations are anthropological in nature without exception. To be sure, the anthropology makes purchase off the central convictions of each of these religions, but none of these religions would claim that their anthropology was their central doctrine or teaching or belief. Has something gone askew? I think so.

Justification can often be treated exclusively as soteriology. It is a means to some benefit. The focus often runs on the right appropriation of the means, upon anthropology more than theology, existentialism[6] more than confession, epistemology[7] more than testimony. Soteriology pulls itself up, so to speak, by its own bootstraps. There is, to speak of the Christian case, a weakly functioning *propter Christum*. Clearly this is the case with James Dunn's definition above. So long as there is the presence of faith, all is well.

I think, for instance, of a student some three or four years ago. In class she spoke very highly of a Buddhist Pure Land nun who was a religion faculty member at one of our Lutheran colleges. She was deeply impressed every time this Buddhist nun spoke in chapel; in fact, she would always want to be in chapel when she spoke. I suspect that what we have at hand here, not for the student, but for the Buddhist nun, is a case in which she had discovered a soteriology that was essentially indifferent to whether the topic under discussion was the crucified Jesus or the Amida Buddha. It worked equally well in both places, so that she ended up as a Buddhist preaching a more convincing "gospel" than supposedly "Christian" professors and clerics.

For many years I have had difficulty bringing the doctrine of justification into the context of interfaith reflection. I think I now have a sense of where the problem lies. Soteriology can become so self-important that it can lose a clearly articulated link with its referent, the rootings of a faith. Justification is not simply a soteriology, it is inherently a doctrine of God. With that it rises or falls. What happens, then, when these defining rootings are brought into the conversation? I explore this in the next section.

Distinctive Understandings

Now we have before us five religious commitments — Jewish, Christian, Muslim, Hindu, and Buddhist. How do we proceed? Let's begin

---

6. Defined as "what sort of experience we undergo in the process."
7. Defined as "what mode of knowing is involved."

with a question. Is justification a case of a new knowing *(gnosis)* or is it an event? If it is an event, what sort of event?

In the "Universal Declaration" above, justification was clearly a case of a way of knowing that applied to all alike without specific regard to a referent. As for the referents at stake, they represent quite a diversity. In the case of Hinduism and Buddhism, the referent is a gnosiological one, something that belongs to the realm of knowing rather than an event as such. In the case of Judaism, Christianity, and Islam, the referent is clearly an event that has ramifications for knowledge. That is to say, the events were events in time and space, our ordinary historical world — the Exodus and Covenant, the crucifixion and resurrection, the sending down of the Qur'an.

The above reflections suggest that in addressing the question of referent it might be helpful to explore first the Hindu-Buddhist outlook in relation to the Christian, and then explore the Christian understanding of justification in relation to Islam and Judaism.

The Other (Buddhism)

I remember well the remarks in Kyoto, Japan, by a Pure Land Buddhist monk speaking to a group of theological students I had brought there some years ago. The story of the Amida Buddha upon which the doctrine of salvation by faith is based is of course strictly mythological, with no basis in actual history. The monk was addressing the question of the antithesis between the imaginary and the actual that he knew was in our minds. To do so he offered a third term. He asked, "Is the Amida Buddha imaginary, or actual, or real? Cannot something be real without being actual?" I understand by this that real means something that has a genuine efficacy even if not historically actual. Whatever has the power to change our circumstance must thereby be real, not simply imaginary.

Now, this is no trivial question or claim. Moreover, this is spoken in the full knowledge that there is a trinitarian-like formula in the Buddhist doctrine of the Three Bodies *(trikaya)* of the Buddha.

To what does the Three Bodies *(trikaya)* refer? It refers to the historical Buddha *(nirmanakaya)*, who is singular; it refers to the imaginative and mythopoetic realms of the countless Buddhas whose only history is in the mind of the devotee *(sambhogakaya)*; it refers to the ultimate, absolute, and unchanging reality of the Buddha mind itself in which all multiplicities are vanishing moments in an eternal collage of changeless change *(dharmakaya)*. What then are the ontological relations amongst these three bodies? The imaginative Buddhas and the historical Buddha are simply manifestations at grosser levels of the absolute body of the Buddha, the shape, so to speak, that enlightenment takes at these lower levels of the imaginative and physical realms.

It does not take long to see that the Three Bodies of the Buddha and the Trinity have little in common either formally or materially.

- The Three Bodies are three modes of manifestation and are infinite in number, while the Trinity refers to three loci of identity that own their identity precisely because they are in relation.
- The Three Bodies dissolve history into realms of a higher and timeless truth, whereas the Trinity implicates the highest reality, God, in the historical and contingent, the timely — God undergoes something.
- While both Buddhists and Christians in their doctrines of Three Bodies/Trinity are giving account of a historical narrative, the narratives are important for different reasons — the gnosis the Buddha discovered, the crucifixion and resurrection Jesus underwent.

The Amida Buddha of Pure Land Buddhism fits into this Three Body scheme. For the Amida Buddha is only one of the innumerable Buddhas in the realm of imagination. By reliance upon this Buddha I am brought into the sphere of this Buddha's influence and salvation. The ultimate outcome is eschatological. My mind becomes identical with the mind of Amida, and I attain the level of enlightenment this Buddha attained.[8] What in the imaginative realm appeared to be an other with whom there can be a faith relationship, in the real realm of enlightenment becomes an identity of mind devoid of relation.

Now, there are many interesting questions that those who affirm a doctrine of justification might want to discuss further with the Pure Land Buddhist. For example, how is human failure (sin) understood?

8. It might be noted that in Shinran's Pure Land, the Amida Buddha is exalted to the highest level, becoming himself the Absolute Buddha reality.

How is faith understood? How is mercy or grace understood? How is salvation understood? We have no time here to explore these questions.

The one point that concerns us is the status of the referent. In the Buddhist case the referent is an apparent other, a skillful means *(upaya)*, that provides the saving point of reference for the one who is totally enmeshed in his or her own karma. Without that external light of mercy shining in and awakening faith, the encasement could not be penetrated and cracked. When the full enlightenment comes, the fiction of the skillful means is transcended. In the Christian case the referent is a genuine other, with whom a genuine relationship is established in faith such that what happens to the other — death and resurrection — now happens also in, with, and for the person of faith. The oneness-in-otherness of the relation remains forever.

The Likeness (Hinduism)

As we view the Vaisnava school of piety within Hinduism, we will look briefly in two directions — first in the direction of Krishna as a manifestation *(avatar)* of the supreme deity Vishnu, and then in the direction of images as bearers of the divine image.

Surely one of the high points of all religious literature is the eleventh chapter of the Bhagavad Gita (Song of the Lord). In this chapter Arjuna, a warrior, begs Krishna, a charioteer, to reveal his true form to him. Conversation with Krishna has led Arjuna to suspect that Krishna must be in some sense the divine incognito. Krishna obliges. The theophany is breathtaking. Suddenly the cosmos opens up to the most terrifying spectacle imaginable as the "hidden God" *(deus absconditus)* of Luther, so to speak, manifests itself. Faced with the divine wrath Arjuna is in utter despair and calls on Krishna to abort the theophany. Krishna obliges, and things return to normal. Krishna then consoles Arjuna, saying that only to those whom he loves will he so manifest himself. He learns that it is only by love that Krishna, i.e., God, can be known. This is the first direction.

Surely one of the most charming aspects of all religious practice is the devotion paid to images in the Hindu tradition, our second direction. Mark Twain put his characteristic slant on the subject when he wrote of his visit to India: "And what a swarm of them there is! The town is a vast museum of idols — and all of them crude, misshapen, and ugly. They flock through one's dreams at night, a wild mob of nightmares."[9] Well, maybe it wasn't charming for him, but if one looks more closely at what is really going on the charm might well appear.

Images of the gods are admittedly made by humans. But all of reality is in some sense a manifestation of God, whether natural or crafted. A properly consecrated image is a fitting medium for a sacramental kind of divine presence. As such, the most characteristic form of Hindu worship is the act of *darsan*, seeing God and being seen by God. The image makes God palpable to the senses, so to speak. Fittingly, it receives all the attention that we would give to any honored guest. It receives gestures of respect and signs of obeisance; daily needs are cared for as if it were a living person. As if it were a kind of "dollhouse" religion, the image is awakened, bathed, dressed, fed, entertained, put to sleep. Characteristically this worship, or *puja*, may be done in a shrine at home, but also in a temple.

The charm becomes theological when we read this interpretation by a thirteenth- to fourteenth-century Indian theologian of the Sri Vaisnava movement:

> This is the greatest grace of the Lord, that being free He becomes bound, being independent He becomes dependent for all His service on His devotee. . . . Behold the supreme sacrifice of Isvara [the Lord], here the Almighty becomes the property of the devotee. . . . He carries Him about, fans Him, feeds Him, plays with Him — yea, the Infinite has become finite, that the child soul may grasp, understand and love Him.[10]

One could well hear the later rhapsodizing of Luther over the *finitum capax infinitum* of the babe born in Bethlehem.

Here in Krishna and the image we have a profound sense of the

---

9. Mark Twain, *Following the Equator* (Hartford, Calif.: American, 1898), p. 504, as cited in Diana L. Eck, *Darsan: Seeing the Divine Image in India* (Chambersburg, Pa.: Anima, 1981), p. 15. See my discussion in *Families of Faith*, chapter 9 on our Hindu neighbor and chapter 17 in the section "Image Is Not Incarnation."

10. The theologian is Pillai Lokacharya, whose dates are variously put at 1205-1311 or 1264-1369. Bharatan Kumarappa, *The Hindu Conception of the Deity as Culminating in Ramanuja* (London: Luzac, 1934), pp. 316-17, cited in Eck, *Darsan*, p. 15.

divine accessibility. Nevertheless, in both cases we have a divine presence that in Christian terms can only be spoken of as docetic. The human flesh of Krishna and the crafted body of the image are vehicles for the divine manifestation, but in no sense do they qualify deity itself. When Krishna dies, it happens purely of the flesh. It is as the relationship between soul and body, as Krishna expounds it to Arjuna. While urging Arjuna to engage in just battle, he at the same time tries to rob the carnage and death of its sting:

> As leaving aside worn-out garments
> A man takes other, new ones.
> So leaving aside worn-out bodies
> To other, new ones goes the embodied [soul].
> Swords cut him [the soul] not,
> Fire burns him not,
> Water wets him not,
> Wind dries him not.[11]

In the case of deity, even more so than for the soul, there is no mixing of the two. Here a hairsbreadth of difference equals an infinity of distance. A fraction is a fracture. Such applies also to the image. There is finally no mixing of the two — the divine and the earthly. The manifestations in avatar and image are in principle infinite.

In the case of these two "gentile" religions, Buddhism and Hinduism, we have seen some striking similarities to the soteriology associated with the doctrine of justification. At the same time, in both cases, we have also seen a striking difference in terms of the referent that roots the separate soteriologies. In the case of the Buddhist, we saw the absence in the end of a distinguishable Other; in the case of the Vaisnava Hindu, we saw the absence of an implication of deity in the stuff of its manifestation.

The Vulnerability (Islam)

With Islam and Judaism we come into very different religious territory. With the Christian they share a belief in creation, in One God, in God's

---

11. *Bhagavad Gita* 2.22-23.

revealing activity within history, in God's universal and free mercy and forgiveness, in a final judgment. Yet, our referents differ significantly. Again here, as with Buddhism and Hinduism, we can make only brief reference to one aspect of the issue.

Some years ago I was invited by the Muslim community in the Twin Cities to engage in a public dialogue at the University of Minnesota with Dr. Jamal Badawi, a Muslim scholar from Canada.[12] It was an event to mark the end of the month of Ramadan, the month of fasting. For me it was the Saturday between Good Friday and Easter. Christians were also invited to participate.

Some four to five hundred people, mostly Muslim, gathered at the Great Hall in the Student Union for some three hours. I began with a presentation on the Bible and the Qur'an. Dr. Badawi followed with a similar presentation. We then engaged each other in conversation. A microphone was then placed on the audience floor and people were invited to ask questions. A long line formed. The first to ask a question was, I believe, a West African Muslim, judging from his dress. With a loud shout he asked, "Why are you Christians so violent?" Quite a way to begin a conversation!

I thought for a moment, and then responded to the effect that, yes, we Christians talk a lot about God's love, but we fail often, if not most of the time, to live it. I then referred to the typical concerns — the Crusades, colonialism, the creation of Israel. This was just before the Gulf War.

Then I paused, concluding: "I believe that Muslims too have done much that is wrong. That is why we, both Christians and Muslims, need a God of mercy!" The silence of the gathering was displaced by an audible "ahh . . . ," as if the whole assembly was in assent.

What a deep affinity we have. The most common reference to God in the Qur'an is of God as gracious and merciful. But mercy is not yet love. Wherein lies the difference? Mercy is always the prerogative of power. Love never is.

One thinks of the parable[13] in which a slave owed the king 150,000 years of wages! The king demanded payment. The slave

---

12. Paul Varo Martinson, *Families of Faith: An Introduction to World Religions for Christians* (Minneapolis: Fortress, 1999), p. 219.

13. Matthew 18:23-35.

begged for mercy. The king granted it. Then, as it turns out, the slave caught a fellow slave by the throat who owed him one hundred days of wages, demanding immediate payment. The other slave pleaded patience and mercy. But he would not relent and cast that slave into prison. When the king heard of this, he summoned the first slave and demanded to know why, when he had been treated so kindly, he acted so cruelly. He then cast him into prison. Here we see an explication of mercy. Only the one who has power over another can extend mercy. Mercy is never given on demand but only freely by the one in power. It can also be withheld.

Such is not the case with love. Love is never free, for it is by nature a self-imposed bondage, so to speak. And it is never the prerogative of power. It is always at risk, vulnerable, active only in weakness. Parents who love their children will know what I mean. Friends who love their friends will know what I mean. Perhaps even spouses will know. It is intrinsic in parenthood, friendship, and marriage to love. Love, however freely chosen, is a bondage.

Here lies the issue of the referents in Islam and Christianity. In Islam, God is always power and therefore also always free to exercise mercy if he so wills. In the Christian faith God is power, yes, but also broken power — love. God's power is made perfect in the weakness of the cross. Here was displayed the divine love at its riskiest and weakest. Such a conception of divine condescension is not possible in Islam.

The End (Judaism)

As we have engaged the question of justification, in each case we have been forced to consider the question of the governing referent. As it turns out, we find some considerable discrepancies. The question of otherness is forced upon us in the conversation with Buddhism; the question of the actual or apparent engagement of the divine in the human and finite is brought to our attention in conversation with Hinduism; and the question of the nature of the divine mercy is unavoidable in conversation with Islam. What is the case as regards Judaism? Might there not be a closer linkage with the Christian since the Hebrew Scripture is integral to the faith of both?

I think it fair to say that for the Christian, and certainly for Paul, the doctrine of justification is an exegesis of the crucifixion. This being said, we immediately sense a profound uneasiness on the part of our Jewish brothers and sisters. It is without question that Paul was the great enunciator of the doctrine of justification and that it was enunciated in conscious self-reflection upon his Jewish heritage. This leaves us no easy way out. Either Paul was wrong, or despite our profound oneness we confront a deep chasm of difference.

How shall we characterize the issue? What was it about Jesus as the crucified Messiah that so incensed the early Saul and so enthralled the later Paul? Clearly the early Saul saw the Christians as blasphemers of God in their worship of, as they supposed, a crucified Messiah. How was it possible for one who is a failure to be the Messiah? How was it possible for one to be Messiah who flaunted both written and oral tradition (Torah) as did Jesus and his disciples, much less question the long-term validity of the temple cult? How could one who is cursed of God be the Messiah? How could one who implicitly if not in so many words claimed equality with God be the Messiah? No doubt these or similar questions were in the mind of the early Saul. He hints at some of them. He accepted the obvious conclusions and persecuted the Christians as a dangerous new cult. In the later Paul's vision of the crucified Jesus risen, the whole of his Torah theology collapsed. In its place stood the reality of a righteousness by faith. Torah could not exegete the cross; the cross exegeted Torah. Jesus was now seen as both the Torah's goal and its end. In Jesus the Torah had reached its goal. Once the aim was attained its function was ended. The Torah now measures the distance between any well-intentioned doer of the law and its attainment in the Messiah — it convicts of sin.

Justification affirms that the cross reveals God's face, that the crucified one is the enactment of God's identity, that by incorporation into Jesus we enjoy communion with God. These affirmations distinguish justification by faith from all other religious confessions, whether Jewish, Muslim, Hindu, or Buddhist, whether they affirm a doctrine of grace and faith or not. Attending to the referent in the several traditions, we have ended up discerning a mounting crescendo of distinctives. If the otherness of God becomes optional, if the actuality of incarnation is bypassed, if the vulnerability of deity is rejected, and if the proclamation of the crucified Jesus as the fulfillment of the Torah is denied, we have lost all grounds for a Christian doctrine of justification. This is in fact the case whether or not one takes these denials singly or as a whole.

Implications and Intersections

Given such difference, with what are we left? Mutual denunciations? Hardly. Let us explore what justification might urge upon us.

Justification as a Doctrine of God

A few more words about justification will help us deal with the question of difference. As mentioned above, justification is no mere soteriology, it is a full-scale doctrine of God.[14] Justification is not an idea, it is an event. It is an event in history. It is an event within God. It is a Word event.

In all of these cases the event is relational. It is an event in history. Insofar as cross and resurrection are happenings in human space-time, they are fraught with relational consequences. It is an event in God. The economy of incarnation speaks of God as a community of oneness-in-otherness in which the Father gives all things to the Son, the Son returns all things to the Father, and the Spirit joins this mutual reciprocity in an eternal dynamic of love. In this giving and receiving God continually justifies God's own reality as the one who gives to the other.[15] This divine reciprocity reaches its climax in the cross and resurrection. It is a Word event. As such, justification constitutes us individually as persons put in the right with God.

It is from the character of justification as event and relationship that I address the question of the religions.

---

14. See, for example, Eberhard Jüngel, *Justification: The Heart of the Christian Faith* (Edinburgh: T. & T. Clark, 2001), pp. 74f.

15. Cf. Jüngel, *Justification*, pp. 78, 83f., etc.

Divergence/Convergence of Religious Ends?

How then are we to assess the difference that we discerned in the religions? Of course, besides difference we also need to speak of intersections. We have already seen some of that. In the Pure Land tradition of Buddhism there is a striking emphasis upon human bondage to wrong and liberation from this bondage only through the freely given mercy of the Amida Buddha received in faith. We have seen it in the Hindu emphasis upon the divine accessibility in the human figure of Krishna or the lowly image of human making. We have seen it in the Muslim emphasis upon the forgiving mercy of Allah. With the Jew we share belief in the divine faithfulness. At these points and in countless other ways we see a rich array of intersections with other religious commitments. But in the end, do we diverge or converge? The subject is too big to explore here, but a couple of preliminary comments can be made.

We have indicated that God is to be seen as committed to relationship, both in God's own self and in relation to the world. This relationality of God is multifaceted. This divine reality is also present to the world in a multifaceted way. A fundamental biblical affirmation is the universality of God's revealing activity in the creation. No human, no created thing, is devoid of a relation with God.

Given this common matrix, what are the conditions of divergence? In my book *Families of Faith*, under a section titled "Is there a providential role for the religions?" I wrote: "We should not discount the possibility in God's final future for all things, that even there the other religions have a role to play. We do not know now how multidimensional God's final rule shall be. Perhaps what other religions are insistent about cannot always be glibly dismissed as idolatry. Perhaps the Spirit has enabled certain people to grasp onto some dimension of God's rule that partially eludes us as Christians."[16] That is to say, it should cause us no surprise that apart from Jesus Christ there is a revealing activity of God to which people respond, whether appropriately or inappropriately, and that these responses become part and parcel of human histories outside of ours. The justifying God is lavish in offering Himself in relationship to all peoples.

16. Martinson, *Families of Faith*, cf. the discussion in chapters 1 and 17.

One illustration might be mentioned. In Buddhism there is the doctrine of the interdependence of all things *(pratityasamutpada)*. Buddhism takes this discovery in a very concrete and concentrated way. It leads to the teaching of non-self. That is to say, there is no subsisting self to any entity whether it be a human or a thing. The self we surmise as our own is in fact empty of any substantial being. Selves are only the momentary and passing phenomena that arise at the meeting point of a myriad of conditions. Enlightenment is to realize this, and to live accordingly, not grasping for a self but living in compassion for all who because of their false attachment to self are in a state of bewilderment and suffering. The desired end is nirvana, where this realization is complete.

Does this have any conceivable relation to God's revealing activity? I think it might indeed. It appears to me as a profound discovery of the meaning of finitude. There is no such thing as a self-subsisting entity. There are only relations. I am the phenomenon that arises at one nexus of relations. You are the phenomenon that arises at another nexus of relations. From a Christian perspective, creation is in part a withdrawal of God from immediate accessibility to mind and body. The Buddhist insight to a Christian may now appear as an insight into the radical interdependency of all things (a rightful discovery of horizontal contingency) without a locus of identity of any kind, whether human or divine (a mistaken discovery of the absence of a vertical contingency).[17]

Do we end up with divergence or convergence? We end up with divergence if the Buddhist insight, as is typically the case, makes it impossible to recognize a God who is a genuine Other, not reducible to the interdependencies of the finite world. The Buddhist end, nirvana, is devoid of God. Is this divergence the end for the Buddhist? Such is the Buddhist claim. Does it have a place in God's final kingdom? That is, does the genuine discovery from a Christian perspective of the absence of a self-constituted self in this world against the background of the withdrawal of God from immediate accessibility have some eternal purchase on God's desire to be related to all God's creation? To us

---

17. Contingency conveys the idea of "to touch." By horizontal contingency I refer to interdependence as we commonly consider it. It is a two-way, mutual form of contingency. By vertical contingency I refer to God's free act of creating real others. It is one-way contingency, thus vertical.

it seems that God is after all acknowledged in a partial, even if backhanded way. If it does have such purchase, it is still not Christian salvation,[18] and in that light can only be judged as loss.[19]

Or is there convergence? Here we need to distinguish two kinds of convergence. One understanding of convergence sees it as if many paths lead to the same mountaintop. It is as if the divergent ends affirmed amount to the same thing. Nirvana is just a different name for the kingdom of God. This is not a viable convergence in the light of justification as argued here. The convergence we have in mind is a convergence that finds itself in conversion. It is a situation, to refer to the discussion above, in which the good that one affirms (e.g., the lack of a self-subsisting self) opens one to the Word of the gospel or, perhaps, to the eschatological vision of the lordship of Jesus (Philippians 2:10-11).

Let me take an illustration from ordinary life. After all, God's revealing activity is not confined to religious circles, but is part of the warp and woof of ordinary life. This account was related to me by a colleague of mine who had served many years as a missionary in Madagascar. Early on he took responsibility for chapel in a Malagasy prison. He first knew a certain prisoner as a bedraggled old man sitting as far back as he could in the room. But soon the man responded to the message, was baptized, and moved to the front. He became a very happy person. One day after chapel he stayed and wanted to share more of his story. He had four children and a wife. It so happened that his son had rustled some neighbor's cattle and was held by the police. No one had seen the actual crime. He thought to himself, "My son is young and has a full life yet to live. My life is soon over anyway." He thereupon went to the authorities and confessed to the crime. The son was released and the father was now in prison. When he heard the text and exposition of Isaiah 53:5 that, "he was wounded for our transgressions, crushed for our iniquities; upon him was the punishment that made us whole, and by his bruises we are healed," he knew immediately what it meant. He then reflected on his new situa-

18. For example, even if such insight were described as "righteousness by insight" it would not be an alien righteousness, a concept central to justification and its relational matrix.

19. For a recent and closely argued case for divergent ultimate destinies see S. Mark Heim, *The Depth of the Riches: A Trinitarian Theology of Religious Ends* (Grand Rapids: Eerdmans, 2001).

tion as a Christian in these words: "I thought that I had been sent to the house of darkness (prison or *trano maizina*), but it has become a house of light *(trano mazava)*.[20]

Here, as with Cornelius, there is a response to God's initial reve-lation — through a vision to Cornelius, through a traumatic life experi-ence for this man — which through the hearing of the gospel becomes full convergence. Many can testify to this kind of convergence, having come from another religious commitment. Others will testify to an ex-perience of divergence. Perhaps both convergence and divergence have their eschatological counterparts as well.

The Justified Subject

Justification is an end in itself, not a means to another end. In the event of justification, which embraces all three senses referred to above, the estranged sinner is united with Jesus in his death and joined to his new resurrection life. The sinner enters into communion with the triune God. What greater end is there than this?

Yet, the forgiven sinner is both justified and sinner, *simul iustus et peccator.* The end into which one has been incorporated through Christ becomes effective in one's life, bearing all kinds of wonderful fruit. What follows is growth in depth. What does this mean? Growth is not an upward movement, so to speak, a becoming righteous in empirical fact so that the initial act of justification is thus rendered truly effective or descriptively accurate. It is rather a downward movement. A con-tinual dying and a continual rising. It is a deep penetration into justifi-cation. This dying and this rising bears its own natural fruit.

Concurrent with this is a growth in breadth. Paul enunciated very clearly the underlying social implications of justification: "There is no longer Jew or Greek, there is no longer slave or free, there is no longer male and female; for all of you are one in Christ Jesus." Justifi-cation right-wises us in God, and thereby also with the neighbor. Only as the sinner dies and rises continually through the law and gospel does the new self arise and growth outward to the neighbor and en-emy take place.

20. Shared by my colleague Duane O. Olson.

As regards the other religions for the Christian, both of these dimensions of growth are important. Dying to self, one is conformed to the crucified; and self-assertion, self-importance, and self-despair pass. Humbled, one is open to others in a new and fresh way, including the openness to be instructed by the profound insights and experiences of those from different religious commitments. Freed, one is joyful in sharing the good news of God's justifying love with all. Loved, one is moved to serve others whatever the cost, making no distinction between the worthy and unworthy.

The Alchemy of Grace

Caroline J. Simon

"At the right time, Christ died for the ungodly." "While we were enemies, we were reconciled to God." This is the gospel — the good news
— of justification in Christ. We have spent many hours thinking hard
together about the subtleties of what justification in Christ entails. It is
time to ask: Have we begun to understand this gospel? Do we *believe* it?

"While we were enemies, we were reconciled to God." If we are not
amazed by these words, then we are fooling ourselves if we think we understand them. The gospel of justification in Christ rests on the alchemy
of grace — the power of grace to transform enemies into friends, to take
the ungodly and put them on the road to godliness. If we have begun to
take grace for granted, if we have stopped being dumbfounded by it, we
have stopped understanding the gospel and stopped believing it.

Ananias was flabbergasted by grace. The writer of Acts does not
seem to think that we need to know much about Ananias except that
he was a disciple. Ananias was a follower of Jesus; he knew that Christ
had died for him, and Ananias sought to live his life in the light of that
truth. Maybe that seemed to be going fairly smoothly, but then
Ananias had a vision.

Here we need to pause and think about what this would have

This sermon, based on Acts 9:1-20, 26-27 and Romans 5:6-11, was preached at the
July 2002 conference "The Gospel of Justification in Christ: Where Does the Church
Stand Today?" held at Luther Seminary in St. Paul, Minnesota.

been like. We are used to reading about people having visions in the Bible. "The Lord said to him in a vision" can seem mundane in a biblical context. But what if *you* were praying and you heard what seemed like the voice of God, saying, "Get up and go to Alexandria, Virginia, to the detention center and ask to speak to Zacarias Moussaoui. At this moment he is praying, and he has seen a vision of you laying hands on him so that he might regain his sight"? Would you believe that *you* had heard the voice of God, or would you think that you were having some vivid hallucination? Which would be harder for you to believe: that God was speaking to you or that God was planning to heal, reconcile, and use Zacarias Moussaoui? Have you heard the reports of Moussaoui's rantings and threats against Americans? Moussaoui has pled guilty to being a terrorist, or at least trying to be one, and has certainly proved himself to be at least verbally belligerent. Maybe God would tell you to go lay hands on Martha Stewart or Ari Fleischer or even John Walker Lindh. But Zacarias Moussaoui?

Are you surprised, then, that Ananias seems much more startled by the content of his vision than about the fact that he is hearing the voice of God? It is not hearing the voice of God that seems to throw Ananias. Perhaps God spoke audibly to Ananias pretty often. Perhaps God usually said things that seemed to make more sense. Ananias wonders whether God is less than fully informed about this Saul of Tarsus. "Did you know, Lord, that this man is an evildoer? He hasn't just done harm, he has done evil. Do you know how many good people Saul has killed? Do you know that he has come to Damascus to kill people just like me?"

Ananias wants clarification. That is understandable. But then God says something that makes even less sense than instructing Ananias to go heal this Saul, this enemy of God.

God says, "Saul is an instrument that I have chosen."

God knows who Saul is and God has chosen him anyway. God has chosen to turn an evildoer into an instrument of grace and reconciliation. And God has chosen Ananias to be an instrument in this alchemy of grace. All Ananias has to do is believe in this gospel of grace and believe that God can choose and change whomsoever God wills.

Of course, believing this gospel is not some theoretic exercise for Ananias. God does not ask Ananias to speak about the gospel at a conference or even to preach about it. God asks him to act as if he believes this gospel, but to do that he has to take his life in his hands. The text tells us only, "So Ananias went and entered the house." That sounds simple enough, but how much faith did the simple act of going to the house where Saul was take? How much courage? After all, Ananias had every reason to be terrified of Saul and to be furious with him.

Did the sensible side of Ananias lead him to debate with himself as he walked to the street called Straight? Did he ask himself on the way, "Was that really the voice of God? How powerful is this grace anyway? Will I live to tell about this or am I on my way to my death?" As he walked, did Ananias think about the disciples that he may have known whom Saul was responsible for killing?

Whatever doubts Ananias may have had, he chose to act on his belief that God is a Lord who can choose and change even evildoers and bad guys.

Ananias believed in grace. And so he went to restore the sight of this evildoer and enemy. Years later, when Saul, who has now become Paul, is writing to the Christians at Rome about the gospel of grace through faith in Christ, do you think that Paul might have had this quiet scene in Damascus in mind?

"While we were enemies, we were reconciled to God through the death of God's son." Where did Paul first learn this gospel? Not on the road to Damascus. On the road to Damascus, Paul learned that he was an enemy of God. "Who are you, Lord?" "I am Jesus whom you are persecuting." Up to that point, Paul thought he was a friend of God, a righteous person who was on God's side. What horror must he have felt when he heard that the Lord was Jesus — that he had been persecuting God — that he'd been dead wrong about who the enemies of God were? The enemies of God deserve death; Paul had lived his life on that firm truth. On the road to Damascus Paul learns that he is an enemy of God. Perhaps Paul took his blindness as a mercy because he could not bear to look at himself after this revelation.

If it was on the road to Damascus that Paul learned that he was an enemy of God, it was in the room on the street called Straight that he began to understand that while we were enemies Christ died for the ungodly. Paul began to understand this amazing truth because he met someone who believed that. The first word that Paul hears from Ananias is "Brother." This word of grace, the good news that enemies can become brothers, comes to Saul not in a blinding vision but in the gentle voice of a stranger.

The Justification in Christ conference has asked the question "Where does the church stand now on this gospel of justification in Christ?" Does the church understand this gospel? Do we have the faith and courage to believe it?

Paul believed this gospel because it was the story of his life. Paul had lived a large part of his life blind to the fact that he had no idea who the good guys and the bad guys were in the world. He lived the early part of his life with very clear ideas about what evildoers deserve. Evildoers deserve death. Paul never stopped believing that, but on the street called Straight he learned the rest of the story. On the road to Damascus Paul is only told that he's been persecuting all the wrong people and that he will be told what he is to do about that. The logic that had informed Paul's life up to that point had a clear answer to what Paul should now do — enemies of God deserve death; Paul is an enemy of God; therefore, Paul should die. Is it any wonder that he gave up eating and drinking? Did Paul spend those hours before Ananias arrived expecting his own imminent death? But God's world was infinitely stranger than Paul had thought it was. On the street called Straight, Paul had his eyes open to the utter strangeness of a world in which instead of killing enemies God dies for them.

Does the church today believe that reality is this strange? Then the church must become a community of reconciliation. And in Acts we see how very difficult it is for the church to become such a community. The church can become a community of reconciliation only if the church stops being sensible and stops second-guessing whom God can use and whom God will call.

The disciples in Jerusalem had much more sense than Ananias did. When Paul showed up in Jerusalem and attempted to join his brothers and sisters in the Lord, they were a long way from being willing to call him "brother." They did not believe that Paul was one of them. Why would they? Even if they'd heard that Saul had been preaching the gospel in Damascus, wasn't it more likely that this was a clever ruse than that God could or would save an evildoer like Paul?

Fortunately for Paul and for the future of the church in the world, there was one person in Jerusalem who believed that the alchemy of grace had worked in Paul's life. Barnabas believed the gospel, and evidently he also believed Paul's story about the Lord speaking to him on the road to Damascus. The text gives us no clue about what explains

Barnabas's ability to believe what the rest of the disciples in Jerusalem were not ready to believe. Ananias at least had his vision and the voice of God to go on. Why did Barnabas believe that God could seek and save even Paul, this persecutor of Jesus, this enemy of God?

Here we can only speculate, but let me offer this guess. Notice how important the pronouns are in Paul's letter to the Romans. While *we* were weak, while *we* were enemies of God, Christ died for us the ungodly. Is it possible that Barnabas believed that Paul could become a friend of God because Barnabas remembered that he himself had been an enemy of God? Is it possible that the rest of the Jerusalem disciples had temporarily forgotten that they were once alienated from God?

Perhaps the greatest challenge that the church faces in sustaining its life as a community of reconciliation is that it is so much more comfortable to see ourselves as dispensers of grace than debtors to grace. As H. Richard Niebuhr so astutely observed,

> As Christians we want to be the forgivers of sins . . . new incarnations of Christ, saviors rather than saved; secure in our own possession of the true religion rather than dependent on a Lord who possesses us, chooses us, forgives us. If we do not try to have God under our control, then at least we try to give ourselves the assurance that we are on [God's] side facing the rest of the world; not with the world facing [God] in infinite dependence, with no security save in [God]. (*Christ and Culture* [New York: Harper & Brothers, 1951], p. 155)

There can be, Niebuhr observes, an ungodliness in "the piety of those who consciously carry God around with them wherever they go" (154). Maybe the disciples in Jerusalem were carrying around this sort of ungodliness and it was giving them spiritual amnesia about how they themselves came to be reconciled to God. Maybe Barnabas was less prone to carry God around with him wherever he went and more prone to ask where God would be carrying him next.

So here we are, a small part of Christ's church. Where does the church stand on the gospel of justification in Christ? We cannot answer that question without asking where *we* stand on this gospel.

Sisters and brothers, where do you see yourself in this story? Do you see yourself in Saul — that zealous but wrongheaded enemy of God lambasted by grace? Do you see yourself in Ananias and Barnabas — those perhaps trembling but breathtakingly courageous believers in the alchemy of grace? Or do you see yourself among those disciples of Jesus who have a hard time remembering that they cannot second-guess grace or carry God in their pocket?

My twenty-year-old son is an adult sponsor for a church youth group. Some of the older adults who act as sponsors probably look at him as just a kid himself, but he is beginning to learn the challenges of trying to contribute to a community of reconciliation. He recently returned from a mission trip that this youth group took to help another church in Brooklyn, New York. Their group spent a week running a vacation Bible school for seventy children from the mainly Jamaican neighborhood. My son, who loves basketball, was excited to find that there were hoops in the gym in the church's basement. During the course of the week he met some young men in the neighborhood and invited them to come by some evening to play basketball with some of the other people from the mission trip. When my son and his friends needed to go upstairs to a worship time, they left their guests to continue playing ball in the basement. Sometime later, the woman in charge of the church facility came to get the pastor who had come with the youth group. She asked him to go downstairs and ask the young men from the neighborhood to leave immediately. Unbeknownst to my son, he had violated a rule against having non-church members in the church without seeking official permission. No telling what trouble these unauthorized strangers might cause. A kind of angry incredulity crept into my son's voice as he went on to say, "While those guys were being asked to leave the church we were sitting there singing 'They'll Know We Are Christians by Our Love.' Can you believe that?"

Where does the church stand on the gospel today? Probably where it has always stood, wavering between belief and half-belief and semi-despairing pleas to help our unbelief.

Wherever we see ourselves in these stories, our Christian calling is, as it has always been, crystal clear — and utterly beyond us. In Christ we are called to believe that the God who died for us and is transforming us from enemies into friends has mercies that are wider than we can fathom. We are called to believe that God can seek and save evildoers and bad guys. We are called to believe that the stranger that we fear isn't any less redeemable than we are. We are called to repent and to believe the gospel. May God grant us the grace to do so.

The Doctrine of Justification
and the Cure of Souls

Katherine Sonderegger

"We do not presume," Archbishop Cranmer wrote in prayer, "to come to this, Thy Table, O merciful Lord, trusting in our own righteousness, but in Thy manifold and great mercies. We are not worthy so much as to gather up the crumbs under Thy Table. But Thou art that same Lord whose property is always to have mercy. Grant us therefore, gracious Lord, so to eat the flesh of Thy dear Son, Jesus Christ, and to drink His blood, that our sinful bodies may be made clean by His body, and our souls washed through His most precious blood, and that we may evermore dwell in Him, and He in us. Amen."

Few doctrines in our tradition are as deeply personal and inward as the doctrine of justification by grace, through faith alone. There are, to be sure, pastoral dimensions of many Christian *loci*, from the doctrine of creation, to the doctrines of election, sacraments, and Trinity. Indeed, it is in the doctrine of the Divine Triunity that much Christian anthropology and cure of souls is being written today. But I think we might say that these doctrines are *patient of* such pastoral application; they can be *put to use* in this way, or read in this light. For this very reason we are inclined to speak of their "pastoral *dimension*," or encourage others to be awake to their role in the care and cure of souls — but in just this way, we acknowledge that their scope, matter, and object are otherwise. And this is no liability in Christian doctrine. The recovery of the freedom, independence from human awareness, and the realism of doctrine — its objectivity, as this feature is sometimes called

166

— was the preoccupation of the great Protestant theologians of the twentieth century; and this recovery was a hard-fought battle, never entirely won. I say, "Protestant theologians" in this great work of recovery, because I believe this struggle for theological realism fell upon Calvinists, and Lutherans above all, for reasons intimate to the Protestant revolution itself.

Martin Luther held that the Church stands or falls by a single article: the doctrine of justification by grace through faith alone. This is the heart of the gospel, the truth of Christian deliverance, the triumph over sin, death, and the devil, the hope of the desperate and the happy song of angels. Whatever we may hold about Luther's relation to the medieval Church that shaped him — and that is a story for another day — we may agree that Luther prized the justification doctrine above all else, and to his descendants, whether in Wittenberg, Geneva, or Canterbury, this doctrine must be defended against all enemies, for it is just here that the great cause of grace is summed up and exhibited in a fallen world. Now *this* doctrine is supremely "pastoral." It does not have pastoral application, use, dimensions, or extensions; rather, it simply *is* that meeting of the Redeemer with the lost, the Shepherd with those He seeks and finds, the Object of faith with its subjects. This intimacy of the Divine with the human later theologians would call "communion" or, rather more technically, "coinherence." Now, I would *not* say that the summary of the Christian faith offered by the Protestant liberal, Adolf von Harnack — God with the soul; the soul with its God — is *Luther's* doctrine. Perhaps we should say it is an inversion or, even, a parody of it. But from our place within the Church, and the history of doctrine, we can trace out the line from Luther to his liberal descendants, and we can see why the Luther revival, above all, fueled the form of Protestant liberalism that sent Karl Barth and his early allies to their battle stations. The doctrine of justification by faith alone is the most pastoral, subjective, and deeply inward of Protestant dogmas. That is its danger — but also its great glory.

But for all that, the justification doctrine is not simply a Protestant dogma; it is rather a dogma of the whole Church, in all its forms, from the gatherings in Chloe's and Prisca and Aquila's houses, to the medieval and modern communions, in cathedrals, storefronts, and the coal fields of Wales. The recent Joint Declaration on Justification is testimony to its catholicity. Alister McGrath has called the

167

Iustitia Dei — the righteousness of God — the centerpiece of Christian proclamation in all times and places, and no gospel can be proclaimed apart from it. These are bold claims — too bold perhaps in places, and certainly not popular in all places — but I believe McGrath is right in the main: in the justification doctrine we stand before the central axis of the Christian faith, or, more properly, we bow down before the unitary, majestic act of God, to judge and deliver his own. There can be no more incisive word to us creatures than this: that in the right season, Christ died for the ungodly. We would be cold-hearted pastors and theologians indeed if we could not hear this Word as an arrow or sword that cuts to the heart, the very heart and inwardness of human life. The cure of souls, in our parishes, schools, cities, and homes, must spring from this source — though of course it must say many things with or beyond this — that a righteous God has to do *with us*, with just these very sinners, in our folly, pride, timidity, and sorrow. *This God* with *this creature*, Karl Barth was fond of saying, is the core of the gospel, *the* great Light cast on us from beyond.

Thomas Cranmer, Henry Tudor's archbishop and confessor, caught sight of that light; his prayerbooks for 1549 and 1552 are his testimony to it. When Henry VIII died, the long-suffering archbishop suddenly found himself free to draft the liturgy he had longed to write: a unified prayerbook for the English people, composed wholly in English — and what glorious English! — and designed to instruct, deepen, and form English Christians in the patterns and ways of the Reformation. Few prayers in those prayerbooks match the Prayer of Humble Access — the name for the prayer with which I began this paper — for its eloquent and moving summary of the Lutheran doctrine of justification by faith.

Much in Cranmer's prayerbooks, to be sure, remains traditional: he drew heavily from the rite that had dominated English worship in the medieval church, the Salisbury liturgy — or "Sarum Use" in Anglican parlance — and he shows the influence of his long study of patristic liturgies, new Continental worship books, and Eastern rites. Cranmer's liturgical work rested on careful, archeological research into the past. Ashley Null, in a book on Cranmer's doctrine of repentance, outlines how Cranmer's liturgy is shadowed in his "commonplace" books. Into these commonplace books was poured the research and commentary on Patristic theology, the ongoing polemics with traditionalists like Stephen Gardiner and John Fisher, and the close scholastic study of Augustine and Luther. Cranmer's prayerbooks fused, in matchless renaissance style, the scriptural idiom of prayer, confession, and praise, the received liturgies of several churches, the learning of the early church, and the central mystery of the magisterial Protestants: justification by grace through faith alone. Cranmer's eucharistic liturgy, styled "the administration of the Lord's Supper or Holy Communion," retained much that was familiar to his congregations: the Sursum Corda, the Sanctus, prefaces, consecration and words of institution, and the Lord's Prayer. Yet Cranmer transformed and made new everything he touched.

The Prayer of Humble Access, like many of the daily collects, came from Cranmer's own hand. He did not, as with other prayers, reorder and rework traditional elements; rather, this prayer is his, out of whole cloth. He placed this jewel in different settings within his rite, reflecting his developing views on the Supper, but in each case it is marked off from the surrounding material by an air of great solemnity and dignity: "the priest kneels by the Table," the rubric in the later prayerbook has it, "to say it in the name of all them that shall receive"; in the earlier book, it is said by all communicants, "meekly kneeling" after a lengthy exhortation and penitential rite. Ashley Null concentrates on these penitential movements in the rite, tracing Cranmer's doctrine from its medieval formulation in the threefold doctrine of penance — contrition, confession, and satisfaction — to his Lutheran and then Reformed formulation of justification of the ungodly, apart from foreseen merit, by grace alone, through faith in Christ. We may safely assume, then, that we see deep into Cranmer's heart when we look into the Prayer of Humble Access — and that, as many of you know, is no easy thing to do. The archbishop offers a sterling example of Churchill's famous diagnosis of the Russians: a riddle, clothed in a mystery and wrapped in an enigma.

It is only fair, I think, to say that the archbishop has had a checkered career in the judgment of his critics, early and late. His own integrity, and commitment to the Protestant cause in England, or indeed to the English Church itself, has been roundly abused by his critics. Cranmer has been viewed as a "time server," a pliant or perhaps cowardly defender of the Royal Supremacy, or, at best, a cipher, unknown to others, uncertain to himself. Cranmer recanted his Protestant views under Mary Tudor, some say, because he never made common cause with Lutheranism to begin with. Or he recanted because his only principle was the Protestant maxim; the Prince must always be obeyed. Or, others say, he was never a Lutheran — or perhaps only so for a brief moment — but was rather a Calvinist, or more serious still, a Zwinglian. But such criticism, however severe, actually pales before the rebuke delivered by an Anglican monk, Dom Gregory Dix.

As liturgists in our audience know well, Dix was the architect of much of the modern "liturgical renewal movement," *the* dominant force in worship these days on both sides of the aisles. And little wonder. *The Shape of the Liturgy,* Dix's most celebrated work, is magisterial: beautifully written, deeply learned, delightfully polemical. But there is pathos in it as well. To read Dix's rapier assessment of Cranmer's rite in *The Shape of the Liturgy* is to grasp just how explosive liturgical change truly is, how deep and convulsive the reaction to the radical innovations of Cranmer's prayerbooks. In removing elements of the ancient rite, Dix charges, or in radically reordering them, Cranmer manages to destroy the very heart of the Eucharist, its power to effect not merely the sacrament, but the Church itself. The "fourfold action" of the Eucharist, Dix writes, stems from the earliest days of the post-resurrection Church: to take, bless, break, and eat. Even these, Cranmer could not leave alone. His early prayerbook does not even include a fraction, or breaking of bread, and the oblation — the proper work, Dix holds, of the laity as an order of the Church — has been reduced to the collection of alms for the poor, with no eucharistic action at all. The 1549 prayerbook is not in fact a way station for Cranmer, Dix warns; it no more teaches a doctrine of the Real Presence of Christ in the Eucharist than does the later one. But the 1552 Prayerbook, the work completed under the child-king Edward, preserves Cranmer's deepest and most troubling achievement: it is, Dix writes, "the only effective attempt ever made to give liturgical expression to the doctrine of "justification by faith alone'" (SL, 672). Now that is not the happy ending for Dix that it happens to be for me; but we may at least agree that he is right. And the Prayer of Humble Access, I would say, is this doctrine in its clearest, most inward, and moving form.

Cranmer begins his prayer with what we might term the "dispositions," the aims, attitudes, and tendencies of the self toward the objects of its awareness. We might pause here a moment before this little word, "dispositions," and my assimilation of it to Cranmer's prayer of contrition and trust. Indeed, these very words — contrition, trust — are themselves, in my view, dispositions as much as — no, more than — they are acts, even acts of the will. Dispositions are long-standing conditions or properties of the self, a way of being-in-the-world that I believe St. Thomas might call "habits." Now such tendencies or characteristics are not altogether separate from acts, but they are distinct from them. In analogy, we might recall the traditional philosophical example of a natural property like "fragility": glass is fragile, whether broken or not; but we can assure ourselves that a particular water glass has this property by hurling it on the floor. The act confirms, exhibits, and conforms to the property of fragility.

Now I think dispositions are characteristics something like this natural property of glass — but only something like. We should not consider human properties, even those only held in reserve, as "natural" or "constitutional" in the way some inorganic dispositions are. Whatever we may think about the role of biology and genetics in human character — and I would say the jury will be out on this for a very long time — human dispositions are not written into our embodied life the way hardness is in diamonds. Rather, human habits are shaped, received, and impressed on us by the language, community, history, and practice that surround us. These "life-worlds," to borrow an older idiom, may have such power that in conforming to them we believe we bow to something like a force of nature; but they remain customary and pliant, a living pattern in a living self. Dispositions are not acquired overnight. It is this feature of the disposition that marks it off from a simple act of will, or even a tendency to act in one way or another. Rather, the human quality of "being disposed" takes up residence in us over many months and years; over time it burrows deep in us and takes hold of our very identity or self. We quietly acknowledge this sovereign power of dispositions when we say that our friends — or, more strongly, ourselves — do not seem like themselves today; or that their actions, or ours, are not what that person would do, though to be sure they have done it. That is just not like them! we exclaim. She couldn't have done it! we say; and by that exclamation we acknowledge her doing that very thing. There is a pattern to a human life, a way and shape of it, that stamps it as our very own, such that even those things we have in fact done cannot be our very own. These long-term habits, engraved in us over time, are admixed in the mystery of human inwardness, an inwardness that is built up, conserved, and cultivated and in just this way becomes inextricably — we might even say, "naturally" — ours. So much for general or philosophical comments on dispositions.

But human dispositions are hardly the sole province of philosophical debate; they go right to the heart of the justification doctrine, from St. Paul's anguished letter to the Romans, to St. Augustine's polemic in *On Nature and Grace,* to Luther's trumpet blast in *The Bondage of the Will,* to Molina, Trent, Dort, and beyond. Dispositions belong to the justification doctrine most simply because they are cultivated and not given to us by birth; dispositions are not inevitable, or inescapable, but are a new creation in the life of faith. Dispositions are not powers or "faculties" as is "the will" or the "ability to do otherwise" — if that indeed is what the faculty of will is all about. Rather, dispositions are something like "acquired nature" — or as we so often say, "second nature" — so that they cannot help but remind us of the Apostle's wrenching analysis of a divided self, and the "good that I will, yet I do not." They do not fall neatly under the single and unified rubric, "nature," that Pelagius conflated with grace. Yet in their habitual character, part sought out, part in-bred, they do appear to fall under just those acts of individual effort that sparked Augustine's anxiety over the "cause of grace," and, later, Luther's and Calvin's opposition to congruent merit and the task of preparing for the gift of saving faith, so vital to the late medieval West. And, as if that is not enough, the later pietist and Protestant scholastic debates over faith and the assurance of election turn on just the gifted yet acquired nature of Christian dispositions, especially those of repentance and trust. These are the subjective and inward puzzles that Christian dispositions present for the justification doctrine — puzzles that all pastors know from their hours in the pastor's study, from the delicate work of applying the spur and relaxing the terrors that is the art of the cure of souls. We will return to these puzzles; but first, more Cranmer.

In the Prayer of Humble Access, Thomas Cranmer offers several Christian dispositions for our incorporation: unworthiness, lack of presumption, beseeching, and, above all, trust. "We do not presume," he has us pray, "to come to this Thy Table, trusting in our own righteousness, but in Thy manifold and great mercies." Now we recognize here the claim by the Continental Reformers that Christians have no preparation to undertake before the Sacrament, no work of meritorious contrition and satisfaction, in order to present a work that God in his ordained mercy may treat as worthiness before Him. We recognize too the compressed footnote to Luther's attack upon works of human righteousness apart from Christ. Cranmer clearly has dogmatic ends in view here. But this is not a theological diatribe under the guise of prayer, not a "talky prayer" of the kind we hear all too often, which signals another sermon under a different name, an ambassador without portfolio. No, this is Cranmer at his most sonorous and reflective, a full act of prayer before the Almighty. Cranmer's opening sentence offers for us, above all, a scriptural disposition or attitude — the centurion's appeal to the healer, Jesus — and reminds us with quiet power that we come before Christ as those who are desperate, who lie exposed before the enemy, death, and who seek healing, not of some minor trouble but of life itself.

Cranmer follows this biblical allusion with another: "We are not worthy so much as to gather up the crumbs under Thy Table. But Thou art the same Lord whose property is always to have mercy." Here again we are offered a biblical attitude to adopt — the Syro-Phoenician woman — but this time Cranmer shows greater freedom over the text. It is Jesus himself, we remember, who sternly warns the woman that she is left only the crumbs under the table; not for her the children's food. And in accepting Jesus' word, she wins her contest with him: even the dogs eat the leavings. Great is her faith, our Lord declares: our confession of unworthiness is an act of great faith, a bold confidence that even the outcast will be fed here. We must be fearless in our petitions, both Luther and Barth counseled. To trust in God's righteousness, and not in our own, to confess our unworthiness before the Redeemer, is not morbid self-loathing but rather a step into the sphere of freedom, the liberty of God's sons and daughters, where our unworthiness is met with mercy and abundance, and we are fed the food of angels.

But most important of all, Cranmer offers to us in the conclusion of his prayer the disposition and biblical attitude summed up in the Gospel of John: the hope "that we may evermore dwell in Christ, and He in us." The mutual indwelling of Christ and the believer, so richly elaborated in the Johannine Supper Discourses, and so remarkably likened to the indwelling of Father and Son, Spirit and Son, mark the institution of the Holy Meal in John, and lay out what it means to feed on Christ in one's heart, by faith, with thanksgiving. To be sure, Cranmer — in two versions in the two prayerbooks — twins this communion of Christ and believer with language from the John of the Apocalypse: that we are to be washed in the blood of the Lamb, our sinful bodies cleansed by his righteous body. And perhaps we are to hear echoes of the "hard saying" in the Gospel, where we are told that we must feed on Jesus' flesh and blood to enter the kingdom: and who can receive this? But these resonances seem to me to take second place to the indwelling of the Lord in his friends, promised in the Supper Discourses. Again and again, throughout Cranmer's whole eucharistic liturgy, we are reminded of this great hope, aim, and disposition of the Christian life: that we may expect and rest confident that, apart from our worthiness, Christ will dwell in us, and we in him.

The young Luther famously described this gift of communion of Divine Object with human subject under the image of marriage: as the groom Christ becomes one flesh with the bride, our sinful selves, and in this intimate union his righteousness becomes ours, and our debt, sin, and suffering become his. Lutherans have called this the "gracious exchange," and it is a sign of its mystery that this very *indwelling* and *intimate exchange* is not the figure for *innate* or proper righteousness — the righteousness we possess — but rather for the *alien* righteousness, the righteousness Christ alone gives and retains as his sovereign grace. We may take the measure of how distinctive Luther's teaching is here by its use in one of his liberal descendants, Friedrich Schleiermacher. It is the maxim of Schleiermacher's soteriology in *The Christian Faith* that "Christ's act becomes ours"; that is the distinctly redemptive side of the general Christian pattern, that "the supernatural becomes natural." Notice here that Schleiermacher, in a doctrine of great subtlety and power, assumes Luther's figure of marriage as the grace of the indwelling Christ, and pays homage to Luther's conviction that Christ's assets become ours, even as our debts become his. But where Luther draws on the gracious exchange to make vivid the doctrine of alien righteousness, Schleiermacher draws on it to show the doctrine of innate and infused righteousness.

We need not settle all accounts with Schleiermacher here, or decide just how faithful an heir of the Reformation he actually was; these are questions for another day, as is the comparison — fruitful, I believe — with the sixteenth-century debates over grace, merit, and the sanctified life. But we can say that in Schleiermacher's doctrine of reconciliation, Christ's act really does become *ours* — our God-consciousness, our deepening dependence on the Redeemer, our own experience of grace, driving back sin, and our own inner testimony to new life where we, with all Christ's disciples, take part in the Church militant, joining in its gradual yet inexorable triumph over the world. Now Schleiermacher was a great student of the Fourth Gospel, and there is little doubt that the indwelling Christ, and the dispositions this "second nature" awakens, are the mainspring of Schleiermacher's theology and, I believe, his Christian piety. But his doctrine is not Luther's, nor, would I say, is it Cranmer's. Schleiermacher's own account of the Christian dispositions, and their root in the justification doctrine, depend upon a different analysis than Luther's of the life of sin and grace, a different assessment of the justified and sanctified self, and a different resolution of the mystery of Christian inwardness. And the pastoral questions, in just these ways, differ from those raised by Luther and, I would say, by Cranmer himself.

Consider once again the gracious exchange as Luther recommends it, as alien righteousness. What we must first say is that Christ stands in our place, and by that, we must first assert that Christ knows our own inwardness, not as the outsider looking in, but rather as *the* insider, as our own "second nature." Christ, St. Paul tells us in Galatians, stands under the curse, has become the curse the Law visits on disobedience — or, in that astonishing verse in Corinthians, he has become sin for us. I propose that we take these verses literally, or, perhaps better, realistically; I believe Luther meant just that. And that is a more radical claim than might first appear. It has often seemed to me that we miss the opportunity to speak a pastoral word in season when we address the justification doctrine. In part, this is so because any doctrine appears at first glance to demand objective treatment as a teaching of the faith, a matter that concerns us, to be sure, but concerns us in the way that, say, any doctrine of citizenship under our constitution would have bearing upon us and our conduct. We can get such a teaching right; and we can also get it wrong. But in even greater measure, I feel that we pass by the seasonable word because we are tempted to believe that the justification of sinners in Christ has to do

175

with a special and discrete problem in dogmatics: how sinners stand before a righteous God. And, like any discrete problem, it has only specific application. But the justification doctrine is at heart the gracious exchange: it is not one problem of the Christian life; it simply *is* the Christian life. For Christ to stand in our place, to become our sin, to bear our curse, to walk the way of our death, is simply to confess that Christ dwells within the far country that just is our inwardness.

As pastors, both lay and ordained, we minister to those who endure grave illness; we hear the confessions that spring from the knowledge of death. Perhaps we have had disclosed to us, during some hardship, or danger, or fleeting moment of great beauty, that our own life cannot last, that we too must enter into the pit, that this very flesh must become dust. Perhaps those we pastor or we ourselves have been given that great grace of shocking honesty where, despite all dodging and evading and turning away, we see death, our death, for what it is: that it is our end. Now it seems to me that it is just here, just in this startling undoing of our own power and invincibility, that the gracious exchange of Christ's justification makes itself heard. We may consider that it has a lesson to teach us — and I would not want to spurn such use. Indeed, the disposition of humility, of dependence upon Another, is certainly to be cultivated in the Christian life. But we may be much bolder than that. This death of ours, this death of our intimates and of our enemies, is what Christ himself knows. He knows it from *within*, from where we stand; he lives in that weakness or indifference or bravery with which we face this last enemy. He is not simply the answer to that enemy. He does not simply stand at the end of it; his name is not simply pronounced as the resolution to a sinner's life. No, Christ *occupies* our death. He is already within its wretchedness, the curse of it. We have all seen our brothers and sisters undone by death — by the stark cruelty of physical unmaking; by the fears, guilt, and bitterness of it; by the callousness, timidity, and shattering grief of those touched by another's death. And we have seen a solemn beauty, courage, and peace emerge from that shriving. But we do not need to *bring* Christ into that godforsakenness; he is already there. For this he came, to occupy just this place.

So too we may have heard, as lay or ordained pastors, the confessions of temptations, warred against or lost. We may have spent those dry hours of anxiety and guilt ourselves, taking our true measure, or fearing it. The stuff of sin is sometimes grand and terrible; so often it is mediocre, empty, a dull ache. As Christians we know this as the exile we are under. It is ungodliness, abandonment. Macbeth longs to pray after he has murdered Duncan; and he cannot. "But wherefore could I not pronounce 'Amen'? I had most need of blessing, and 'Amen' stuck in my throat" (Macbeth 2.2, 30-32). His religious life is an empty show. We could not live long in the Christian Church, or in the world that extends both within and beyond the Church, to know firsthand this ungodliness, this life without God or hope in the world. We are so often tempted to believe we must *bring* Christ into this abandoned world; we must apply him or his teachings in this dry land. And to be sure, the preaching of justification *is* the speaking of this name, the proclamation of forgiveness through his own work, and the reconciliation of God's enemies through his own loving sacrifice. This proclamation is the ground of our disposition of gratitude, a central grace of the life of faith. But we would not grasp the radical gift of Christ's gracious exchange did we not see that Christ need not be brought to this dryness and curse; he is already there. He came for this. He knows it from our place, in our dullness, fear, anxiety, and emptiness. In our deepest ungodliness he is already within it, assuming it, bearing it, taking it for his own. This is Christ's high-priestly work: he intercedes with the Father not from some lofty altar, undefiled, but rather from within our own disfigured hearts. In just this way, Christ is victor.

So too we must say that the gracious exchange of Christ with the ungodly speaks the pastoral word of judgment, the judgment of this particular grace. Cranmer invites us to pray that Christ may dwell in us, and we in him, and it is this moment of our indwelling him that brings forward the sharp judgment of the sinner. The Apostle Paul excoriates his readers: Do you not know that all those who have been baptized in Christ have been baptized into his death? How can you continue in sin? Again, we are often tempted, in our homiletic and pastoral tasks, to treat these verses in St. Paul as an *application* of Christ's death, or the Church's sacraments, to daily Christian life. And there is no doubt that that application can be made; indeed, St. Paul's hortatory and parenetic sections in his letters amply demonstrate its power. I for one would find welcome stronger preaching and moral instruction on Christ as Judge — and not only of those rulers of this age! Surely the Name that is above every name sits even now in judgment on us all. But I think we may be bolder than such applications. For in the gracious exchange, the dying Christ indwells us, and we in his death: and that just *is* our death, the execution of the Old Adam.

In his magisterial treatment of the justification doctrine, Karl Barth laid stress on God's righteous act of righting wrong. Justification should not be seen as a weak permission of sin, or a turning aside from the destruction of the creature by the chaos of evil. No, Barth writes, God lays claim on his creature; he will defend the creature against its undoing, and make the wrong right. Not surprisingly, there is great realism in Barth's doctrine: God *does* declare the sinner righteous, but in and by the declaration God delivers and makes good what is fallen and despoiled. That is why, Barth claims, the justification doctrine is not Gospel against Law but rather supremely Law — the Law of God's own gracious victory. Barth develops the powerful realism of his doctrine by underscoring the Judge's execution of the sinner. "Man's wrong," Barth warns, "i.e., man himself as a wrongdoer cannot stand in the judgment of God. The righteousness of God means God's negating and overcoming and taking away and destroying wrong and man as the doer of it" (4.1, §61.2, 535). All these sections, again not surprisingly, are hedged about with the stark language of "event" and dialectic: we do not see this in ourselves, *simpliciter,* but rather in the apocalyptic disclosure of the Spirit of Christ. Now, it is no easy thing to argue against Barth — many greater minds than mine have found this out! — and especially on this complex and ramified methodological conviction. But I must say that I believe we can say more about ourselves *simpliciter* and *per se* than I think Barth does here.

I believe we may say that in the gracious exchange we discover in ourselves the marks of our own death, the quiet, tidal sweep of our sinful selves out to sea. As pastors, lay and ordained, we may preach this word also. Again, we need not exhort our parishioners or ourselves to search within for these signs, or to worry over them, or to strive to bring them forward. Rather, we may boldly and simply say that this death just *is* our Christian life. We need not *take up* the cross; it takes us up. Christ's judgment works on us from within, his death in us and our life in his death, such that we are crushed by it. The Christian life is a breaking-down and a breaking-open, a mortification day by day. It is an alien work because it is Christ's own; but it is an inward grace because it is at work on our own flesh. We may speak of this as medicine, as St. Augustine sometimes did. Or we may favor the bearing of the cross, as Calvin did, or of dying to the world, as the ascetics did, or more starkly still, being crucified to the world, as St. Paul did, a man who knew crucifixion for what it was — a state torture, not a pious symbol. In the cure of souls, we will find many eloquent testimonies to this work of judgment, and it will bear the stamp of each individual life. We need not find a single rubric for this sovereign judgment of Christ, for it applies to each of us in our inescapable particularity. It may be our bodily sufferings; it may be rather our vigorous health. It may come in grief, or doubt, or loneliness; or again in our intimacies, our ambitions and success. But in the end, Death says to Everyman: I will be your companion; I will go with you. This conformity to death, the end of all the living, is the breaking-in and breaking-down of all flesh by the shape of Christ; and it is the particular glory of the creature to bear this form. Christians assent to this judgment by Christ; but all will come to this judgment seat. It is God's way of righting wrong.

We may return then, for a brief time, to Cranmer once again, and his recommendation of Christian dispositions. It may seem to some of us, or to some of our congregations, that a prayer filled with such dispositions could not seem like good news to Christians these days. Does it not preach a disposition of self-contempt? Does it not encourage a morbid self-abnegation? Are we not simply falling on our knees all the time here, never to arise? Could we not justify every kind of abuse, ridicule, and weakness by commending such prayers, and such dispositions? By now, you will suspect that I'm not likely to agree with these questions — but I am not unsympathetic to them either. Christianity is the religious practice of sinners, and we have done much in the Church and the world to earn that description. To interpret Cranmer or, more broadly, the Christian faith as a counsel of despair and an embracing of abuse is to caricature and mock the redemption we have in Christ. The dispositions we are to enter into are not a species of self-help, whether banal or profound. They are not advice we should listen to or refuse, nor are they qualities we may adopt by an act of will or pious or deluded striving. Rather, the dispositions of confidence and trust, of humility, unworthiness, and imprecation, are simply gifts. They are *descriptions* — not ideals — of the life of grace, of the gracious exchange of Christ with the ungodly. They are our second nature — partly cultivated, partly discovered — because they are the fruits of Christ's alien work in us, to dwell in us richly, and we in him. To be sure, these dispositions are our own Christian work, the aim of our devotion, and the ends of our wills; they are our own inwardness. But we would not grasp the astonishing good news that Christ stands in our place, and that his righteousness is ours, our sins his, did we not see that "it is no longer I that lives, but Christ who lives in me." The startling fusion of St. Paul's subjectivity with Christ — his odd movement in and out of his own inwardness, to the law of his mind and the law of his members — this interplay of Christ with the believer makes our own dispositions, St. Paul tells us, the gift, judgment, and presence of Christ. This is the mystical union that undergirds Christian doctrines as varied as Christology, ecclesiology, and the sacraments; it is the chief work of the Holy Spirit. When we repeat the Prayer of Humble Access, then, or cultivate the dispositions as our own second nature, we enter into the mystery that is Christ's own grace: that though we are unworthy to gather the crumbs under his table, yet it is his property always to have mercy. In the end, the cure of souls can only be this: that Christ dwells in us, and we in him.

We began with Thomas Cranmer, his English prayerbooks, and his exposition in liturgy of the Lutheran doctrine of justification by grace through faith alone. Perhaps it would be fitting to end not with them, but with the Object toward which they all aimed: Christ in us, the hope of salvation. This is the heart of the justification doctrine, the heart of the cure of souls.

Contributors

Gary J. Dorrien is Ann V. and Donald R. Parfet Distinguished Professor and Dean of Stetson Chapel at Kalamazoo College, Kalamazoo, Michigan. (Episcopal Church in the U.S.A.)

Avery Cardinal Dulles, S.J., is Laurence J. McGinley Professor of Religion and Society at Fordham University, Bronx, New York. (Roman Catholic Church)

Gabriel Fackre is Abbot Professor of Christian Theology, Emeritus, at Andover Newton Theological School, Newton Center, Massachusetts. (United Church of Christ)

George Hunsinger is McCord Professor of Systematic Theology at Princeton Theological Seminary, Princeton, New Jersey. (Presbyterian Church, USA)

Paul Varo Martinson is Professor of Christian Mission and World Religion, Emeritus, at Luther Seminary, St. Paul, Minnesota. (Evangelical Lutheran Church in America)

Margaret O'Gara is Professor of Theology at the University of Saint Michael's College, Toronto, Ontario. (Roman Catholic Church)

Steven D. Paulson is Professor of Systematic Theology at Luther Seminary, St. Paul, Minnesota. (Evangelical Lutheran Church in America)

Michael J. Root is Vice President for Academic Affairs and Dean at Lutheran Theological Southern Seminary, Columbia, South Carolina. (Evangelical Lutheran Church in America)

Caroline J. Simon is Professor of Philosophy at Hope College, Holland, Michigan. (Reformed Church in America)

Katherine Sonderegger is Professor of Theology at the Episcopal Theological Seminary in Virginia, Alexandria, Virginia. (Episcopal Church in the U.S.A.)

Wayne C. Stumme is Director of the Institute for Mission in the USA and Professor of Theology and Mission (retired) at Trinity Lutheran Seminary, Columbus, Ohio. (Evangelical Lutheran Church in America)

Michael E. Tassler is Senior Pastor at Bethel Lutheran Church, Manassas, Virginia. (Evangelical Lutheran Church in America)